MW01147321

MATERIALS DEVELOPMENT CENTER

MODIFICATION OF
BEHAVIOR OF
THE MENTALLY ILL

Publication Number 936

AMERICAN LECTURE SERIES®

A Publication in

The BANNERSTONE DIVISION *of*
AMERICAN LECTURES IN SOCIAL AND REHABILITATION
PSYCHOLOGY

Editors of the Series

RICHARD E. HARDY, Ed.D.
Diplomate in Counseling Psychology (*ABPP*)
Chairman, Department of Rehabilitation Counseling
Virginia Commonwealth University
Richmond, Virginia

and

JOHN G. CULL, Ph.D.
Director, Regional Counselor Training Program
Department of Rehabilitation Counseling
Virginia Commonwealth University
Fishersville, Virginia

The American Lecture Series in Social and Rehabilitation Psychology offers books which are concerned with man's role in his milieu. Emphasis is placed on how this role can be made more effective in a time of social conflict and a deteriorating physical environment. The books are oriented toward descriptions of what future roles should be and are not concerned exclusively with the delineation and definition of contemporary behavior. Contributors are concerned to a considerable extent with prediction through the use of a functional view of man as opposed to a descriptive, anatomical point of view.

Books in this series are written mainly for the professional practitioner; however, academicians will find them of considerable value in both undergraduate and graduate courses in the helping services.

MODIFICATION OF BEHAVIOR OF THE MENTALLY ILL

REHABILITATION APPROACHES

RICHARD E. HARDY

JOHN G. CULL

CHARLES C THOMAS • PUBLISHER
Springfield • Illinois • U.S.A.

Published and Distributed Throughout the World by
CHARLES C THOMAS · PUBLISHER
BANNERSTONE HOUSE
301-327 East Lawrence Avenue, Springfield, Illinois, U.S.A.

© *1974, by* CHARLES C THOMAS · PUBLISHER
ISBN 0-398-03052-9
Library of Congress Catalog Card Number: 73-16497

With THOMAS BOOKS *careful attention is given to all details of
manufacturing and design. It is the Publisher's desire to present books
that are satisfactory as to their physical qualities and artistic possibilities
and appropriate for their particular use.* THOMAS BOOKS *will be true
to those laws of quality that assure a good name and good will.*

Printed in the United States of America
Y-2

Library of Congress Cataloging in Publication Data

Hardy, Richard E.
    Modification of behavior of the mentally ill.

    (American lecture series, publication no. 936. A publication in the Bannerstone Division of American lectures in social and rehabilitation psychology)

    1. Mentally ill—Rehabilitation. 2. Behavior therapy. I. Cull, John G., joint author. II. Title. [DNLM: 1. Behavior therapy. 2 Mental disorders—Rehabilitation. 3. Rehabilitation, Vocational. WM420 M692 1974].
RC576.H32   362.2'04'25   73-16497
ISBN 0-398-03052-9

Dedicated to Mr. E. B. Whitten,
Executive Director of the National
Rehabilitation Association,
outstanding rehabilitation leader
and innovator over many years

CONTRIBUTORS

Thomas-Robert H. Ames: Assistant Professor of Community Mental Health Technology, Department of Health Technology, Borough of Manhattan Community College, City University of New York. Has degrees from the University of Florida and New York University. Prior to joining the City University of New York, he was Executive Director of the Young Adult Institute and Workshop, Inc. Previously he had been Coordinator of the Habilitation Program for the mentally handicapped at the Eastern School, Inc. Professor Ames has served as a consultant to a number of commissions, schools and agencies. He is a Fellow and regional board member of the American Association on Mental Deficiency, President of the New York Metropolitan Rehabilitation Counseling Association, a Fellow the Royal Society of Health, and a member of several other professional organizations. He is the recipient of the 1973 meritorious service award presented by the Northeast Region of the National Rehabilitation Association.

Barry B. Craig, M.Ed.: Director of Rehabilitation, Virginia Department of Mental Health and Mental Retardation. Formerly Rehabilitation Counselor and Casework Supervisor, North Carolina Division of Rehabilitation. He completed the Psychiatric Rehabilitation Program, Department of Psychiatry, University of Virginia Medical School and the Psychiatric Internship Program, Department of Psychiatry, Harvard Medical School. Mr. Craig has lectured on topics in psychiatric rehabilitation and is author of *Psychiatric Rehabilitation: The Client, Treatment and Rehabilitation Methods,* An Independent Study Unit for Rehabilitation Counselors, published by the University of North Carolina.

John G. Cull, Ph.D.: Director, Regional Counselor Training Program and Professor, Department of Rehabilitation, School of Community Services, Virginia Commonwealth University, Fishersville, Va.; Adjunct Professor in Psychology and Education, School of General Studies, University of Virginia; Technical Consultant, Rehabilitation Services Administration, U. S. Department of Health, Education and Welfare; Vocational Consultant, Bureau of Hearings and Appeals, Social Security Administration; Lecturer, Medical Department Affiliate Program, Woodrow Wilson Rehabilitation Center; Consulting Editor,

American Lecture Series in Social and Rehabilitation Psychology, Charles C Thomas, Publisher. Formerly Rehabilitation Counselor, Texas Commission for the Blind and Texas Rehabilitation Commission; Director, Division of Research and Program Development, Virginia Department of Vocational Rehabilitation. The following are some of the books Dr. Cull has co-authored and co-edited: *Vocational Rehabilitation: Profession and Process, Contemporary Fieldwork Practices in Rehabilitation, Social and Rehabilitation Services for the Blind, Fundamentals of Criminal Behavior and Correctional Systems* and *Drug Dependence and Rehabilitation Approaches*. Dr. Cull also has contributed more than 60 publications to the professional literature in psychology and rehabilitation.

Donald B. Derozier, Ph.D.: Received degrees from St. Norbert College, Marquette University and the University of Kansas. He is a Clinical Psychologist in private practice in Oshkosh, Wisconsin. Formerly Dr. Derozier was Chief of the Adolescent Male Service and Staff Clinical Psychologist at the Winnebago State Hospital, Winnebago, Wisconsin.

Thomas C. Dickinson, Ph.D.: Supervising Clinical Psychologist, Department of Psychiatry and Department of Rehabilitation Medicine, Edward J. Meyer Hospital, Buffalo, New York. Psychological Consultant for the New York State Office of Vocational Rehabilitation. Dr. Dickinson has been involved in practicum and internship experiences for students in clinical psychology, rehabilitation counseling, and rehabilitation medicine and nursing. He has made a number of contributions to the professional literature with a focus upon areas of intellectual and psychological evaluation of rehabilitation clients, their demographic characteristics and methods of assessing rehabilitative potential of general hospital outpatients.

Joseph J. Duetsch, Ph.D.: Coordinator of the Alcoholic Treatment Programs at the Salem, Virginia Veterans Administration Hospital. Prior to that he was a Staff Psychologist at Salem and before that a Psychophysiologist, Army Medical Research Laboratory, Fort Knox, Kentucky. Currently he is an instructor at the University of Virginia, Roanoke office; Consultant, Lutheran Church in America, Virginia Synod; Consultant, Lutheran Children's Home, Salem, Virginia. He is a licensed Clinical Psychologist in Virginia.

Alan Frankel, Ph.D.: Recently joined the Veterans Administration as a Research Psychologist. Previously he was Director of the Rehabilitation Psychology Training Program at the University of Portland (Oregon). Before that he was an instructor in the Department of Rehabilitation Medicine at Albert Einstein College of Medicine. He has taught graduate courses in assessment, therapy, community and rehabilitation psychology. He has published on attitude theory, Self-Help groups, and education in rehabilitation. His current interests include hemodialysis, multivariate analysis, Self-Help groups, and behavioral treatment for alcoholism. He is a licensed Psychologist in Virginia.

Deloss D. Friesen, Ph.D.: Has degrees from the Northwest Nazarene College and the University of Oregon. Dr. Friesen is an Associate Professor in the Department of Educational Psychology and Measurement at the University of Nebraska, Lincoln, Nebraska. He has held positions as Counseling Psychologist at the University Counseling Center, State University of New York at Albany; Supervisor of Admission Examinations, State University of New York at Albany; and instructor at the Hudson Valley Community College. Dr. Friesen's particular interests are in the areas of psychotherapy, marital adjustment, and vocational choice.

Robert L. Gunn, Ph.D.: Chief, Day Treatment Center, Sepulveda Veterans Administration Hospital, Sepulveda, California; Chairman, Equal Opportunity Council of Greater Los Angeles Area; Chairman, West Los Angeles Federal College Association. Formerly Coordinator of Program Evaluation staff unit of Veteran Administration. Dr. Gunn has contributed numerous articles to the professional literature in the treatment of the mentally ill.

Richard E. Hardy, Ed.D.: Chairman, Department of Rehabilitation, School of Community Services, Virginia Commonwealth University, Richmond, Virginia; Technical Consultant, Rehabilitation Services Administration, U.S. Department of Health, Education and Welfare; Consulting Editor, *American Lecture Series in Social and Rehabilitation Psychology*, Charles C Thomas, Publisher; and Associate Editor, *Journal of Voluntary Action Research*. Formerly Rehabilitation Counselor in Virginia; Chief Psychologist and Supervisor of Training, South Carolina Department of Vocational Rehabilitation and member South Carolina State Board of Examiners in Psychology; Rehabilitation Advisor, Rehabilitation Services Administration, U.S. Department of Health, Education and Welfare. The following are some of the books Dr. Hardy has co-authored and co-edited: *Social and Rehabilitation Services for the Blind, Vocational Rehabilitation: Profession and Process, The Unfit Majority, Fundamentals of Criminal Behavior and Correctional Systems* and *Drug Dependence and Rehabilitation Approaches*. Dr. Hardy has contributed more than 60 publications to the professional literature in psychology and rehabilitation.

Robert A. Lassiter, Ph.D.: Associate Professor in Rehabilitation Counseling, Virginia Commonwealth University, Richmond and former Director, Rehabilitation Education and Research Unit, Rehabilitation Counseling Program, and Associate Professor, School of Education,

University of North Carolina at Chapel Hill; Technical Consultant to the Rehabilitation Services Administration, Social and Rehabilitation Services, Department of Health, Education and Welfare; Consultant in Continuing Education for the Training and Research Departments, Division of Vocational Rehabilitation in North Carolina and the North Carolina Commission for the Blind. Formerly Rehabilitation Counselor, Florida Division of Vocational Rehabilitation; Executive Director, North Carolina Society for Crippled Children and Adults; State Director, North Carolina Division of Vocational Rehabilitation. Publications include: *Vocational Rehabilitation in North Carolina*, School of Education, University of North Carolina, 1970; "Vocational Rehabilitation in Public Schools," *High School Journal*, 1969; "Help for the Mentally Retarded Person," *North Carolina Education Journal*, 1967.

Joel Martin Levy: Program Director of the Young Adult Institute and Workshop, Inc. Previously Coordinator of the Institute's Residence and Alumni Supportive Programs. He did his undergraduate work in art education and psychology, and his graduate work in psychology at New York University. He was, for a number of years, a high school and college teacher and counselor. He has served as a consultant in rehabilitation to a number of agencies including Opengate, Inc., Somers, New York. In 1972, he was recipient of the National Rehabilitation Counseling Association's Elkins Rehabilitation Counselor of the Year Awards for the State of New York and the Northeast Region of the United States. He is a member of the Executive Board of the New York Metropolitan Rehabilitation Counseling Association, a branch of the National Rehabilitation Counseling Association, Treasurer of the New York Metropolitan Chapter of the National Rehabilitation Association, and an active member of several other professional organizations including the American Association on Mental Deficiency.

Philip Herman Levy: Coordinator of the Residence Program of the Young Adult Institute and Workshop, Inc. Previously, he was Assistant Coordinator of the Institute's Alumni Supportive Programs. Formerly Coordinator of the Metropolitan Young Adult Council of the New York Association for Brain Injured Children. Previously he had served as a group-worker and counselor in several of the Young Adult Institute's programs. He completed his undergraduate work Cum Laude with honors in psychology at Brooklyn College, City University of New York and is presently a doctoral student in Counseling Psychology at New York University. He is a member of the following professional organizations: The National Rehabilitation Association, National Rehabilitation Counseling Association, and the American Association on Mental Deficiency.

Steven Mathew Ross, Ph.D.: Chief, Drug Dependence Treatment Center, V.A. Hospital, Salt Lake City, Utah; Instructor, Department of Psychiatry, University of Utah Medical Center, Salt Lake City, Utah; Assistant Clinical Professor, Department of Psychology, University of Utah; Formerly, Program Supervisor, Behavior Modification Training Center, Salt Lake City, Utah and Staff Psychologist, V.A. Hospital, East Orange, New Jersey. Dr. Ross is very active in research which has led to a number of publications in psychological and psychologically oriented journals.

The following books have appeared thus far in the *Social and Rehabilitation Psychology Series*:

PREFACE

THIS BOOK represents an effort on the part of the contributors to offer a volume which is practical, realistic and oriented toward principles which have broad applicability in rehabilitation work with the mentally ill. The contributors are persons who have had considerable experience in the field of rehabilitation and mental health.

This book should be of considerable value to various mental health professionals who come from a variety of backgrounds. It should offer especially useful information to social workers, beginning psychologists, rehabilitation counselors, and others working in various environments with the mentally ill. The rehabilitation team is generally made up of hospital and rehabilitation agencies' staffs. It is usually composed of psychiatrists, rehabilitation counselors, social workers, psychologists, vocational evaluators, industrial therapists, nurses, instructors, and workshop personnel.

Rehabilitation of the mentally ill requires a very broad base spectrum of services. The role of rehabilitation has become increasingly important during the last decade. Generally, in vocational rehabilitation the process centers around the returning of the patient-client to work. The rehabilitation counselor becomes an important member of the treatment team which provides various services to the client in order that he can achieve adjustment to work according to his capabilities in terms of stress and physical endurance.

The rehabilitation team to some degree continues to follow the client when he becomes an out-patient. The trend toward the development of community base programs for the treatment and rehabilitation of the mentally ill makes the coordinating role of the rehabilitation counselor even more important in order that the client can stay in close contact with those team members whose services are so essential to his total rehabilitation. It is hoped that this book will provide additional clarification of various rehabilitation approaches effective for use with mentally ill persons.

RICHARD E. HARDY

JOHN G. CULL

Richmond, Virginia

CONTENTS

MODIFICATION OF
BEHAVIOR OF
THE MENTALLY ILL

CHAPTER I

WHAT IS MENTAL ILLNESS

THOMAS-ROBERT H. AMES *and* PHILIP H. LEVY

- INTRODUCTION
- SOCIETY'S PERSPECTIVE
- A PSYCHOSOCIAL PERSPECTIVE
- THE REHABILITATION PERSPECTIVE
- CONCLUSION
- REFERENCES

INTRODUCTION

WE ARE ON THE DOWNSIDE of the "Age of Anxiety." The tempo of life has increased to an almost unbearable pace. Although in past centuries, life was certainly not easy, often fraught with dangers and uncertainties, there was a stability, predictability and integrity which gave reassurance and support to the individual and the group in the struggle for a meaningful and satisfying life-style.

The twentieth century has added disruptive elements with such range and dimension that adjustment seems to have become more difficult: Wars disarrange personal, national and even international life patterns as never before; the population explosion has brought profound social tensions in its wake; racial prejudice, dire poverty and unreasoned discrimination breed despair and hatred; environmental pollution erodes and wastes the potential for life on earth; economic crises and technological changes cause social upheaval of mammoth proportions; and the urban social complex with its excessive competition, impersonal bureaucracy, high mobility, and impersonality enhances feelings of isolation, anxiety and disillusionment. Is it any wonder that maladjustment is our country's most serious health problem? In New York alone, the chronic mentally disabled population still accounts for approximately 76 percent of the total hospital census. (Weinstein and Patton, 1970).

So bleak a portrayal of the social condition is a distortion itself of not balanced by a recognition of the myriad positive developments in science, technology and the humanities which give promise for an enrichment of life and resolution of social problems through a more comprehensive understanding of how adequate adjustments are made.

Today, as our society is becoming progressively more complex and heterogeneous, it is extremely erroneous to accept simplistic definitions and labels. An understanding and acceptance of this is paramount to a comprehension of the present state of normality-abnormality, mental health-mental illness, adjustment-maladjustment. All of these concepts are subject to modification in relation to the transformations that society is experiencing. It is thus imperative that we emphatically reject the application of outmoded generalizations to the rich spectrum of individual human behavior. The clumping together of people's behaviors, problems and adjustments is as much a travesty as would be the viewing of Chopin, Dylan and the Beatles as merely music; or of roses, gardenias and orchids as merely flowers. Each is guilty of the egregious error of flagrant over-simplification. Society must view itself as "a tapestry in which individual lives provide the color and contrast." (Holme, 1972). It is peremptory that we accept persons as individuals, not X's and Y's— understanding being the integral part of this acceptance. The scope within this chapter, therefore, is aimed at this and is antithetical to a diagnosis → compartmentalization approach.

SOCIETY'S PERSPECTIVE

The popular view of mental illness is founded generally on the atypical and bizarre. The roots go deep into the past where misinformation, misconception, superstitions and unscientific descriptions abound. Ignorance and fears are still prime ingredients and are often promoted by the reporting style of the mass media.

Various elements in the popular view strongly retard change in society's response to maladaptive behavior: The misconception that there is a sharp differentiation between normal and abnormal behavior; the hereditary stigma attached to mental illness in the popular mind; the equating of genius and insanity; the idea that mental patients are incurable and dangerous; and the stigma of disgrace attached to mental disorders.

There is little understanding that generally the behavior of mentally disabled people, institutionalized or not, is virtually indistinguishable from that of so-called healthy, normal people; and both normal and abnormal behavior patterns are coping or adjustment devices used to meet the demands of one's life situation as one sees it.

The mental patient is also influenced in his view of himself by the popular view and the descriptive, diagnostic label applied by the helping professions. The mental patient is assigned a "sick role" and learns how to live up to the expectations implicit in the role of schizophrenic, drug addict, exhibitionist or mental retardate. The impact of the approved label is to foster a devaluation of one's self-concept and to mark oneself in all aspects of social interaction and opportunities for self-expression and achievement.

Who decides who is abnormal or mentally ill; and, further, what are the criteria they employ to arrive at such a conclusion? Merely because an individual displays peculiarities in behavior does not justify the appropriateness of labeling as mentally ill. Would this classification not imply organic damage or dysfunction and neglect the truth that a significant value judgment is involved? The cultural relativists would have us believe that "abnormality" should simply be viewed as deviations from the social norms of behavior. Much human difficulty not only arises from an inability to adapt to the norms of society, but also from the rigid structures imposed by society with which the individuals' life-styles are expected to be consonant. The statistical approach to abnormality considers only the frequency with which a particular behavior occurs—those behaviors exhibited by the majority being normal, and all minority behaviors rendered abnormal. This does not take into account the evaluation of what is desirable or undesirable, beneficial or deleterious, only what is most prevalent. An obvious area where the statistical approach would be inapplicable would be that of intelligence. Mental retardates are no more "abnormal" than geniuses, both being in the minority. Yet the terms certainly are viewed differently and connote definite value judgments. An individual would definitely aspire to one and seek to avoid the other. Thus conformity is being stressed in both the cultural relativist's view and the statistical approach. It is of interest to ponder whether neuroses will not shortly be viewed, in accordance with these theoretical constructs, as normal as the reported rate if incidence increases. The medical model traditionally views health as the absence of symptoms or pathogens. It equates mental pathology with physical pathology, hence giving rise to the concept of mental illness for which medical treatment techniques, parallel to those used in treatment of physical pathology, must be devised and utilized, such as shock therapy and chemotherapy. The concept of illness or referring to an individual as a patient purports a biological deficiency or impairment. The question then arises "For whose benefit are these classifications pronounced?" For too long we have accepted the notion that we diagnose and label for the therapeutic welfare of the maladaptive individual. Is it not true that out of an inability to cope with these individuals, we have created counselors, therapists and a variety of other practitioners to whom we have assigned the goal of alleviating mental disorder; but are they not, in reality, rendered powerless to do so, by pressuring the congruence with norms as the underlying desire, while presenting them with an all-permeating role of "protector of society from those feared deviants?" There is a strong body of opinion in the mental health field that most patients remain hospitalized for extended periods because appropriate alternative treatment plans are unavailable.

An example of the dangers inherent in current diagnostic procedures is provided by a recent experiment conducted by Dr. David L. Rosenhan in which eight "normal" individuals feigned mental illness in order to gain admission to various mental hospitals. After admission, they behaved "normally" and attempted to convince the medical personnel of their mental health to no avail. The personnel of the twelve hospitals involved did not detect the experiment and often viewed the pseudo-patients' efforts as symptomatic of the imagined illnesses which had been diagnosed.

A PSYCHOSOCIAL PERSPECTIVE

There is a viable alternative to the previously professed theories, that being the need for the term *maladjustment* superseding the use of sick or abnormal; and the recognition and acceptance of normal or adaptive behavior being that which contributes to the growth and fulfillment of the individual and the group. Behavior is only maladjustive when it does not achieve these essential components of mental health. We do not intend to deny the existence of an overlap between the tenets of the cultural relativists and ourselves in recognizing that some behavior which is not consistent with the norms of society is also maladjustive, but we completely disagree with any postulate suggesting that all behavior that is not consonant with society's mores and norms is maladjustive. Careful consideration must be given to the possibility of certain behaviors required or accepted by society as normal or abnormal, and even whole groups or cultures being considered as maladjusted. One can be sure that by this we do not suggest an upheaval of all present cultures, but only an analysis of what has been accepted blindly. Behavior must be congruent only with reality.

An illustration of the need to rethink what is accepted as abnormal or normal behavior was reported by the *New York Times* in its February 9, 1973, issue. So conservative a professional group as the American Psychiatric Association is now struggling with the need to modify some of its concepts of mental disorders. The reported instance is that of the A. P. A. Committee on Nomenclature seriously considering a recommendation that homosexuality be eliminated as a sexual deviation in the Association's *Diagnostic and Statistical Manual of Mental Disorders.*

The psychosocial view to which we adhere is based upon several theoretical constructs: the major ones being *Gestalt psychology, existential psychology, self-theory,* and *behaviorism.*

Gestaltists believe that it is essential that man understand that he is unique and accept this uniqueness. The theory sees man as having the ability to be himself and the responsibility to accept whatever the consequences may be. Man is envisioned as being capable of realizing his greatest potential if he so desires.

In most instances man's destiny is self-determined. Man must work to achieve individuality; then, once realized, he must accept himself as he is and others as they are, accepting the inevitable disparity. Thus mental health is not contingent upon conformity, but upon the realization of as close to 100 percent of man's potential as possible. The achievement of manhood is an ongoing, dynamic and evolutionary process which pervades the individual's lifetime growth.

The overriding sovereign principle of growth in Gestalt theory is that there is a desire in each person to grow, to push, to develop from a lower, diffuse, undifferentiated organism, dependent upon others for satisfaction of all needs, to an integrated, self-actualized person. Perls (1971) states that "the process of maturation is the transformation from environmental support to self-support (the utilization of inner resources)."

Gestalt theory is not naive enough to view man as living in a vacuum; rather central to their theory of personality is the notion that the individual is imbedded in a larger context (his environment), ". . . man is not considered as an isolated animal. All contact that man has is creative adjustment of the organism and environment." (Perls, 1971). Man's formation of dependence upon his environment for support, rather than on himself, yields the development of "character—a rigid, fixed way of responding to the world." (Perls, 1971). The greater the magnitude of character, the less potential one is able to utilize. These preconceived, conformist behavior patterns do not facilitate mental health due to the movement away from individuality and self-actualization. Change, as well as progress towards mental health, takes place only "if one takes the time and effort to be what he is." (Kagen and Shephard, 1971). This will counteract the precipitating forces of neurosis, which are a great number of unfinished situations. Change occurs when one becomes what he is, the abandonment of his ego ideal in favor of self-acceptance, self-expression, assimilation and the ability to extend awareness to the averbal level.

Self-theory, as professed by Rogers, stresses the flexibility and capability of the individual. Rogers also believes that man is basically a positive creature. He sees from his own experience that people have a basically positive direction and that when they are accepted, they move in certain directions—they are constructive, moving toward self-actualization, growing toward maturity socialization.

The difficulty, according to Jourard, commences with man's attempts to conceal his real self behind a mask. People hide their true feelings in an attempt to avoid criticism or rejection, but inasmuch as this concealment is universally practiced, our view of others is based on partial understanding and is consequently false. This results in individuals living in a world of strangers with little understanding of others' actions. The major difficulty is that man is unfortunately unique in his capability of being one thing while seeming, from his actions, to be something else. "Man can attain health and fullest development only if he can be himself with others and find goals with meaning." (Jourard, 1971).

The decision to disclose ourselves or to be secretive is a very important one, since mutual ignorance is the root of many problems between groups as small as families or as large as nations. A person will permit himself to be known if he believes his audience consists of men of goodwill. Self-disclosure follows from an attitude of love. Healthy personalities display ability to make themselves fully known to other healthy persons. A person's self grows from being known, as people stop growing when they repress themselves. A maladjusted person struggles to avoid becoming known by another person. This causes a stress which produces patterns of an unhealthy personality and a variety of physical ills. Hope, purpose and a meaning for life produce a state of health. Demoralization by events leads to ills. Those events, relationships or transactions which give people a sense of identity, worth or hope and a purpose for existence are inspiriting; while those that make a person feel unimportant, worthless, hopeless, low in self-esteem, and isolated in their existence are dispiriting.

Self-theorists view normal behavior in the form of conforming to usual social patterns, as yielding social acceptability, status defense, minimal gratification of body needs, and occasional illness. "Normal" people seldom know great joy or enthusiasm while seldom producing very much. Other important aspects of mental health are healthy interpersonal behavior and a willingness to be known (self-disclosure).

Existential philosophy, as expressed by Kirkegaard, desires for men to come to an understanding of their souls and their destiny. This, as do self-theorists and Gestalt points of view, emphasizes the need for individuality and a thorough understanding of one's self. The existential view of death is consistent with the need for individual appraisal, as opposed to generalization and labeling. Heidegger states that the authentic meaning of death—"I am to die"—is not an external and public fact within the world, but is an internal possibility of one's own Being. (Barrett, 1962). Each person has to die and suffer his death for himself; no one else can die for him. Heidegger states that only when one takes death *into* himself, does an authentic existence become possible for that person.

Sartre denies that there are any fixed or external values for man. Man is free, but this leads to grave responsibility. Man can become what he wills and works for. The mature man is the man who is courageous enough to realize that man is what he makes himself.

May recognizes the world as a structure of meaningful relationships in which a person exists and in the design of which he participates.

Horney believes that neurotic conflicts (maladjustive behavior patterns) begin when we are children, not suddenly:

> Why not help children deal with these conflicts before they become neurotic trends? I would suggest compulsory and comprehensive group counseling throughout the child's school life in order to have children share similar problems and learn the dynamics of their conflicts as well as methods of appropriate responses. This is an alternative to waiting for the overt manifestation of the neurotic conflict. Self-awareness could have individuals increase their understanding of themselves and their environment. (Levy, 1973).

Behaviorists reject not only the classification system of pathological behaviors, but other diagnoses in which operational definitions cannot be given in behavioral terms. Categories such as "aggression," "anxiety" and "fear," unless operationally defined, are useless labels. Behavioral counseling has its goals formulated in terms of greater insight, self-understanding and self-organization. Most significant though is the realization that individual needs must be considered paramount, while labeling and classification are to be avoided.

The unifying factor relating to the four previous theories is the emphatic conviction that evaluation ought to be based upon the consideration of what promotes the individual's well-being and that of his society. The optimism engendered in such a perspective impels us to consider the client's potential for self-actualization.

THE REHABILITATION PERSPECTIVE

Over the past fifty odd years the process of rehabilitation has been applied first to the physically disabled and more belatedly and grudgingly, in recent time, to the mentally and/or socially disabled (always, however, within a vocational or occupational context). No doubt the frame of reference has been the *work ethic* and the restoration of one's sense of adequacy and improved self-concept measured by the ability one demonstrates in vocational adjustment.

To the traditional elements of determining feasibility for services, vocational planning and counseling, coordination of rehabilitation services, selective job placement, and short-term follow-up with case closure as rehabilitated, there must be modifications made and other elements added if the rehabilitation process is to adequately meet the needs of the mentally disabled. The emphasis on exclusion of those not fitting a narrow and rigid set of feasibility criteria must be replaced by a focus on the individual's potential as a human being. The centralized office as the locus for dispensing services must give way to a concept of "out-reach" which brings services within easy access of clients within their own communities. Vocational planning and counseling must be enlarged to cover the client's life-style and life adjustment. Work should not be the only valid rehabilitation goal. As the client reenters the mainstream of community life, various transitional services can facilitate adjustment. For some, supportive services may be requisite in helping maintain adjustment. Follow-up needs to be broadened to allow for periodic evaluation, and the development of "community resources centers" where clients can avail themselves of requisite services such as developmental counseling and preventive counseling as well as the transitional and supportive services mentioned above.

Life adjustment implies ongoing growth and change. Our perspective of rehabilitation must evolve into a more dynamic concept and be viewed as open-ended. The goal will then cease to be satisfactory performance of a particular job and emphasize the total rehabilitation of the individual.

CONCLUSION

In this chapter we have tried to suggest a broader, more functional concept of the various maladjustment problems which plague mankind than is conveyed by that of mental illness.

We have proposed a psychosocial view of adjustment and malad-justment based on elements of various current psychosocial models. We accept the idea that human behavior can be viewed as a con-tinuum from very well adjusted at one extreme to very maladjusted at the opposite extreme.

The emphasis, in both our treatment of the maladjusted or mental-ly disabled and the rehabilitation process, must be focused on the development of adjustment skills and the provision of a variety of services which will promote their well-being and that of society. It is our contention that in the past there has been an overemphasis placed upon the welfare of society to the neglect of the individual. We hope this imbalance can be redressed.

REFERENCES

Adams, Henry B.: Mental illness or interpersonal behavior? *American Psychologist, 19*:191-197, 1964.

Allport, Gordon: *Pattern and Growth in Personality.* New York, HR&W, 1961.

Ames, Thomas-Robert H.: Training and supportive services for the mentally handicapped adult. Unpublished manuscript presented before the California chapter of the American Schizophrenia Foundation, Oakland, California, November, 1968.

Barrett, W.: *What Is Existentialism?* New York, Grove, 1964.

Bloom, Jean L.: The severely emotionally disturbed child. In Roucek, Joseph S. (Ed.): *The Difficult Child.* New York, Philos Lib, 1963, pp. 170-190.

Cantril, H.: A fresh look at the human design. In Bugental, J. F. T. (Ed.): *Challenges of Humanistic Psychology.* New York, McGraw, 1967, pp. 13-20.

Carson, R.: *Interaction Concepts of Personality.* Chicago, Aldine, 1969.

Combs, Arthur W., Avila, Donald L., and Purkey, William W.: *Helping Relationships: Basic Concepts for the Helping Professions.* Boston, Allyn & Bacon, 1971.

Holme, Richard: Preface. *Abnormal Psychology Current Perspectives.* Del Mar, California, Communications Research Machines, Inc., 1972.

Jahoda, M.: *Current Concepts of Positive Mental Health.* New York, Basic Books, 1958.

Jourard, Sidney: *The Transparent Self.* New York, Van N-Rein, 1971.

Kagen, Joen, and Shepherd, Irma: *Gestalt Therapy Now.* New York, Har-Row Colophon Books, 1971.

Kaplan, A.: A philosophical discussion of normality. *Archives of General Psychiatry, 17*:325-330, 1967.

Kanfer, Frederick H., and Saslow, George: Behavioral analysis: an alternative to diagnostic classification. *Archives of General Psychiatry, 12*:529-538, 1965.

Kaufman, Walter: *Existentialism from Dostoevsky to Sartre.* New York, Mer. World Pub, 1956.

Keil, Ellsworth D.: Follow-up programs for emotionally restored patients: Some issues and considerations. *Journal of Rehabilitation, 36*:32-42, May-June, 1970.

Kelly, G. A.: Psychology of personal constructs. In (Ed.): *Clinical Diagnosis and Psychotherapy,* New York, Norton, 1965, vol. II.

Kromboltz, J. D., and Thorensen, C. E.: *Behavioral Counseling: Cases and Techniques.* New York, HR&W, 1969.

Levine, Murray, and Levine, Adeline: The climate of change. In Levine, M., and Levine, A. (Ed.): *A Social History of Helping Services: Clinic, Court, School and Community.* New York, Appleton, 1970, pp. 11-21.

Levy, Philip H.: A critique of Horney's theory of neurosis. *American Journal of Psychoanalysis,* publication pending.

MacLeech, Bert: A forward looking concept in rehabilitation. In MacLeech, Bert, and Schroder, Donald R. (Eds.): *Seventh Annual Distinguished Lecture Series in Special Education and Rehabilitation.* Los Angeles, U. of S. Cal. Press, 1969, pp. 19-30.

May, Rollo: *Existence.* New York, S&S, 1958.

Milgram, Norman A.: M. R. and mental illness: A proposal for conceptual unity. *Mental Retardation, 10*:29-31, December, 1972.

Mosher, Loren R., and Feinsilver, David,: *Special Report: Schizophrenia.* Rockville, Center for Studies of Schizophrenia, National Institute of Mental Health, 1971.

Opler, Marvin K.: Schizophrenia and culture. *Scientific American,* August, 1957, pp. 3-7.

Patry, Frederick L.: Mental health: What is it; how to hold on to it. *Journal of Rehabilitation, 29*:19, July-August, 1963.

Paul, Norman L.: Helping the mentally ill: Failure and progress. *Journal of Rehabilitation, 29*:43-44, March-April, 1963.

Perls, Frederick S.: *Gestalt Therapy Verbation.* Lafayette, Bantam (by arrangement with Real People Press), 1971.

Reiff, Robert, and Scribner, Sylvia: Rehabilitation and community mental health: Employability and disability issues. *Journal of Rehabilitation, 36*:11-15, May-June, 1970.

Rensberger, Boyce: Psychiatry reconsiders stand on homosexuals. *New York Times,* February 9, 1973.

Roe, Ann: Community resources centers. *American Psychologist, 25*:1033-1040, 1970.

Rogers, Carl: *On Becoming a Person.* Boston, HM, 1961.

Rosenhan, D. L.: On being sane in insane places. *Science, 179*:250-258, January 19, 1973.

Szasz, Thomas S.: The myth of mental illness. *American Psychologist, 15*:
113-118, 1960.

Weinstein, Abbott S., and Patton, Robert E.: Trends in chronicity in the
New York State Mental Hospitals. *American Journal of Public Health,
60*:1071-1080, June, 1970.

Wylie, Ruth C.: The present status of self-theory. In Borgatta, Edgar F.,
and Lamber, William (Eds.): *Handbook of Personality Theory and
Research.* Chicago, Rand, 1968, pp. 728-787.

Zax, Melvin: Recent innovations in dealing with mental health problems in
the U.S.A. *Dansk Psykolognyt, 18*:3-7, 1967.

CHAPTER II

THE USE OF BEHAVIOR MODIFICATION TECHNIQUES WITH THE MENTALLY ILL

DeLoss D. Friesen

■ Introduction
■ Basic Ideas of Behavior Principles
■ Setting Up the Behavior Modification Program
■ Philosophical Objections to Behavior Modification
■ Suggested Reading

INTRODUCTION

A FEW SHORT YEARS AGO the mention of behavior modification divided people fairly sharply into two camps: for or against. Those trained in, or at least introduced to, a psychodynamic or phenomenological explanation of the human personality were usually opposed to manipulating the patient's behavior. On the other hand, the person embracing learning theory as the better explanation of human behavior (according to the medical or disease model) was usually comfortable with behavior modification.

Behavior modification is a process through which human behavior is altered directly by rewarding desired behavior and not rewarding unwanted behavior. This approach is based on the notion that behavior which is rewarded will increase and behavior which is not rewarded will decrease.

Behavior is the effect or the result of some deeper process or illness. Therefore, treatment of the behavior alone is superficial. When behavior is maladaptive it is often considered to be a symptom of some deeper problem. The medical model indicates that an attempt to cure a problem by changing the superficial behavior is analogous to an attempt to cure a brain tumor by treating the patient's headache, and is perhaps fraught with as much danger. Even if not dangerous, treating the symptom without dealing with the root cause may prove to be fruitless. The medical model further argues that since the root cause is not removed, a second symptom would take the place of the first. Therefore any attempt to change behavior directly is at best a waste of time due to the patient's substituting one symptom for another and is at worst dangerous. Using this premise, many workers in the mental health field have not used the technique of behavorial modification.

Other behavioral scientists feel that the medical model, while appropriate for most of medicine and for those psychological problems that are clearly organic in nature, does not fully explain the psychology of man. Such behavioral scientists believe that man learns his behavior whether it is a skill like tennis or a psychotic behavior such as pulling out all of one's hair. If behavior is learned rather than caused from some deep source, then it can be unlearned and some new more appropriate behaviors can be acquired.

Many mental health professionals attempt to resolve the conflict between the psychodynamic purist and the learning theory purist by using multiple treatment approaches. Severe psychotic symptoms respond to major tranquilizers; hassles in the family are reduced by family therapy, with traditional counseling and psychotherapy producing insight, more mature problem solving and changes, and clarification of values and attitudes.

It is true that as the patient's overt psychotic symptoms are brought under control by medication, his family starts to understand him better through family therapy and he understands himself better because of psychotherapy—then his behavior begins to improve. But the behavior has not changed enough. In other situations the patient's behavior itself is such a problem that other forms of treatment cannot be successfully employed. Some psychoanalytically oriented psychiatrists are using behavior modification to reduce the severity of symptoms so that regular analytical therapy can be effective. Modifying the behavior of patients is seen more and more as an important part of the treatment package, whether used with other treatment modalities or separately.

Some patients, particularly the mentally retarded or those institutionalized for many years, have not responded well to treatments other than chemotherapy. Chemotherapy may reduce agitation or decrease hallucinatory behavior, but no drug has been discovered which increases politeness, coming to work on time, responsibility, or personal cleanliness. Behavior modification techniques may not increase the I.Q. or decrease strange ideations, but if the patient's speech, dress and manners become more appropriate, his probability of surviving outside the hospital is surely increased.

Behavior modification works! It does change behavior, but it takes some continual effort on the part of everyone who interacts with the patient: staff, family, employer, etc. Suppose, for example, that patient H.J. has had a psychotic break and now is recovering. H.J. does not dress neatly and lacks personal hygiene. His shirt is not tucked in or buttoned, his fly is unzipped, and often he reeks of urine. Even when all the psychotic symptoms subside, he is not welcome in many homes or in places of employment. But the staff develops a rather complex program and in a few weeks has shaped his behavior to where he is now acceptably neat before breakfast (he may earn his breakfast by neatly dressing himself), does fairly well in the workshop working on a repackaging subcontract, and comes back to the ward to be praised for his neatness. In the evening he is able to spend some of his points at the canteen that he has earned during the day for being careful whenever he urinated. His progress is being maintained by verbal praise and spendable points from the staff.

Contrast the patient H.J. to a normally developing small boy who has personal hygiene problems with unzipped pants, polo shirt on backwards, and is careless while urinating. He learns just the same way as H.J. The boy gets reinforced positively: rewarded for good behavior and punished for bad behavior. The difference between H.J. and the little boy is that little boys grow up. They develop an internal system of reinforcement. The little boy turned young man wants to be appropriately clean because he feels better that way and people respond more positively to him. No one praises a young man for having his shirt tucked in or for not having body odor, but subtle reinforcers in the environment plus internal feelings maintain the behavior. Unfortunately this is not so for many of the H.J.'s. If H.J. is moved to a board and room home staffed with those who do not use or understand the principles of behavior modification, his behavior may quickly revert back to its original state. This illustration cautions the user of behavior modification techniques to remember that behavior must be reinforced for it to continue to occur. If a patient's behavior is successfully shaped in a hospital environment but reverts to its original state when the patient returns to the family environment, the conclusion is not that behavior modification is ineffective but rather that the patient's behavior was not sustained by his environment. It does little good to use staff time to alter the behavior of a patient if it is known that the environment to which the patient will return is dedicated, even unintentionally, to keeping the patient ill.

BASIC IDEAS OF BEHAVIOR PRINCIPLES

Two similar schools of psychological thought have influenced greatly the psychotheropeutic world: the works of Ivan Pavlov and B. F. Skinner. Pavlov's system, called classical conditioning, holds that learning takes place by the associating of a new stimulus to an already established stimulus response pair.

Classical Conditioning

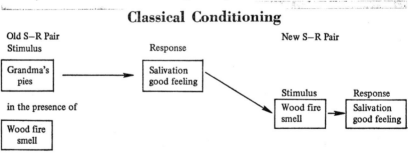

Figure II-1

The response to the pies is a natural one. After eating grandma's pies several times in the presence of the wood fire odor, the wood fire takes on the capability of producing some of the same kind of sensations as when the pies are present. You can imagine an adult with this background frequently enjoying a fire in the fireplace. Another example:

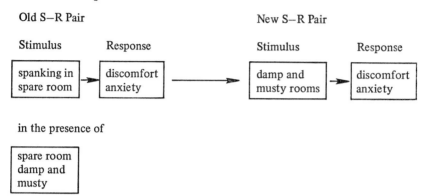

Figure II-2

This kind of association is very common. Phobias seem to be explained very well by this classical model. We tend to remember an event such as a severe spanking, but we forget the other cues that were present. Phobias often seem to be unexplained because we have been trained to look for symbolic meaning when, in fact, the explanation may be simple association, a case of classical conditioning.

Operant Conditioning

The second system, even more widely used as a theoretical base for behavior modification is Skinnerian, or operant, conditioning. Operant conditioning uses a slightly different model. Instead of a stimulus followed by a response, operant conditioning posits a response which is followed by a reinforcement.

As examples: (*See Figure II-3 on next page*)

The operant approach does not ignore the stimulus but concentrates on the response and the reinforcement of that response. There are many factors which affect the rate at which one acquires learning using the response → reinforcement model.

The most general concept of operant conditioning is that *behavior which is rewarded or reinforced is likely to occur again*. A puppy which is purposefully ignored each time he whines soon emits a low level of whining behavior, but a puppy which is given

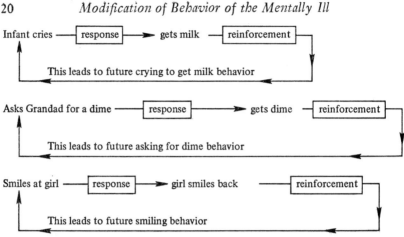

Figure II-3

attention (reinforcement) through food, petting or even mild scolding continues or increases whining behavior. Behavior must be reinforced to occur repeatedly and on cue. Politeness, personal hygiene, work habits, punctuality, etc. are all behaviors which must be reinforced to occur consistently.

A second concept states that *the more quickly a behavioral response is reinforced the more likely the future occurrence of that behavior*. It is far more effective to praise a patient for having made his bed immediately upon completion of the task than to do it at the end of the day. A week later has almost no effect on future bed making. This is a difficult problem to manage in behavior modification programming. Immediate reinforcement does not occur after rounds, or at morning or evening reports, or meals, or after Mrs. Brown is restrained, or after inventory is finished. And yet there are times when nurses, psychiatric technicians, social workers and rehab counselors cannot take the time to properly administer immediate reinforcement.

It is also important that staff be aware of the effects of inconsistent reinforcement. If cleaning a ward or workshop for inspection takes precedence over reinforcing some newly emerging positive behavior of a patient, then the staff clearly finds the approval of the administration more reinforcing than the progress of a patient. There will be situations, of course, which demand action, but the staff should be aware of the results of their behavior and behave in the direction with the most positive outcomes.

Points to Remember in using Behavior Modification
Know What the Reinforcers for Your Patients Are

Most people respond to primary reinforcers such as food with the result of nicknaming behavior modification the "M&M Therapy." For many adults snack type foods such as potato chips and pretzels have value as reinforcers. Tobacco is frequently used. Alcohol, where legal for treatment purposes, is an effective reinforcer. Many behaviors improve with the anticipation of a couple of short beers at the 5 p.m. ward bar. Some treatment facilities have constructed questionnaires which list a large number of items with potential reinforcement value. The patient then identifies those items which he would like to enjoy. While this approach has usefulness, it is often inaccurate. Patients may mark items as reinforcers which they care nothing about and omit ones they do care about. The best method for identifying reinforcers is to observe the patient. Things that the staff does not consider reinforcing may be powerfully reinforcing for the patient. For one patient to sit in a certain chair, watch a particular TV show, go for a walk, or have a nap may be reinforcing while a cigarette, a movie or ice cream is reinforcing to another patient. Some tasks, such as work, are drudgery to be endured by one person but pure pleasure for a different person.

The Power of Any Reinforcer Varies

Satiation and fatigue also influence the potency of reinforcers. Many favorite foods have high reinforcement value because they are available infrequently. The Christmas plum pudding would lose much of its reinforcement value if it were served many times during the year. Even patients who like ice cream would grow tired of ice cream if given it ten or twelve times each day. If you are very tired, a long walk is not appealing regardless of your desire for walks. If a patient has just had a big meal, a candy bar loses much of its power to reinforce. It is important for the mental health worker to have several items, tasks or privileges available as reinforcers. By varying the reinforcers the patient will retain a high interest in the program. A common complaint regarding staffs operating behavior modification programs is that the reward works and the patient improves, but then the patient gets worse. Usually the patient has grown tired or lost interest in the reinforcer.

PRIMARY AND SECONDARY REINFORCERS: With more normal patients, both in terms of symptoms and intellectual functioning, a secondary reinforcer differs from a primary reinforcer in that a secondary reinforcer is learned and is often symbolic and irrelevant. A primary reinforcer is immediate and direct. For example, a patient makes his bed so he can have a piece of candy or has worked well at the bench for two hours to earn a cup of coffee. Money is a good example of secondary reinforcement—one does 50 units of work to earn $5.00. Secondary reinforcement can be immediate, but it is not direct. One cannot eat $5.00, but it can be exchanged for something edible. Money, poker chips, stars on a chart, punches on a card, or tokens are all examples of this kind of secondary reinforcement. This economy system is discussed more fully later.

Secondary reinforcement has several very positive aspects as a therapeutic tool. It allows the mental health worker to reinforce desirable behavior immediately without having to be a walking general store. Because the tokens or chips are cashed in for something reinforcing, the patient usually has a variety of reinforcers to choose from, hence he may vary the reinforcer. If he tires of soda pop, he may buy a game of pool. The most important long-range aspect of secondary reinforcement (in some forms referred to as a token economy) is its normalizing effect. It allows the patient to get an immediate symbolic reward while training him to delay immediate gratification. Decisions must be made whether to buy candy and soda pop today or to save for a week and go out for pizza and beer. The concepts of working for a paycheck and then budgeting one's money are concepts which can be more easily taught within the structure of a token economy.

THE USE OF SOCIAL REINFORCEMENT: Another type of reward is social reinforcement. Praise, greetings and salutations, smiles, affectionate behaviors, touching, and other verbal and non-verbal events are social reinforcers. They are learned reinforcers rather than natural reinforcers like food. Using Pavlov's model, a baby learns to associate the mother's smile with milk. Later, the mother's smile procides pleasure without the milk being present. Still later, through a process called stimulus generalization, a smile from any valued person will give pleasure. Social reinforcers are very important in that almost everyone can learn to respond to attention from others. The problem with some psychiatric patients, especially those from deprived environments, is that they have not learned to respond positively to positive attention. These patients can be taught to respond to social reinforcers by pairing praise, attention, smiles, etc. with such primitive reinforcers as food.

Schedules of Reinforcement

While behavior must be reinforced to assure its re-occurrence, this does not mean that an act should always be reinforced every time. Let us first consider continual reinforcement. *To become learned, a newly emitted behavior should be reinforced continuously.* If a chronically depressed patient is observed smiling, the smile is to be reinforced immediately and every time it occurs. It is important for the patient to associate the response (smiling) with the reward. If the behavior emitted is only occasionally reinforced, the organism will not make any association between the reward and the desired behavior. Once the person makes the response-reinforcement association, the behavior will continue at a high rate (if the reinforcer retains its potency). If, for example, ward and sheltered workshop personnel working together on Mary's smiling behavior have reinforced her continuously, she will be smiling at a high rate. But if she goes home for a weekend where no one reinforces her smiling, her smiling behavior will decrease to about zero when she returns. This process of a once learned behavior decreasing to near zero is called *extinction*. While the fastest way to learn a new behavior is to have that behavior reinforced every time it is emitted; continuously reinforced behavior also extinguishes rapidly. It has been found that when established behavior is maintained on an intermittent reinforcement schedule, the behavior will continue long after reinforcement ceases. Fishermen, for example, have been known to continue to fish many hours or even days without reinforcement. The task in designing a schedule of reinforcement is really two-fold: using continuous reinforcement to establish the behavior, then switching gradually to intermittent reinforcement to make the behavior more resistant to extinction. John's coming to work on time has been reinforced every time it occurs and John has been on time the last nine out of ten mornings. On the 11th morning his punctuality is not reinforced and he may or may not be on time the 12th day. The next day, if he is present on time, reinforce him to re-establish the desired behavior. Reinforce for several days and then skip a day or two. The reason for switching to an intermittent schedule where reinforcement is given on an irregular basis is not to do away with the necessity of reinforcement, but to decrease the necessity for continuous reward. This is normalizing in that while the real world is based on rewards, tangible or intangible, rewards are not handed out every time a behavior is emitted. Every smile is not responded to and few people will comment on pressed pants or shined shoes. There must be a minimal amount of reinforcement to maintain behavior; otherwise people would not fall out of love, change political parties, or find new friends.

Shaping Appropriate Behavior

Sometimes a behavior is desired that is not being performed by the patient. It is possible, by operant conditioning, to produce a behavior which is currently not in the person's behavioral repertoire. *Successive approximation is a method to bring behavior closer and closer to the desired pattern through a series of progressive steps, each made possible by selectively reinforcing certain responses and*

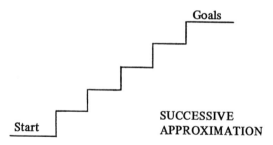

Figure II-4

not others. Thus responses which are closer approximations to the goal are reinforced and all other responses are not reinforced. Successive approximation is used in teaching any skill, from combing hair to skiing or piano playing.

Suppose that Jane has not learned to comb her hair but appears to possess the motor and intellectual skills necessary to do so. Let us further suppose that Jane likes corn chips and can hold the comb. The task now is to shape her behavior through successive approximation. First, reward her with the corn chips and praise only when she holds the comb with the teeth pointing down. After that behavior is well established (repeatedly reinforced) move on to the second step: reinforce her only if the comb is brought within eighteen inches of her head. At first she will be confused, as she is accustomed to being reinforced every time; but it will not take many attempts, and she can be reinforced. If eighteen inches is too difficult a step for her, make the goal easier. When she consistently brings the comb closer to her head, move to the next step: shape bringing the comb closer, perhaps moving from eighteen inches to twelve inches then to six inches and finally to touch the hair. The last steps will be to move the comb into the hair, learn to comb in the right direction, and to learn to style her own hair. These last steps may take as many as ten to twenty discrete steps.

While it is possible to teach Jane to comb her hair through shaping alone, it would make it much easier if the process of combing hair were demonstrated or modeled for her. *Modeling is observational learning.* Imitative behavior through modeling is an excellent shortcut to acquiring new behavioral skills.

Positive or Negative Reinforcement and Punishment

Behavior is also learned through negative reinforcement as well as positive reinforcement. Positive reinforcement involves a reward, whereas negative reinforcement is the avoidance or termination of a painful or annoying stimulus. Swatting a fly is an example of negative reinforcement. The response of swatting is reinforced by the cessation of the buzzing. Paying attention to an unruly patient so he will quiet down is also negatively reinforcing for you. The problem is that your behavior is positively reinforcing for the unruly patient, for he has learned that the best way to get your attention is to be unruly.

Punishment is not negative reinforcement because there is nothing reinforcing about punishment in itself. *Punishment does not change behavior, but merely suppresses it temporarily.* Punishment teaches the subject to avoid getting caught rather than teaching behavior change. Instead of using punishment to control undesirable behavior, it is much better to reward positive behavior. Rather than to punish swearing behavior on the ward, it is much better to reward positive conversation. Another problem in using punishment is that it must be given by someone. If a patient is desiring attention, a verbal tongue lashing may be highly reinforcing. Most people would rather be given negative attention than to be ignored. If punishment must be used to prevent a dangerous behavior from occurring, it should be done as quickly and with as little personal contact as possible. Fifteen minutes in a stimulus free, quiet room would have fewer negative results than a ten minute lecture or being belted to a chair in a public day room.

One type of problem frequently seen by the family of mental patients is inappropriate social and personal behavior. Greeting everyone that walks into the canteen may not seem strange to the hospital staff, but the same behavior at the local dime store will earn a phone call to the ward. The ward is often seen as one big, happy family with every patient, except the withdrawn ones, knowing everyone else's business. This behavior may be functional for those people who will be spending the rest of their lives in the hospital setting, but it is not functional for those who are planning to leave. A method similar to shaping and successive approximation is discrimination learning. This is a high level process which tells us that behaviors are appropriate only in context. When a staff is getting ready to move a patient slowly from the ward into the community, it is very useful to observe the patient in a workshop setting or at home or on a shopping trip. With the contextual cues altered, the patient's behavior can more clearly be judged appropriate or inappropriate. Then the process of discrimination can be taught, but it usually is necessary to involve in the learning process the mental health professional who is in the intermediate phases of rehabilitation. Behavior must be shaped and reinforced in the setting where it occurs as well as back on the ward.

SETTING UP THE BEHAVIOR MODIFICATION PROGRAM

There are four simple points which serve to outline the behavior modification program. The acronym PAIR is spelled from (1) problem, (2) antecedents, (3) intervention and (4) results.

The first task is to scientifically define the *problem*. What exactly is the behavior in question? Not only what is the behavior, but when and how frequently must be asked as well. Behavior is lawful and occurs for a reason. The knowledge of when and how much behavior, along with other events in the environment, can be used to find the cause for negative behavior. It is important to know how much behavior because (1) the patient may be really emitting the behavior less than you think; (2) he may be doing more; and (3) his average rate must be known to determine the effectiveness of your intervention.

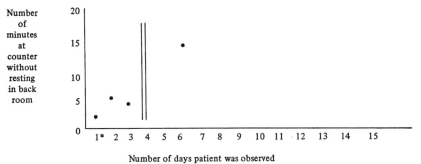

Number of days patient was observed
*Mean number of minutes from three daily observations.

Figure II-5

Let us suppose that Mary is staying at a halfway house and is working at a coffee shop run by the house. Mary has trouble with "nervous spells" and must go to the back of the room for a rest. She works a 4½ hour shift and gets a ten minute break after each 1½ hour period. It was decided to observe Mary three times each day, twenty minutes each at the beginning of the shift and after each break period. The problem is being able to work at the counter. The graph shows an average time at the counter of two minutes the first day, five minutes the second, and four minutes the third. Mary was able to stay at her work station less than five minutes on each trial.

The second letter in PAIR represents *antecedents*. In this situation antecedents are those events which have occurred just prior to and immediately after the client's inappropriate behavior. This takes more observation. Having the patient keep records if he is able to or at least tell you verbally contributes to your data. It is important to know what has happened in the environment or at least what the patient thinks has happened. In our example, Mary was watched both at her work station and in the back room. The following things were observed: (1) Mary had very poor eye contact and never smiled at the customer; (2) the customers often stared at her; (3) Mary reported that the customers were sending evil thoughts into her mind; (4) Mary was worse after a very blatant staring; (5) Mary always laid on the cot in the back room; and (6) Mary complained to the other girls about her problem, and they conforted her.

The third letter in PAIR stands for *intervention*. The strategy for intervention is determined by the data collected in the first two steps. It appears that the customers stare at Mary because she appears to be so frightened. This staring makes her even more frightened. She enjoys the back room as she gets to lay down and she gets attention. She likes the break time also. With this information a program is set up to modify her behavior. The conditions are now (1) for every customer she looks at when taking the order or smiles at just once she gets a tip (poker chip) worth one minute extra break time; (2) the cot is removed; (3) if she leaves the counter because of nervousness she goes to the storeroom and sits where no one can listen to her story; and (4) break periods can be taken in the back room with the other girls where it is permissible to visit. Along with this the coffee shop manager observes any behavior Mary emits while with a customer or other employees. Whenever she does something positive, he immediately reinforces her for what, however small, she does. This helps her calm down after dealing with a particularly obnoxious customer. The task now is to follow through on the strategy and to record the patient's progress and any other data that would be useful.

The fourth letter in PAIR represents *results*. Now look at the progress and evaluate where to go from here.

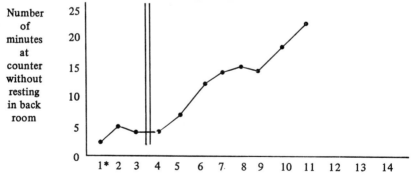

Number of minutes at counter without resting in back room

Number of days patient was observed

*Mean number of minutes from three daily observations.

Figure II-6

It appears that the strategy works. The reinforcements seem appropriate for shaping new behavior, and the settings that were reinforcing inappropriate behavior have largely been removed. The scientist may want to know what part of the program was responsible for the change, but that it works is most important to the practitioner.

If the changes in the hypothetical case of Mary had not been as positive, a different strategy would be tried until progress was made. Even though, as in this example, the behavior moves along nicely, you not finished. Usually you have followed a continuous reinforcement schedule. It is not practical to consider long-term behavior maintenance on other than a variable intermittent schedule. So you substitute verbal praise once in a while for a token. Also you hope that the environment will begin to provide some reinforcement of its own. Some real tips and genuine smiles may take over. The end of the chart doesn't mean the end of the program. Modify it to suit the patient's needs.

Think Positively

A natural tendency is for the staff to shape behavior by rewarding appropriate behaviors and punishing inappropriate ones. If this style of treatment is used, the staff will try to find good behaviors (by the staff's definition) to reward and poor behaviors to punish but will usually find far more negative than positive behaviors. Aversive (selected punishment) is an effective form of treatment for certain psychiatric problems in the hands of a competent professional. But if the whole staff uses aversive conditioning freely, the attitude of negativism reduces the acquisition of positive behaviors. Besides, except in special situations, punishment does not change behavior —it only suppresses it.

The question is what to do with negative behavior. *Most negative behavior should be ignored.* The greatest amount of inappropriate behavior continues to be emitted by the patient because it is reinforced by social attention. Psychotic, aggressive, annoying, self-destructive, etc. behavior usually causes some commotion. A fire in the waste basket gets more people involved than a hundred good work passes. While the staff is the greatest giver of attention, much is also given by the family and the other patients. The cooperation of the family and others should be gained if the negative behavior is to cease quickly.

In addition to ignoring inappropriate behavior, another part of the procedure is to shape a positive behavior which is incompatible to the negative behavior. If a person is getting reinforced for reading, playing cards or watching TV (acceptable behaviors) he can not be pacing the floor (unacceptable behavior).

If the patient is about to do something destructive to himself or someone else, place him in a stimulus free room (no bed, no chairs, no pictures, etc.) until the behavior has subsided. Use as little force as necessary to decrease the importance of this event in the patient's eye and as much force as necessary to get the patient under control quickly. In summary, use positive reinforcement for desirable behaviors, ignore negative behavior, and introduce and reinforce positive behaviors that are incompatible with the negative behavior.

The Reinforcement Economy

One of the most useful techniques in encouraging the patient is reinforcement economy. This is a system by which a patient earns points, funny money, or tokens and then spends them for the necessities and luxuries of life. The economy has a normalizing effect in that the patient experiences many of both the positive and negative consequences of their behavior.

The basis for any economy is income and expenditure. The patient must earn enough to pay for his necessities. He should be able to, by working harder or longer, earn enough for some luxuries. He should not be allowed to earn too much or establish a large bank account too easily, as this weakens the system. The unit of exchange (money, points or tokens) should not be loaned by the bank (staff) to the patients or from one patient to another. This practice teaches some patients begging behavior rather than work behavior.

It is best if the entire building, or at least ward, are on the same economy, since everyone gets the same pay for the same job and is charged the same price for the same privilege. If possible, the economy should be extended into the work setting and into the living setting if the patient is not full-time at the hospital.

The economy in a hospital, like that of the real world, is based upon supply and demand. Jobs that everyone wants, within reason, pay less than those no one wants. If apples are more desirable than oranges, apples cost more. Spending is encouraged. The more people spend, the more beneficial behaviors they will perform to earn the currency.

All appropriate personal, social and working behaviors can earn points. Bed making, tooth brushing, showering, clean underwear, smiling, "good morning," reading newspapers and magazines, proper use of fork, taking small bites, staying at the work station, number of items assembled, coming back from coffee break on time, and remembering meals are some of the many behaviors which can earn points. Patients spend points purchasing things that have a high reinforcement value to them. Examples include coffee, cigarettes, soda pop, candy, snack foods, regular meals, a bed (instead of a cot), TV, newspaper and magazine, games, and walks, swearing, laying on bed during the day, inappropriate dress, sleeping late, or crazy talk.

Some of the items to be purchased, such as food, universally have a high reinforcement value. Other behaviors, like newspaper reading, will earn some patient points and cost others points. The difference is at what level the patient is performing that behavior. A college graduate who refuses to read a newspaper or magazine might get paid for it, whereas someone who reads excessively, neglecting social interaction, may have to pay for his reading.

In the spirit of trying to keep things on a positive note, fines are generally avoided as such. People are allowed to eat cigarette butts, hallucinate in the corner, or crazy talk to a technician; but these behaviors cost them money. The question of semantic game playing is valid here, but there is more than just that. If the staff tells the patient he can talk to the clock for twenty points, the patient often finds the behavior less desirable if it is permissible and if it costs something. If talking to the clock is really important, there are other gains because the patient has to perform other desirable chores to earn the twenty points which allow him to talk to the clock.

A token economy can follow one of three models: (1) everyone receiving the same income and outgo for the same behavior; (2) everyone on a highly individual program tailored to his own needs; or (3) everyone following the same basic system with some individual programs for problem behaviors. The first type is the easiest to administer, the second type leads to the greatest change, while the last type is a functional compromise.

Common Behaviors that can be Increased or Decreased using Behavior Modification

Recognition of Environment

A common complaint is that mental patients are lost in a fantasy world. This is made worse by not attending, at least verbally, to their surroundings. Patients should be reinforced, (verbal praise, points, tokens, stars etc.) for knowing what day it is, for addressing people by name, and being aware of objects in and changes of the environment. Teaching appropriate behavior in context is the task. It is appropriate to compliment a nurse on her new dress once. Any comment more than once should be ignored. Similarly Dr. Jones may appreciate a "good morning" from Tom the first time but finds it inappropriate more than once the same morning.

Improved Social Interaction

Rewards should be given for all positive forms of communication. One experimental program is the model interview. This interview is a fifteen minute discussion between the patient and the same technician, nurse or counselor occurring several times a week. The purpose is to teach discussing things meaningful to both the patient and a normal adult. Crazy talk or psychosomatic complaints are ignored. The patients are encouraged to watch the news, other TV shows, or read the paper for a discussion focus.

A technique with a similar goal is to have a patient government with appropriate participation and good decision making being reinforced. Patients can work in small groups planning ward activities and giving suggestions to the staff useful in treatment programs for other patients. The quantity and quality of the group's decisions and recommendations determine the points earned.

Work Behaviors

The most typical work behaviors which are reinforced are: coming to work on time, staying at the work station, working while at the station, self-supervision, responsible use of rest room, amount of work, quality of work, and accepting orders and criticism. Points as reinforcement which can be used with points earned on the ward are the most effective as the consequences of work behavior are coupled with those of living behavior.

Personal Habits

The bladder, unless there is organic damage, can be brought under control. Positive reinforcement for dry clothes and a ten point charge for clean clothes in the event of an accident is often effective. For bed wetters, the pad which rings a bell at the first drop of urine is very useful. This wakes the patient up while they still have a full bladder. They can then be led to the bathroom (reinforced, of course). After repeated trials, most people will learn to awaken with a full bladder before the bell sounds.

Table manners are a problem. As usual, good manners are reinforced, but other problems occur here with chronic patients particularly. They often have developed disgusting eating habits. A shaping procedure is useful. This takes a lot of time, as each patient must be worked with almost individually. When the patient slips in his behavior, his food can be removed. Eating as best as he can is the prerequisite for having the food. Some mental health settings use small tables with white linens and flowers for the best mannered. The poorest mannered eat from steel trays with several steps for intermediate manners in between. As one improves, he moves from one group to the next until he is at the white linen table.

Sitting and Sleeping

These are usually behaviors which should be decreased rather than increased. Charging rather stiff fees for daytime bed and chair use helps. Making the ward a noisy place after last "get up" call discourages late sleepers. Chairs moved from back corners into busy day halls lose some of their appeal for chronic sitters. Of course, having activities which interest patients (incompatible responses) make staying awake better than sleeping.

Actions That Annoy Staff

Every social worker, rehab counselor and nurse has experienced the patient who has endless complaints and/or questions. Ignoring unimportant or fabricated concerns is usually enough. If it is not, questioning can be purchased on a sliding scale. Several free questions per day with an increasing fee schedule for the dependent patient may control this problem. Not only will this slow down the questions, but for the patient who hates to make decisions, independent behavior should be shaped for the dependent patient. At first reinforce making any kind of decision. When decision making is well established, start reinforcing only those choices which are good ones.

Crazy Talk

The relating of hallucinations, delusions and strange beliefs is one of the most self-defeating of all behaviors. A patient can look normal and have good work skills; but if he cannot be on a new job ten minutes without telling everyone of his delusioned system, he is immediately suspect and avoided by others. This usually produces even stranger behavior in the patient. A decrease in crazy talk can be effected by ignoring it in any conversation and reinforcing those thoughts which are sensible. Discontinue any conversation which contains mostly crazy talk.

Aggressive Behavior

Mild, appropriate aggressive behavior is encouraged as a normalizing function. Inappropriate behavior has consequences. Swearing can be decreased by placing the patient in a stimulus free room, rent charged of course, for unlimited swearing. Striking behavior can be handled in a similar fashion: a purchase of fifteen minutes with a punching bag not only makes the anger cost something but shows an alternative way for handling anger. A very low fee for the punching bag prior to overt aggression encourages hitting the bag rather than a fellow patient.

PHILOSOPHICAL OBJECTIONS TO BEHAVIOR

While many issues could probably be raised, two points of objection are frequently aired: control of human behavior and bribery.

Behavior modification is seen as the control or manipulation of the patient. The behaviorist would not deny this, but would say the patient is being controlled already by reinforcing his current behavior; and it is causing the patient trouble. The family and hospital staff pay attention to his hallucinations. They reinforce his crazy talk. Ignoring his schizophrenic gibberish is not cruel, but humane. To reinforce schizophrenic behavior *is* cruel, as it causes people to avoid him and decreases his chances for independence.

The second most frequent objection is that behavior modification constitutes bribery. Bribery is the act of causing someone to do something against their own and/or society's best interests. A reinforcement schedule helps someone to do something toward their own and/or society's best interest. Except with the most disturbed patient who already has most of life's choices made for him, most patients agree with the intent of a good behavior modification program. They want to get better. We all respond to reinforcement. Few of us would continue to work very long if our employers ceased paying wages. We would stop being friends to those we love if they gave us no social reinforcement.

Behavior modification could be used in a controlling, authoritarian fashion; but in the hands of sensitive humanitarian mental health workers it is a powerful and beneficial tool.

SUGGESTED READING

Ayllon, T., and Azrin, N.: *The Token Economy*. New York, Appleton, 1968.

Diebert, A. N., and Harmon, A. S.: *New Tools for Changing Behavior*. Champaign, Res Press, 1970.

Gardner, William I.: *Behavior Modification in Mental Retardation*. Chicago, Atherton, 1971.

Reese, E. P.: *The Analysis of Human Operant Behavior*. Dubuque, Wm. C. Brown, 1966.

Shaeffer, Martin: *Behavior Therapy*. New York, McGraw, 1969.

CHAPTER III

BEHAVIORAL GROUP THERAPY WITH ALCOHOL ABUSERS

STEVEN M. ROSS

- ■ TECHNIQUES AND TERMINOLOGY
- ■ PRE-GROUP PREPARATIONS
- ■ GROUP MEETINGS
- ■ CONCLUSION
- ■ REFERENCES

THIS CHAPTER is an attempt to present a broad spectrum behavioral approach to group treatment of alcoholism. The emphasis will be on practical techniques which the reader can use regardless of his theoretical orientation. Theory, technical vocabulary and academic arguments will be kept to a minimum, while references will be provided the reader to obtain more detailed information of various techniques, the research literature and other sources.

The approach to be described is based on the assumption that alcohol abuse is a learning problem in that patients learn to either escape or avoid unpleasant events or gain access to pleasurable events through excessive drinking.

If patients learn to respond in these ways to various life events, it is possible to teach them to respond in ways other than drinking. The task of the group is to provide a setting where other behaviors can be learned, practiced and strengthened. Unless there is more to be gained by not drinking than by doing so, drinking will persist. The group must, therefore, also help in generalizing the behaviors learned in the group to situations where they are most needed outside the group, namely, in the community.

The group has special advantages for accomplishing these very difficult tasks, advantages which individual therapy lacks: (1) members are able to learn from each other via observation and imitation; (2) members learn that their problems are not unique, and they are not alone; (3) new behavior can be practiced and strengthened in the presence of a variety of people which more closely approximates "real life"; (4) group censure and support can exert more pressure to bear for change and strengthening of new behaviors; (5) patients learn that they are able to trust and help others; (6) more efficient use of the leader's time is made; and (7) more facets of problems and more problem solving techniques can be gained from group discussion.

Naturally, the total treatment of the alcoholic cannot occur in one therapy group. There are often medical, vocational and recreational problems which must be left to other members of the treatment team. Often individuals must be prepared to function in a group, and this preparation itself may take the form of one-to-one counseling or therapy. The leader must decide with each potential group member which problems should be brought up in group and which are better dealt with elsewhere. The key to this problem lies in pre-group preparations, namely, deciding on the kind of group (composition, goals, commonalities of members, time limitations, size) and the assessment of prospective members (identifying behavioral assets, deficits, excesses).

In the sections to follow we will examine these pre-group functions in greater detail, but first it may be helpful to define a few terms which will be used, trying, of course, to adhere to my original promise of keeping technical vocabulary to a minimum. It is more the purpose of this section to provide the reader with a "cookbook" of techniques which he can draw upon regardless of the type of group he runs than it is to teach a foreign academic language.

TECHNIQUES AND TERMINOLOGY
Baseline Rate

This term refers to the frequency, duration or magnitude with which a particular behavior occurs naturally before any type of treatment takes place. Obtaining baseline rates before treatment provides us with some indication of how successful our treatment is, providing we continue to get data on the same behavior in the same way after treatment begins and ends. If someone drinks a fifth of scotch every day prior to treatment, their baseline drinking rate would be a fifth per day (magnitude). Another way of measuring pretreatment drinking behavior might be to observe how frequently a patient pours a drink during a particular time sample. The third possibility, duration, might be determined by measuring with a stop watch how many total minutes during a time sample the patient had a drink poured for himself.

It is not necessary to obtain all three measures on any given behavior. For any given behavior—whether it be drinking, talking about family problems in group, or number of A.A. meetings attended—there is usually one best measure to obtain. A general rule of thumb is if a behavior occurs frequently and lasts only a few seconds, e.g., fidgeting, eye contact, using a particular word, it is probably better to measure frequency of response. If the behavior occurs for several hours or minutes, e.g., tardy for group, feeling depressed, talking in group, it is probably better to measure duration of occurrence per session, per day, etc. Magnitude is probably best used when the behavior already is in some quantified form, e.g., number of ounces of wine consumed in a day or week, how fearful someone rates themself on a scale from o to 100. A much more detailed description of data collecting is provided by Jackson and Della-Piana (1972).

While it is not always feasible to obtain baseline rates and subsequent data on all problem behaviors for all patients because of the practical limitations of time, personnel, cost, etc., it is possible to a greater degree than one might imagine, especially in a hospital or clinic or through home visits. At the very least, patients themselves can obtain data on their own behavior, even if it is something as gross as counting empty bottles. In addition, many friends, family members, employers and relatives are willing to help as collateral sources of data and general functioning. By comparing several baseline rates we can determine how reliable the measure is, providing the two observers do their data collecting independently of each other. The help of collaterals should never be enlisted without the full knowledge and consent of the patient lest his trust in the treatment program be undermined.

Functional Analysis

A functional analysis of behavior is an assessment of what cues set the stage for certain responses to occur and what happens immediately after the responses have occurred which strengthen (reinforce) them or weaken them. All of the behavior we emit which has some effect on ourselves or our environment is controlled by that effect. To change this behavior we must change the effect it has, or we must practice new responses to the old cues. These notions are worth pondering for a few minutes because they are very important but very difficult to achieve.

Consider an individual who claims that he does not know why he drinks. He even says that if he knew why he drank he would not be asking for our help. It is very likely that this individual is telling the truth. He may be unaware of many events that lead to drinking and what the drinking "does for him." If he were to keep records of his drinking, including: What Occurred Just Prior to Drinking; the Date, Time, Place; Alone or With Whom; Amount Consumed; Type of Beverage; What Happened After Drinking, very definite patterns would emerge which would yield much information as to what cues the drinking and what functions the drinking serves. I have had copies of the above information made which I give to people seeking treatment and individuals they list as collateral sources of information. I call these data sheets the *Intake Record* and often require waiting list patients to complete them in order to qualify for treatment when a vacancy arises. This does not mean that if they have already stopped drinking they must start again to provide pretreatment baseline data. However, if they do drink or even have an *urge* to drink they are to record the information as accurately as they can.

The patterns which emerge from intake data of this type are often very informative and can be very helpful in setting goals and generating group discussion. For example, an individual reports coming home from work tense and needing a drink to "unwind." Upon arriving home he finds his wife yelling at the kids and asking him to punish them for misbehavior. This may further upset him because he may not want to punish them for something that happened hours earlier and did not even involve him. Instead of having one drink he may have three. Instead of having the drinks *with* his wife and kids while chatting about the events of the day, he may bring the bottle to a secluded location of the house in order to escape the battle. His wife may then turn on him for shirking his responsibilities which results in another three drinks to drown her voice. By now dinner is ready but he is in no mood to eat and has a few more. He and his wife may sleep separately that night. He probably wakes up with a hangover (late because the alarm clock is in the master bedroom and he slept on the couch). Feeling terrible, he has a few to get him going and to give him courage to face the boss who is angry because he is late. At work people look at him twice because he is disheveled. He feels they are staring at him and talking behind his back. His job may be in danger which adds to the pressure he feels he is under. He may try to be a model employee and perform perfectly that day. If he makes a mistake he becomes extremely upset with himself. At lunch he "has a few to steady his nerves."

This individual may be starting a binge or he may be in the middle of one. We could go on to describe the rest of his day, but let us stop at this point and look at a functional analysis of his behavior. His Intake Record shows that he first reported an urge to drink upon arriving home in order to unwind. There are two possibilities at this point. Does arriving home *itself* function as a cue for drinking or does the feeling of needing to unwind? Perhaps both do. Careful inspection of his intake pattern might reveal that he automatically drinks whenever he arrives home regardless of how he is feeling and regardless of how well he and his family are getting along. Perhaps he has learned to drink upon arriving home because so much of the time his wife has a drink waiting for him or because the family squabbling makes arriving home an aversive event. Pre-group discussion might focus on these possibilities: what else he might do instead of drink, how the group might be of assistance if he brings the problem up in group, and the fact that other group members can be expected to ask for his help for similar kinds of problems.

The second urge to drink or actual drinking that he probably reported on his Intake Record was the additional drinking which occurred after his wife accused him of shirking his responsibilities. Again, inspection of his Intake Record over time might reveal that he almost always drinks after being criticized. Furthermore, the criticism-drinking association is not limited to his wife. The pattern may also reveal that even when his own children criticize him, not to mention his boss, co-workers and friends, he drinks or has a strong urge to drink. Criticism, then, may also function as a cue for drinking of which he may not even be aware. The drinking which follows criticism may enable him to calm down and forget the criticism which had been bothering him. In addition, the drinking may give him courage to tell the criticizer to shut up. The section of the Intake Record which asks "What Happened After Drinking?" might, in fact, support these hypotheses by showing that the individual feels more relaxed and forgets about the criticism or tells the criticizer off. Careful questioning by the group or by the leader prior to the group's starting might reveal difficulties in assertion and extreme sensitivity to criticism. Both of these problems would lend themselves to group treatment quite well, and we shall provide some concrete examples of how in later sections.

The third and fourth drinking episodes in our example were drinking instead of eating dinner and drinking to get him going in the morning. Let us examine number three. If our patient or our home observer is keeping accurate records, he would have recorded under the column, "What Occurred Just Prior to Drinking?", "wife called out, 'Dinner is ready!' ". Then, he would have recorded the date, time, and specific room in his house for the place. Under the next column, "Alone or With Whom?," he would have recorded, "with family." Next he would have recorded an estimate of the "Amount Consumed" and then the "Type of Beverage." Finally, he would have recorded something under the last column, "What Happened After Drinking?" He might have recorded something in this last column such as "I wasn't bothered by her voice anymore and I was glad she had cooked for me for nothing. Served her right." Again, looking at his intake pattern over time might demonstrate similar ways of escaping aversive stimulation, that his appetite diminishes when drinking, and that he uses alcohol to help him punish others, even when such punishment is not warranted (if his wife deserved punishment for anything, and that is debatable because of insufficient information, it would be for telling him to punish the kids when he arrived home and then punishing him when he failed to do so. Instead of counter-punishing her or asserting himself, however, he ended up punishing her surreptitiously for cooking dinner which was an appropriate behavior that he should have reinforced).

The fact that he had a drink or two the following morning "to get going" is not uncommon. The hangover sets the stage and functions as the cue. The drinking itself allows the patient to escape the aversive headache, nausea, criticism, etc. It is also not uncommon for alcoholics to continue drinking to avoid the onset of withdrawal symptoms entirely.

The last drinking episode mentioned, having several at lunch to "steady the nerves," was cued by making mistakes on the job, by people looking at him, and by worry over his job being in danger. Examining his intake pattern would probably show that each of these is sufficient to act as a cue for drinking. Group discussion could focus on steps he could take to increase his job security and how he could be desensitized to making mistakes and having people look at him.

While we have been discussing an individual who claims that he does not know why he drinks, all of what we have demonstrated ap-applies equally well to those who *can* tell us why they drink. Often, large discrepancies exist between what the patient thinks alcohol is doing for him and his actual behavior just before and just after drinking. In addition, cues which set the stage for excessive drinking may be unnoticed; it is easy to attribute the reasons to things which may have little to do with the total amount of drinking that goes on.

Reinforcement and Contracting

To reinforce is to present some verbal or physical reward after a response occurs. Anything is potentially a reinforcer. The only way one can be sure is to see the effect it has on the response which it follows: if it makes the response more likely to occur again under the same conditions, it is strengthening the behavior and is, therefore, a reinforcer. On the other hand, if a consequence to a response produces some verbal or physical event which decreases or suppresses the response, the event is punishing the behavior and is an aversive event. If drinking is followed by an antabuse reaction, drinking is punished by that very aversive event.

It is easy to show that what may be reinforcing for one person in a group may be aversive to someone else. Someone who loves to talk and be the center of attention, for example, will probably talk at a very high rate (talking response strengthened) if the leader and the rest of the group sit and reinforce the talking behavior with rapt attention, continuous eye contact, nods of agreement, and requests for more detail. Another individual who finds talking in group aversive would probably talk as little as possible under the same conditions. Therefore, one should not assume that a reinforcer *is* a reinforcer until the effect has been observed.

Extinction refers to the process of withholding reinforcement from a response which has ordinarily been given reinforcement. The purpose of extinction is to diminish the response. If the group ignores an individual who has previously gained a great deal of attention by telling people how much liquor he can drink, two things will happen. First, his rate of such talk will probably increase (this can be expected and is called the extinction burst); but if the group remains steadfast, his alcohol talk will soon begin to decrease, especially if the group gives him attention when he speaks of other, more appropriate topics.

Reinforcement is most effective when it is delivered immediately. When a response is new and still weak and unpracticed, reinforce each time the response occurs. To make the response durable, however, the schedule of reinforcement should be *thinned* and reinforcement should be given every second or third time the response occurs. At the same time, patients need to learn how to start programming their own reinforcers for themselves as part of improving self-control.

A convenient vehicle for teaching patients to program their own reinforcers as well as for teaching realistic goal setting is a written contract. Homme, *et al.* (1970), Knox (1971), and Stuart (1971) have described the procedure in detail on a one-to-one counseling basis. It is possible, however, to make the same kinds of commitments to a group or to bring up a contract negotiated on a one-to-one basis in the group and to discuss the commitment.

Several steps are involved in teaching patients to write their own contracts. First, the therapist or group leader and the patient decide upon some specific problem behaviors which can be improved on a daily or weekly basis. A level of performance is then agreed upon which *both* parties agree is fair, easily attainable, clear and worthwhile. Next, consequences in the form of reinforcement are agreed upon for performing the behavior at the specified level. Both parties must agree that the reinforcer(s) is acceptable in that it is given consistently and a short time after the performance. The contract should also be positive in the sense that the parties are saying, "If you do this I'll do that" vs. "I will not do this if you do that." The contract is considered fair if the amount of work required of both parties or the amount of performance and the amount of reinforcement are of equal weight.

The second and third stages of teaching patients to write their own contracts either with themselves or with family members involves showing them how to specify target behaviors clearly so that there is no doubt or room for argument as to whether they occurred or did not occur. The same is true for teaching the patient to identify reinforcers which are all around him but which are unnoticed and taken for granted. The patient is then given guided practice in writing contracts specifying first the behaviors and then the agreed upon consequences.

Exchange contracts between husband and wife are variations of self-contracting. They seek to teach partners how to reciprocally give in order to get, and take the general form, "I'll do this if you'll do that." This is in contrast to a coercive or arbitrary form of interaction, for example, "Do it or else" or "Do it because I said so."

Contracts should be written, signed by both parties, and dated. The period for which the contract is in effect should be specified as well as when the contract will be reviewed for changes or extensions. In addition, there should be some provision for record keeping of the behaviors to occur. If the contract is negotiated between an individual and the group, all should sign and have access to copies. Progress toward performing the behaviors should be discussed in the group and support for following the contract given. Often it is helpful to provide fines or other consequences for failure to follow the contract in addition to the positive consequences for meeting the terms.

By writing and completing a series of short-term contracts, patients move toward specifying and attaining longer-term goals. Therefore, a fourth stage in contracting is teaching the patient to specify long-term goals and the methods by which he can attain them. While progress toward short-term goals is reinforced almost immediately with small rewards, this same progress and the same rewards are, in fact, serving the purpose of rewarding progress toward long-term goals. When a series of short-term or "mini" contracts is fulfilled, that in itself may be a long-term goal; the reinforcer should, therefore, be of greater magnitude than for each of short-term contracts. To illustrate, a wife might want to redecorate or paint a house. The husband would like her to stop nagging him to do it. Both would like to take a vacation in a few months. A series of short-term exchange contracts might be as follows: Husband: "I agree to paint for one hour during the week and at least four hours a day on weekends if my wife does not mention painting that day and if she gives me a choice of dinners for that evening." Wife: "I agree to give my husband a choice of dinners and to not mention painting to him if he paints for one hour a day during the week and four hours a day on weekends." Additional consequences might also be specified in case of default: "If my husband fails to paint the required number of hours on any day, he will prepare his own dinner and do his own dishes." The husband might add: "If my wife mentions painting or does not provide a choice of dinners, I will not be required to paint that day." Both the husband and the wife may then agree to a longer term goal: "If the house is completed by (date) we will take a week's vacation in Canada."

Shaping, Fading and Prompting Responses

Shaping refers to a procedure in which a new response is learned by rewarding rough approximations to the desired response. An individual who has never been in a group before and who is unable to discuss intimate material can be reinforced initially just for talking. As time goes on, however, he can be prompted by the leader (who also prompts the rest of the group to do the same) for talk which comes closer and closer to the desired areas of discussion. As the desired responses are made and strengthened through group support and reinforcement, the leader fades his prompts out of the picture and lets the natural contingencies of reinforcement take over.

Psychodrama Techniques

A variety of techniques using principles of social learning theory have evolved. Many have been with us for years under different names. Moreno (1966), for example, has developed several techniques within the general context of psychodrama. Sturm (1970, 1965) has translated these techniques into a behavioral format. While space does not permit a full discussion of all Moreno's techniques, some of the more frequently used techniques as they relate to a behaviorally oriented group will be presented.

Warm-up is a period in which the leader attempts to elicit a great deal of reinforcing interaction (smiles, acceptance, physical touching, attentive listening) and to discourage punishment or extinction (bored stares, disapproval, withdrawal). An atmosphere is created in which participation in the group and the group itself is seen as reinforcing and in which people can be spontaneous without fear of punishment.

Problem-presentation begins with the leader reinforcing the members' attempts to reveal personal problems which they are asking the group to help solve. Usually a problem is focused on that which the group agrees is relevant to their own lives. Often the leader serves as a model for members to imitate by stating that everyone, even he, has problems with which to contend.

Self-presentation is the next step in which the individual describes the setting and characters in detail in which the problem has most recently come up. The leader may also ask the individual to enact the various roles so that all present can get a better understanding of the cues which set the stage for various responses and what the consequences are.

Role-playing techniques are probably the most widely used of all those to come from psychodrama. They enable group members to model appropriate behavior for others to imitate, to selectively prompt and reinforce each other for improved performance, and to see oneself from others points of view.

After self-presentation of the problem, the leader asks the patient to choose members from the group to play the major characters. In choosing the auxiliary cast, the patient is asked to choose, whenever possible, on the basis of an actual resemblance to a real character. In addition the auxiliaries are told to incorporate their own reactions into the role. If they are not quite sure of how to play them, additional detail is given and several trial runs are made. Often the patient is asked to reverse roles, either to show how the character needs to be played or to show the patient the other's position or point of view. When roles are reversed again to their original positions, patients often have new ideas of how best to respond to the other individual, taking into account the other's expectations and perceptions.

Not only does role-reversal enable patients to understand better the behavior of others, but it also provides an opportunity for the patient to interact with "himself." By stepping back and looking at himself, patients are often surprised at their own behavior and are often quite receptive to prompts and suggestions from other group members as to how to handle the problem differently. These alternate ways of handling situations can then be rehearsed and re-rehearsed with the group providing feedback as to how comfortable, convincing and appropriate the patient seems in performing the new behaviors.

Sometimes it is apparent that the patient is responding to cues or consequences which other members of the group feel are not there. Or it may be that the group senses that the patient is avoiding saying or doing certain things which would be most appropriate. A technique for giving this feedback immediately and at the same time modeling the appropriate behavior is *doubling*. The leader asks one or more group members to play directly alongside the patient and to first mimic his responses in order to start approximating his character. The next step is the dropping of simple mimicry when the auxiliary is ready and saying and doing what the patient is not saying and doing under the circumstances. The patient stops his enactment to observe the double and then imitates the double's behavior. He then observes the consequences of the new behavior on the character with which he is interacting. He can also reverse roles at this point to compare his old behavior with the new behavior learned from the double.

While the double provides instant and simultaneous feedback of new behavior to be learned and imitated, the *mirror* is the original "instant replay" developed long before video tape equipment. The patient is asked to leave the stage or area where role-playing is occurring and to watch while an auxiliary plays parts of the performance just enacted. The patient can then evaluate his performance while not in the midst of some other role. The auxiliary may also be requested by the leader to extend the new behaviors to new situations so that the patient can see the adequacy of his new responses in a variety of settings. In *future projection* the patient and other group members anticipate problems and practice solutions using the new behaviors for future events which are likely to occur or which the patient would like to see occur.

Sessions are usually brought to an end with additional reinforcement for the patient who enacted his problems and for the group as a whole. This is accomplished through *group participation* in which group members are called upon to share what they have learned about their own problems while observing the enactments and providing feedback. In this way tangible progress is made public and the patient is reinforced for his efforts by knowing that he has helped others in the group.

Assertion Training

This technique, developed by Wolpe (1958), involves training patients to appropriately express both positive and negative feelings. It is common for many of us to say nothing rather than to stick up for our rights or to tell someone off because of fear. Either we are afraid of hurting their feelings or we are uncomfortable because we do not know quite how to say it. Often feelings of resentment keep building and the fear of losing control and "blowing up" develops. In these cases alcohol enables the individual to either relax and forget the resentment or to tell the person what he thinks of them (with guilt and apologies often following when sober).

Assertion problems are frequently apparent when group members seem timid, relate experiences in which they did not know what to say, and have trouble expressing positive feelings such as love and respect as well as annoyance, irritation and expressions of the opinion that their rights as human beings have been infringed upon. Role-playing techniques can be extremely useful in assessing the problem and treating it.

The leader, for example, can openly ask the group if any members have difficulty telling people how they feel or if they "keep things inside." If no one volunteers such information, standard scenes can be enacted with group members taking turns in the various roles and giving each other feedback as to how they came across. Wolpe asks patients to respond to such standard scenes as: walking out of a shop and finding you have been short-changed one dollar; someone pushing in front of you in line; ordering a steak rare and the waiter brings it well done. Wolpe and Lazarus (1966, p. 41) provide a more complete list of possibilities. Additional scenes can be used depending on the actual experiences of group members once it has been established that some members really do have an assertion problem.

Desensitization

Systematic desensitization is another technique developed by Wolpe for the treatment of a specific problem, namely, excessive fear which prevents appropriate behavior from occurring. While the technique was originally employed in individual therapy as was assertion training, it has been successfully used in groups on many occasions. We must, however, make a distinction between groups formed purely for desensitization, assertion or some other specific problem and more heterogeneous groups which include these techniques for some members. It is probably unwise to spend very much group time on a problem which has relevance only for a very few members; therefore, unless the problem involves a theme which is troublesome for other members, too, and can be treated in a few sessions of role-playing, it is better to form another group for individuals just having that problem. An alternative would be to deal with it in individual therapy.

As originally developed, systematic desensitization involves first, pinpointing precisely what it is about the situation which is causing the fear, and what factors seem to make it better or worse. For example, a patient might become panicky if criticized by his boss in front of co-workers but only a little uncomfortable if criticized about his bowling score by friends. A hierarchy of scenes is drawn up ranging from the first scene which causes no discomfort at all to the last scene which makes the patient the most frightened which that problem has made him. To insure that steps between hierarchy items are not too great, the patient is asked to rate each scene on a subjective 100 point scale. The zero point represents absolute calm and 100 represents the most frightened he has been. Hierarchy items, according to Wolpe, should not be any more than fifteen units apart.

Patients are then taught *deep muscle relaxation* which is believed to be a response incompatible with fear and which is a very useful technique in its own right for individuals who have trouble relaxing. After relaxation is achieved the patient imagines himself actually engaged in the first scene on the hierarchy. The scene is imagined several times, first three to five seconds, then six to eight seconds and then usually ten to twelve seconds. Relaxation is reinstated between each imagining. If no anxiety is signaled while imagining, the process is repeated with the next scene until the entire hierarchy is negotiated, a process which usually takes several months.

Often relaxation training and a small amount of *in vivo* desensitization can be easily incorporated into a group which has not been formed specifically for those reasons. Desensitization often is a by-product of role-playing almost any new behavior until it feels comfortable and can be accomplished by shaping and rewarding approximations to the goal behavior. For example, an individual with a fear of criticism can construct a hierarchy with the help of the group and then role-play each scene until it no longer causes discomfort. Each step in the hierarchy represents approximations to the final scene which may be a goal to then achieve outside the group. The group may actually give individual members homework assignments to carry out between meetings. One of these can be reporting on doing those things outside the group which the member has been working on in the group. It is important, however, not to give assignments which the member is not ready for or which will lead to failure. Members should not go beyond the hierarchy scene they have successfully completed in group.

Another way of doing systematic desensitization, assertion training, and relaxation training in groups is to carefully select group members who have one of those problems and work only on that problem in that group. Lazarus (1961, 1968), for example, describes group desensitization and assertion training. More recently Suinn and Richardson (1971) have developed an extension of relaxation training to provide a general competency for new anxiety-provoking situations. These groups are time-limited and highly specific. The members all have the same problem, although they may be heterogeneous in other respects such as age, educational background, etc. For example, in a desensitization group, all the members might have a fear of height for which they are seeking treatment. In a ward of alcoholic patients there may be a half-dozen or more who have fears of failure or other specific fears. Often highly specific groups can be run simultaneously with other groups and individual therapy in a general ongoing alcohol treatment program. Frequent staff meetings are necessary to insure continuity of care across modalities.

Relaxation Training

First introduced by Jacobson in 1938, the procedure is relatively straightforward and can be mastered by most people in a few hours of training. There is considerable overlap with hypnotic techniques, especially some of the suggestions which some clinicians use to deepen the state of relaxation achieved. Each of the major muscle groups in the body is first tensed and then slowly relaxed beginning with the hands and forearm. The fist is clenched and the patient is asked to concentrate on the feeling of tension and to learn to discriminate when it is present in varying degrees in each muscle group. Similarly, he is asked to concentrate on the feeling of relaxation which seems to "flow into the muscle" when, after being held tense for about five seconds, it is slowly relaxed. The upper arms are usually done after the hands and forearms: the triceps by pushing the hands against each other very hard and gradually relaxing and the biceps by clenching the fist and tensing the upper arm and gradually relaxing. The muscles of the upper back, neck, face, stomach, thighs, calves, and ankles are all done in like fashion. If any tension remains in any muscle the patient is instructed to redo it until it feels quite relaxed. A calm, relaxing voice on the part of the therapist is required, as is a quiet room with no distractions. While a reclining chair or couch is optimal, I have relaxed groups of eight patients on hard folding chairs by having them get as comfortable as possible by leaning way back with the legs outstretched, head back and eyes closed. No muscle tension should be required to sit or recline while listening to the instructions, and arms should be resting comfortably at the sides.

After the muscles have been relaxed, additional suggestions are given. For example, patients can be told to concentrate on their breathing: "Breathe deeply . . . (pause while patients inhale) and slowly . . . calm and relaxed. Muscles loose . . . no hurry . . . enjoying the relaxation you have achieved. Notice how you seem to get heavier in the chair and muscles seem to relax more each time you exhale." Another common suggestion is to ask patients to imagine lying in the sun and to feel the warmth of the sun on their skin. "Your muscles feel warm and relaxed. You may find yourself getting a little drowsy. Perhaps you can hear water lapping against the side of a pool." Another useful technique is to ask patients to think of a word which they can associate with the pleasant state of relaxation (not an alcohol related word) and which they can think of when they are beginning to feel tense. Patients are told to practice relaxation between sessions in order to achieve it more rapidly. When proficiency is gained the patient merely thinks of his word or tells himself to relax.

In concluding this section on techniques and terminology several words of caution are needed. It should be obvious to the reader that we have merely scratched the surface of techniques and procedures about which many volumes have been written and into which many years of research and development have gone. Readers should have some knowledge of the existence of these techniques from the foregoing section, but they are urged to consult both the references listed and other practitioners who have some experience using the techniques. No technique is effective if used incorrectly.

PRE-GROUP PREPARATIONS

Selection

There are many opinions as to whom to select for a group and whom to exclude. Almost all writers agree that at the very least, members should be able to listen to each other and be able to talk to each other. Aside from this basic and obvious starting point, group leaders differ markedly. Some prefer only highly motivated and highly verbal members having a great deal of similarity in problem areas. Others prefer the most heterogeneous group possible. In dealing with alcoholism, the author's preference is for a heterogeneous group in regard to age, sex, educational level, length of alcoholism and related problems, marital status, and verbal ability. On the other hand, extremes in socio-economic and educational areas are probably best avoided.

Usually the author will form a homogeneous group when, as mentioned earlier, several individuals are found to share a very specific problem such as assertion or relaxation. The homogeneity centers around the problem area itself rather than around personality characteristics of the members.

When in doubt about the composition of a group and the selection of members, it may be useful to run a larger trial group first (Stone, Parloff, and Frank, 1954). Members for smaller groups can then be drawn based on the performance of individuals in the trial group and the leader's criteria for membership.

Size

The author has found that a group of from six to eight members is optimal. Other writers would tend to agree (e.g., Goldstein, Heller, and Sechrest, 1966).

Assessment

Closely related to the selection problem is the problem of assessing individual difficulties which might be effectively dealt with in a group setting. We have already discussed several important aspects of assessment, a functional analysis of behavior and objective data on the frequency, duration or magnitude of appropriate and inappropriate responses. The goal is to identify behavioral assets as well as deficits and excesses and to get some indication of functioning in these areas prior to treatment.

Several other instruments and procedures are used in addition to the Intake Record. First, there is probably no substitute for a thorough interview. The author uses an intake interview which asks for four collateral sources of information for reliability and validity checks, demographic information in terms of number of days worked, highest monthly income, number of days spent in jail or in a hospital for alcohol related problems, how serious a problem alcohol is, and family history and living conditions for the six months prior to entering treatment. This information is later compared to what is occurring six months after treatment. The information also tells a great deal about the individual factually and in the way he answers the questions.

Frequently the Fear Survey Schedule (Wolpe and Lang, 1964; see Tasto, *et al.*, 1970, for an updated version with norms) is administered. The schedule is a checklist of 122 items which sometimes arouse fear or discomfort. Patients are asked to indicate how much discomfort they would feel to each item on a five point scale ranging from "Not at All" to "Very Much." Often the schedule provides information regarding fear arousing cues or situations which lead to heavy drinking. Areas covered include social situations, medical procedures, and small animals and insects.

Another paper and pencil technique which is sometimes used is the Reinforcer Survey Schedule (Cautela and Kastenbaum, 1967). The schedule, which by no means exhausts all possibilities, attempts to identify activities (other than drinking) which patients might enjoy. Group discussion can often focus on these other possibilities.

On occasion, particularly when there is question of thought disorder, some traditional diagnostic tests such as the MMPI, Memory-for-Designs, and Proverbs might be used. However, if thought disorder fails to appear in the hour-long intake interview, it is doubtful that there is enough present to preclude an individual from participating in a group. Kanfer and Saslow (1969) provide a more detailed discussion of behavioral assessment techniques used in conjunction with more traditional methods.

Time Limits

Depending on the context in which the group occurs, there are probably advantages to both time-limited and time-unlimited groups. Time-limited groups are often useful when maximum gains are sought in least amount of time, when progress and goals are explicit, waiting lists long, when treatment needs to be standardized (as for example, in process and outcome research), and problems are not so severe as to be expected to take more than two to six months to resolve. Time limits may also bring pressure to bear on individuals "to start shaping up" as the end of therapy approaches and slower members see tangible gains made by other members in the group.

An alternative approach which combines an ongoing group format with time-limited therapy is one in which individuals enter and leave the ongoing group when they have reached their criterion levels of performance or the goals they set for themselves with the help of the leader and the rest of the group. Thus, in the pre-group asssessment and specification of problems, a timetable of expected progress and termination can also be tentatively formulated. This does not mean that goals and timetables cannot be revised as new problem behaviors become apparent in the group. Nor does it mean that other group members cannot assist in revising goals, problem solving strategies, and timetables once the group has begun. On the contrary both are desirable and should be prompted and reinforced.

GROUP MEETINGS

Initial sessions are usually spent establishing ground rules or, re-iterating those discussed in pre-group meetings with the leader, re-fining assessment techniques and problems to be worked on and restating the implied or written treatment contract.

Common ground rules include such matters as promptness, the expectation that members will try to help each other, that what goes on in the group is confidential*, that relationships among members outside the group should be discussed in the group, that assignments outside the group will be completed and reported on in the group, and that private meetings with the leader can be requested at any time, but that what is discussed should be brought up in group either by the patient when he feels he is ready or by the leader when he feels the patient is ready. Another ground rule is often that members cannot attend group if they have been drinking, but that urges to drink are appropriate to discuss in the group†. This is more frequently a needed rule with outpatients rather than in-patients.

Additions, deletions and modifications to these rules are often the topics of the first meetings. They can be used as vehicles to get members "warmed up" to talking in the group. By reinforcing and prompting this somewhat impersonal but interesting and constructive material, the leader begins making the group itself more attractive. As the attractiveness of the group increases, so does its potential for helping through reinforcement of appropriate within- and extra-group activity. During these initial meetings the leader also prompts and models much verbal behavior which emphasizes the commonali-

---

*Confidentiality can be a problem in regard to other staff within an institution who are responsible for the patient but who may not be members of a particular group. Sometimes patients will not discuss material which they are afraid will be entered in charts for others who are less familiar to them to read. Often these fears can be allayed by assuring patients that other staff are professionals who are there to help, or that the information will be charted in very general terms or not at all until the patient feels he is ready to share it with those staff.

†While problems which result in urges to drink are discussed, "drink talk" *per se* is discouraged, at least in later sessions. Examples of "drink talk" would be humorous descriptions of events which happened while drunk, favorite beverages, or boasts of how much liquor one can hold. This type of material contributes nothing construc-tive except, perhaps, to remind us that the individual needs to develop social skills in other areas.

ties among the members and avoids or discourages interactions which might be aversive (see earlier section on warm-up).

Unless members begin discussing problems spontaneously, the leader begins prompting the group to start doing this. He may ask someone to begin who seems quite willing to share his problems with the group in pre-group meetings. The individual may be asked to recount some of the problems he and the leader have discussed, perhaps Intake Record data or perhaps a contract he is thinking of negotiating with his wife. This, in turn, leads to discussions of whether or not others in the group have similar problems, how they are typically handled, how they can be handled differently, and how group members can help. The leader, meanwhile, should be prompting and modeling problem solving strategies and reinforcing the group for generating solutions to problems. Potential solutions are role-played with the group providing feedback as to how adequate and comfortable the characters appeared. As the leader prompts and reinforces the group for appropriate behavior, the group imitates him, especially if this process is made explicit and the group is encouraged to do so. As the group imitates the leader's behavior, the leader can begin fading his prompts and reinforcements and allow the group more and more autonomy. Sessions can be closed with a review of progress and assignments to try some of the rehearsed behavior outside the group and to record the results.

Later meetings can begin with a summary by a member of what happened at the last meeting. This in itself may create fruitful discussion since other members may have different perceptions and remembrances of what occurred. Next, a presentation of what occurred outside the group since the last meeting usually ensues with questions directed at those who had assignments to carry out in the interim. Throughout, the leader must keep the group on its course —the generation and maintenance of new behavior.

It is not uncommon for individuals to begin manifesting behavior within the group which serves the purpose of allowing the individuals to avoid certain subject areas. Fidgeting, extreme nervousness, pacing, lateness, very much or very little talking, monopolizing the group, competing for the leader's attention, long discussions of personal history, complaints of mistreatment, are some of the typical group behaviors which may cause the group to drift off course. Usually bringing these episodes to the group's attention brings censure to the individuals responsible. The inappropriate behaviors may then decrease or they may be denied. In either case, the wishes of the group can be made explicit, and the guilty parties can then be asked by the group for a commitment to decrease those distracting behaviors while increasing other appropriate behaviors. These within-group behaviors also provide additional information for problem areas to be worked on. Cases of extreme nervousness or too little talking, for example, might indicate the need for relaxation training or assertion training.

As the group progresses, new goals might be substituted for those originally discussed. As the new behaviors are learned and practiced outside the group, it becomes obvious that the group becomes less and less necessary for certain individuals. The fact that someone is getting ready to terminate should be explicit. This gives the group a chance to provide feedback to the individual as to the progress they have seen him make and to reinforce the individual's self-confidence. The individual, in turn, can give the group feedback on how they have helped him. Rather than terminating abruptly, it is probably better for most individuals to gradually phase out by attending less and less frequently, using the group to support and reinforce the new behaviors being carried out outside the group, and by functioning as a model for other patients to imitate.

CONCLUSION

Many techniques have been presented within a behavioral context. These techniques can be used regardless of the reader's theoretical orientation simply by translating the terminology into language with which the reader is most familiar and using those techniques that seem to make the most sense in a given group situation. It would probably be most effective for the novice group leader to choose a few techniques at first and become thoroughly proficient with them before trying to master a large number. Otherwise, the resulting groups will be a hodgepodge of technique while common sense and just plain listening will be minimal.

REFERENCES

Cautela, J. R., and Kastenbaum, R. A.: A reinforcement survey schedule for use in therapy, training and research. *Psychological Reports, 20*:1115-1130. 1967.

Goldstein, A. P., Heller, K., and Sechrest, L. B.: *Psychotherapy and the Psychology of Behavior Change.* New York, Wiley, 1966.

Jackson, D., and Della-Piana, G.: Establishing a behavioral observation system: A self-instruction program. Unpublished manuscript, Bureau of Educational Research, University of Utah, 1971.

Kanfer, F. H., and Saslow, G.: Behavioral diagnosis. In Franks, C. M. (Ed.): *Behavior Therapy: Appraisal and Status.* New York, McGraw, 1969, pp. 417-444.

Lazarus, A. A.: Group therapy of phobic disorders by systematic desensitization. *Journal of Abnormal and Social Psychology, 63*:504-510, 1961.

Lazarus, A. A.: Behavior therapy in groups. In Gazda, G. M. (Ed.): *Basic Approaches to Group Psychotherapy and Counseling.* Springfield, Thomas, 1968, pp. 149-175.

Moreno, Z. T.: Psychodramatic rules, techniques and adjunctive methods. In *Psychodrama and Group Psychotherapy.* New York, Beacon, 1966.

Stone, A. R., Parloff, M. B., and Frank, J. D.: The use of "diagnostic groups" in a group therapy program. *International Journal of Group Psychotherapy, 4*:274, 1954.

Sturm, I. E.: The behavioristic aspect of psychodrama. *Group Psychotherapy, 18*:50-64, 1965.

Sturm, I. E.: A behavioral outline of psychodrama. *Psychotherapy: Theory, Research and Practice, 7*:245-247, 1970.

Suinn, R. M., and Richardson, F.: Anxiety management training: A nonspecific behavior therapy program for anxiety control. *Behavior Therapy, 2*:498-510, 1971.

Tasto, D. L., and Hickson, R.: Standardization and scaling of the 122-item fear survey schedule. *Behavior Therapy, 1*:473-484, 1970.

Wolpe, J.: *Psychotherapy by Reciprocal Inhibition.* Stanford, Stanford U Pr, 1958.

Wolpe, J., and Lang, P. J.: A fear survey schedule for use in behavior therapy. *Behaviour Research and Therapy, 2*:27-30, 1964.

Wolpe, J., and Lazarus, A. A.: *Behavior Therapy Techniques.* New York, Pergamon, 1966.

CHAPTER IV

GROUP COUNSELING WITH PEOPLE WHO ARE MENTALLY HANDICAPPED

ROBERT A. LASSITER

INTRODUCTION

For our generation there is no such thing as life without trouble. There are only good kinds of trouble and bad kinds of trouble. How can we preserve our aspirations (without which no social betterment is possible) and at the same time develop the toughness of mind and spirit to face the fact that there are no easy victories.

JOHN W. GARDNER

59

THE REHABILITATION WORKER who is involved in the use of group counseling with people who are mentally handicapped—either at work in a facility or in a community based program—experiences "no easy victories." Gardner's usual skill in communicating a particular dilemma faced by the helping professions is applicable to the hundreds of rehabilitation workers who must quite often choose from alternatives in small group work that appear to be equally amorphous.

Three major difficult and perplexing problems are perceived by rehabilitation workers as they use small group methods in working with clients who are labeled as mentally handicapped:

1. A lack of solid evidence that group counseling produces a satisfactory work adjustment for people with serious mental problems.

2. Usually an awkward or discomfiting feeling on the part of the rehabilitation worker who assumes responsibility for group leadership, and the accompanying anxiety and apprehension he experiences as he begins to interact with his clients.

3. An inability to apperceive a clear pattern of organization or a systematic framework within which the client and the counselor can work together toward the goal of freedom for the client through the medium of work.

Purpose of This Chapter

The goal of this chapter is to examine these three areas of concern to the rehabilitation worker and the mentally handicapped client. *First*, a review of the professional literature is made. The purposes here are to assist in gaining historical perspective and to share in the search for circumstances which point to behavior indicating group counseling may be beneficial. *Second*, a rationale for the role of the rehabilitation worker performing as a leader or facilitator in group counseling is presented in conjunction with a list of tentative requisites for prior experience and training which appear to be needed by the rehabilitation worker in the field of mental health. And, *third*, general guidelines are postulated in an effort to offer rehabilitation personnel some assistance in the establishment of a systematic pattern to use in group counseling with people who suffer a variety of mentally handicapping conditions.

REVIEW OF THE LITERATURE

The use of group counseling or psychotherapy methods in the treatment of mental illness is not a new phenomenon to psychologists, psychiatrists, social workers and other professional people involved in the rehabilitation process, in an institutional setting, or in a community mental health clinic. However, this approach or method has not been widely associated with the work of the rehabilitation counselor, work evaluator or other rehabilitation staff, except in recent times (Rudd and Margolin, 1969). At the present time, group counseling is not only being chosen by large numbers of rehabilitation agencies and facilities as the *modus operandi* for staff to follow; but the increasing emphasis and importance placed on group work by the general public (and particularly the "mental health public") has had a pervasive effect on the rehabilitation concept as it has emerged in the field of mental health in the past decade.

Walter Neff, in his book, *Work and Human Behavior*, chronicles the shift in rehabilitation techniques from "guidance" to "counseling" in more recent times as rehabilitation staff have turned to the problems of mentally handicapped people with severe conditions—which Neff states "implies an increasing belief that the problems of adjustment to work are, in some sense or other, problems of personality. Where these problems are severe, they cannot be solved by the giving of occupational information or the administration of tests. Some type of reconstruction of relevant areas of the personality appears to be required. The result has been an increasingly intensive search for appropriate methods of treatment." (Neff, 1968)

One method found appropriate in this search appears to be group counseling. Despite the rapid, and at times excessive, production of explanations for group counseling, theoretical and philosophical definitions found in the literature are not very helpful to the rehabilitation worker. A major problem is the inability or unwillingness of leaders in the field of counseling to be more careful than they are in statements such as "Group counseling and group psychotherapy are treated as the same phenomenon except that each has a distinctive setting and a unique relationship to the network of persons in the group. Group counseling takes place largely in educational and social settings. Group psychotherapy is used in hospitals, clinics for mental health and private practice by psychologists and psychiatrists." (Fullmer, 1971). Ohlsen attempts a similar distinction in his book, *Group Counseling*, by concluding "Group psychotherapy, on the other hand, is defined here as a therapeutic experience for emotionally disturbed persons . . ." (Ohlsen, 1970). While we can appreciate the contributions these authors and others are making in the search for a clear definition of group counseling and the distinctions between counseling and psychotherapy, these kinds of explanations are of no benefit to the rehabilitation counselor. Much of the rehabilitation worker's in-service and university education in counseling has provided a "role" for individual counseling based on the counseling model, i.e., the relationship found in the educational and social settings; and, while the rehabilitation practitioner and trainer have usually been able to modify theoretical constructs to fit the pragmatic world of rehabilitation—on the one-to-one relationship in counseling—it is clear that the rehabilitation counselor, for example, cannot follow this model in his work with small groups. The rehabilitation worker is, in reality, asked to conduct group counseling for the emotionally disturbed, the mentally retarded, and clients with serious behavior problems; in fact, these severely handicapped people represent the largest number of clients who now receive some type of group counseling services, from a task-oriented approach to a basic encounter or sensitivity activity. Thus, the clients themselves require a "different" type of group counseling. And, in addition, rehabilitation workers engaged in group work are employed as members of the "team" at a mental hospital, half-way or transitional living facility, or in a community mental health clinic; the professional models they find for group work would certainly be classified as "therapeutic."

A brief survey of rehabilitation training as shown in *The Use of Small Groups in Rehabilitation* suggests that universities and agency training staff have already turned to the basic encounter group or sensitivity training. In one chapter of this handbook, William Schutz, author of *Joy*, states, "Many of our methods come from areas loosely referred to as the human potential movement or the humanistic orientation . . ." (Berzon and Solomon, 1968). It is an understatement to declare that this movement in training for rehabilitation workers in the more affective area of group work has presented serious problems to the rehabilitation practitioner who, with the client, have the responsibility of maintaining a strongly goal-oriented approach to work adjustment, since it is the major component of the rehabilitation process.

As a result of confusion and frustration experienced in this area. it is important for rehabilitation administrators, facility and community rehabilitation staff, and university educators to begin looking seriously at the need for a more precise and parsimonious definition of what "rehabilitation group counseling" really is.

At this point, rehabilitation practitioners are coping with various ways to become involved with the feelings of clients, and at the same time they are emphasizing thoughts or behaviors that will lead to employment. These activities are attempts to blend the affective and cognitive areas in order to provide an opportunity for the mentally handicapped person to learn effective interpersonal and job skills. George Isaac Brown in his introduction to the concept of "confluent education" defines this blending as follows:

> Confluent education is the term for the integration or flowing together of the affective and cognitive elements in individual or group learning, sometimes called humanistic or psychological education . . . a philosophy and a process of learning in which the affective domain and the cognitive domain flow together, like two streams merging into one river, and are thus integrated in individual and group learning . . . It should be apparent that there is no intellectual learning without some sort of feeling, and there are no feelings without the mind's being somehow involved (Brown, 1971).

An important handbook distributed to rehabilitation workers in recent years is *Reality Coping and Employment Adjustment.* This approach to group counseling for mentally handicapped people is based on the concepts expressed by William Glasser in *Reality Therapy.* The "reality coping" goal in group counseling is viewed to be the learning by clients of effective rather than ineffective behaviors. "Needs are 'fulfilled' by the reinforcing properties of environmental conditions. Abilities are simply the responses utilized by the individual to respond to those aspects of his environment which require a 'coping' response. Congruence, then, between needs and environment reinforcing properties and congruence between patient abilities and the abilities required by the environment, will create realistic behavior." (Kramer and Hawkes, 1968).

In this reality coping approach to group counseling, the authors present two models which represent essentially what is to be taught conceptually to participants in a reality coping group. The first, *self improvement,* is concerned with self-involvement, self-evaluation, self-direction and self-achievement. These areas are "taught" to the participants in order for them to reach the goal of *self improvement.* "The emphasis is on *behavior in response to the environment,* i.e., being able to respond" (Kramer and Hawkes, 1968). In the second model, reality coping is portrayed as a set of concepts referred to as *action principles,* based an Glasser's reality therapy viewpoints. The action principle model produces a plan of action: It requires that group members become involved with others and that changed behavior will result in changed feelings and emotions. "This may begin in the group by constantly encouraging group members to support each other in desirable ways, to interact with telephone calls, or going to movies together between sessions, etc. Group members must be encouraged and then taught, where necessary, how to establish contacts with others . . . learning to function better will not be a mystery to group members. They can learn the concepts and learn them well." (Kramer and Hawkes, 1968).

It appears that this model of reality coping and employment adjustment, while established specifically for post-hospital group counseling, contains principles and methods which can be adapted to the general guidelines that are recommended in the latter part of this chapter. And the reality coping model, with modifications made by the rehabilitation worker to suit his own "reality," can be highly beneficial to group counseling with persons who are classified as mentally *retarded.*

In today's world of rehabilitation group counseling, the procedures or techniques used by the practitioner range *from* large group sessions (resembling classrooms), with members engaged in problem solving assignments under the supervision of a rehabilitation worker viewed as a teacher, a director of personnel, etc., *to* the small group approach based on Carl Rogers' basic encounter group, T-Group or sensitivity training, or other small group activities based in the affective area, with the rehabilitation worker acting as a group leader or facilitator who uses an extremely non-directive or group-centered attitude as well as technique (Rogers, 1970). In addition to the *Reality Coping and Employment Adjustment* handbook, there are several references available which include comprehensive descriptions of the great variety of small group methods now being used in rehabilitation and other settings. The T-Group or sensitivity training method developed by the National Training Laboratory in Bethel, Maine; the intensive or basic encounter approach of Carl Rogers established at the Center for the Studies of the Person at La Jolla, California; the rational-emotive marathon groups developed by Albert Ellis' institute in New York City; Big Sur, California's Esalen Institute which was influenced by Fritz Perls' gestalt therapy views; and other small group work which has had direct or indirect effects on the emerging process of rehabilitation group counseling:

Berzon, Betty, and Solomon, Lawrence M.: *The Use of Small Groups in Rehabilitation.* La Jolla, Western Behavioral Sciences Institute, 1968.
Bradford, Leland P., et al.: *T-Group Therapy and Laboratory Methods.* New York, Wiley, 1964.
Cartwright, Dorwin, and Zander, Alvin: *Group Dynamics.* New York, Har-Row, 1968.
Coulson, William R.: *Groups, Gimmicks and Instant Gurus.* New York, Har-Row, 1972.
Fullmer, Daniel W.: *Counseling, Group Therapy and System.* Scranton, Intext, 1971.
Goldberg, Carl: *Encounter: Group Sensitivity Training Experience.* New York, Science, 1970.
Ohlsen, Merle M.: *Group Counseling.* New York, HR&W, 1970.
Rogers, Carl: *Carl Rogers on Encounter Groups.* New York, Har-Row, 1970.
Yalom, Irwin D.: *The Theory and Practice of Group Psychotherapy.* New York, Basic, 1969.

In concluding this general and admittedly somewhat limited survey of the literature which affects rehabilitation group counseling procedures, a statement made by Carl Rogers in a recent interview relates to rehabilitation agencies and facilities as they look to future possibilities in the movement toward greater use of the group counseling approach in rehabilitation (Rogers, 1972):

> (Replying to a question regarding the future of encounter groups) I believe there will be possibilities for the rapid development of closeness between persons, a closeness which is not artificial, but is real and deep and which will be suited to our increasing mobility of living. Temporary relationships will be able to achieve the richness and meaning which heretofore have been associated only with life-

long attachments. Aloneness will be something one chooses out of a desire for privacy, not an isolation into which one is forced.

CARL R. ROGERS

RATIONALE FOR GROUP COUNSELING IN REHABILITATION

One achieves mental health to the extent that one becomes aware of one's interpersonal relationships.

HARRY STACK SULLIVAN

For purposes of this chapter, group counseling in rehabilitation can be defined tentatively as the process in which the rehabilitation worker and a small group (eight to ten members) of clients work together in a rather flexible alliance of affective realms and the more cognitive fields related to action. This approach, combining the area of encounter-type sessions with action-oriented activities, will allow mentally handicapped people an opportunity to acquire appropriate interpersonal skills as well as prepare for a more satisfactory adjustment to life through productive and self-actualizing behaviors—whether the process is designed for those clients with employment potential, or for those who because of severity of disability, age or other factors will perform limited work in activity centers or community programs in independent living.

"One of the major requirements of the adjustment to work is the ability to interact in certain appropriate ways with other people present on the scene" (Neff, 1968). Perhaps this thought expressed by Neff can provide rehabilitation workers with the best rationale for the use of small groups in workshops, centers and other facilities. Existentialism appears to be the philosophical base for this "interaction with others on the scene" concept. For example, in almost all of the group counseling techniques there is the use of an ahistorical approach (the "here and now" views of Fritz Perls' gestalt therapy movement); participants are encouraged to interact on a feeling level, in an honest and open way—giving and receiving "feedback"; and, the reliance on the climate of, and even the "personality" of the group for pressures to change rather than on authoritative pressure for the "right or wrong way." Arbuckle defines the existential psychologist's goal in therapy as one

> to help the individual achieve a state of acceptance, of responsibility for self, thus to be free . . . Man is free—he is what he makes of him-

self, the "outside" limits and restricts [e.g., a handicapping condition], but it does not determine [completely] one's way of life. Existence precedes essence . . . Man is not static, but he is rather in a constant state of growing, evolving, becoming. He is in a state of being, but also non-being . . . Existentialism sees counseling and psychotherapy as primary human encounter . . . The stress is on today rather than yesterday or tomorrow. A real human encounter must be in terms of now, and life and living are in terms of what *is*, not what was or what might be (Arbuckle, 1970).

Another hint of the origin of this philosophical base can be seen in Rollo May's statements:

Therapy is concerned with helping the person experience his existence as real . . . which includes becoming aware of his potentialities and becoming able to act on the basis of them . . . the significance of commitment is not that it is simply a vaguely good thing or ethically to be advised. It is a necessary prerequisite rather for seeing truth . . . decision precedes knowledge. We have worked normally on the assumption that, as the [client] gets more and more knowledge and insight about himself, he will make appropriate decisions. This is a half-truth. The second half of the truth is generally overlooked, namely, that the person cannot permit himself to get insight or knowledge until he is *ready* to decide, takes a decisive orientation to life, and has made the preliminary decision along the way (May, 1958).

There is no question that rehabilitation personnel working with mentally handicapped people can benefit from a thorough study of an existentialist psychology since the rehabilitation concept itself is "an existentialist one." The thoughts expressed by Rollo May and others reinforce the choice made in rehabilitation toward group counseling as one way to help clients have the opportunity to interact with other people in order to make better decisions regarding adjustment to life and to work.

However, the rapidly proliferating group counseling approaches have brought problems to rehabilitation practitioners: the acceleration in group experiences and the prolific writings of research studies in the group process have resulted in a "knowledge explosion" which, in some cases, has prevented the practitioner from assimilating and implementing this knowledge. And, in turn, his frustration is increased by the demands of administrators, supervisors, university educators and the clients themselves for an "instant movement" toward using more and more methods in group counseling—"whatever that means!"

> Encounter groups distort what they are good at, which is a chance for a person to try himself out and make his own value discoveries . . . "You should say what you feel. Say it with directness. No need to hide here what would embarrass you elsewhere." Under that kind of pressure, a person might say and sometimes do considerably more than he means.

> Encounter groups offend as dreadfully as any political collective, yet more immediately, when they roll along on the energy of a crowd, when they call on the individual to perform, when they become a court that decides about him and claims right of access to his secret heart. When that happens, I want no part of them.

> Gimmicks are not necessary. The encounter can happen without them. So it bothers me when *groupers* haul them in. When a gimmick (or game) is going, one can't differentiate between what the gimmick makes happen and what *we* are able to achieve among ourselves.

These excerpts are taken out of context from *Groups, Gimmicks and Instant Gurus, An Examination of Encounter Groups and Their Distortions* by William R. Coulson, a well-known and prominent leader in the development of encounter groups. He is a co-director of the "La Jolla Program," a group training center sponsored by Carl Rogers' Center for the Studies of the Person. Obviously, the man feels positively about the basic encounter approach to group therapy, and yet he expresses the concerns that many practitioners have felt about the intensive small group experience. In his book, he points out the flaws of the group process and at the same time provides his personal views of the benefits that "free" encounter sessions can provide: He asks, what has one achieved ideally, in encounter learning?

> He [the client] has achieved an expanded range of choice. He can be more present to people when he wishes, and more private also when he wishes that. He can be in charge of his life through being more aware of where he is; that is to say, less compelled by his habits, with less need to defend against his experience, with greater sensitivity to the full range of feelings all people have. One of the interesting facts about the long-run effects of encounter groups is that, after going through the considerable kinds of trauma I have been describing, individuals often wind up looking much as they did before the encounter. But with a difference. I know it in my own life:

this time I can choose to be the way I am, and I can sense in myself the real possibility to be other than how typically I am, *if I judge that to be appropriate.* I am no longer compelled to be some one way only. One could not ask for more (Coulson, 1972).

Just as one could not ask more of the person who is mentally handicapped and is working toward a new adjustment to life and work.

Charles B. Truax of the Arkansas Rehabilitation Research and Training Center comments on the group process in rehabilitation:

> . . . there is abundant evidence available indicating that genuineness (honesty and realism), warmth and interpersonal contact, and empathy or listening for the person inside the other are indeed significant sources for therapeutic personality and behavioral change . . . While we at present do in fact have more research evidence, both solid and suggestive, than is being utilized in practice or in training, it is also clear that research will forever lag behind innovation in practice . . . I would like to reiterate the importance of *outcome* research over *process* research. In a sense our training institutions, state licensing boards, and professional board examinations have also been process rather than outcome oriented. In view of the mounting evidence demonstrating conclusively that the practice of [group] counseling and psychotherapy is, on the average, ineffective, a focus on therapeutic outcome is vital to the development of our field (Truax, 1968).

In the development of a rationale for the role of the rehabilitation worker to perform effectively as a leader or facilitator in group counseling, it seems important to review the critiques by Coulson and other group leaders on how group counseling is being distorted and sometimes abused, and equally important to study carefully the comments and suggestions made by counseling leaders such as Truax in regard to research. "Outcome" research, or a study of what happens to our clients after group counseling is completed, is not only a more realistic approach in research in this field, but it is one that students working in a practicum in a university setting and rehabilitation workers in the field can perform without a great deal of excess work in the office and without the expert skill and knowledge required in process research.

> With regard to it (the theory of relativity) science and research owe much to intuition and to "being sympathetically in touch with experience"—I came to it by continuing to ask myself questions about space and time that only children ask.　ALBERT EINSTEIN

It is difficult to answer the question posed by many practitioners in the rehabilitation field in regard to minimum qualifications for counselors and other personnel who work with mentally handicapped people in small groups. *Assuming* that the professional person assigned to group work or who is responsible for setting up group experiences for clients has already met the "generally accepted standards" for performance as a rehabilitation professional person and that he has an understanding and accepting attitude toward his clients (and toward the disability label, too) then the following suggestions are made:

1. A master's degree in a rehabilitation field or its equivalent (as indicated in recent certification statements made by the National Association of Rehabilitation Counseling).

2. At least one experience as a member of a basic encounter or sensitivity training group.

3. One or two introductory courses in social psychology emphasizing the research studies in group dynamics.

4. Selection of a consultant (or co-leader)—one who has wide experience in group work and possesses a positive professional reputation among his peers. In other words, "check him out." A Ph.D. is not, in itself, a reliable criterion for selecting a competent supervisor or consultant in this field.

5. *Read* all books, articles in professional journals, reports of conferences, etc. which are available.

(The dilemma here: there are professional people who are extremely effective in group work who may not meet all of these suggested "requisites" and there are rehabilitation workers who meet all the above suggestions for competency and have additional "credentials" who are not successful in helping clients through this approach.)

Before we begin to look to the development of general guidelines for establishing some systematic pattern to follow in the use of small groups with mentally handicapped people, a final statement is taken from an article appearing in *Rehabilitation Record*, "Group Counseling with Rehabilitation Clients" (Gust, 1970):

> While I would not call it a panacea, group counseling—both leader-less and counselor-led—appears to offer to the rehabilitation client the opportunity to learn to adjust to his role as a handicapped person through an experience in positive social interaction for long-term

usefulness. In rehabilitation we are concerned with some type of reintroduction of the client into the typically able-bodied or non-handicapped community. This is one common bond which most rehabilitation clients share. (And), there are many other common concerns for the handicapped client which make group counseling an appropriate choice . . . Being able to experience and work through real feelings encountered in group interaction is probably the most unique and beneficial aspect of group as compared with individual counseling.

TIM GUST

A PATTERN TO USE IN GROUP COUNSELING IN REHABILITATION SETTINGS

This pattern of organization of small group work in rehabilitation will require modification by the practitioner to meet the reality of his particular work situation. While the plan is based on empirical studies and abstract philosophical theses, "outcome" research suggested by Truax is limited to one experience, altered to meet specific needs of a group of students; therefore, the activity schedule should be viewed by the group leader as a flexible guide and *not* a formal plan that has received the blessings of "process" research. In fact, it is perhaps more important for rehabilitation workers to remain open to the group movement, and while using the group method, follow Truax's suggestion of each student and practitioner utilizing an "outcome" research plan. This practice can be beneficial not only to the rehabilitation group leader; but, if shared with others, it can provide the basis for an orderly, evolving systematic approach which can help more mentally handicapped people become productive.

OUTLINE OF AN ACTIVITY SCHEDULE

One Week	During the first week, eight to ten mentally handicapped people are selected for group membership
	Rehabilitation worker and client meet in individual conferences for orientation
	Rehabilitation worker distributes the plan to all concerned
	First meeting of the group devoted to instruction related to small group dynamics
Four Weeks	Four encounter type small group sessions—one hour per week for the four-week period
One Week	Individual conferences with clients—thirty minutes to one hour each for the one-week period

| Three Weeks | Three task-oriented or problem solving sessions—one hour per week for this three-week period |
| One Week | A PLAN is prepared by the client and the rehabilitation worker related to adjustment to employment —through individual conferences—thirty minutes to one hour each for the one-week period |

Total:
Ten Weeks:

I. Introduction:

A. The rehabilitation worker arranges for eight to ten clients to meet in a small group setting. One hour per week for the group counseling, and thirty minutes to one hour per individual session—this allows for seven weeks of one hour group counseling sessions and three weeks for personal interviews.

B. The rehabilitation worker interviews each client selected for the program during the first week as the schedule begins. Participants are told in this conference about the overall plan for the group and individual meetings, the meeting places, time, others involved, and the specific reason for the use of the group approach. Each client has as opportunity to clarify for himself the purpose of the small group work and the rehabilitation worker will be able to gather new data about the individual which may help to facilitate the client's learning about himself in relation to others in the world of work.

C. Also, in the first week of the schedule, the rehabilitation worker should inform all administrators and colleagues of the plan and have copies of the schedule of activities distributed to other members of the staff. It is important for the counselor to make clear the need for maintaining confidentiality in regard to the group sessions and to explain the importance of this "keeping quiet" attitude until each client, with the assistance of the group leader, prepares and distributes a progress report on himself to all staff, other agency professional personnel, or to employers (at the end of the sessions).

D. One final activity is suggested for the facilitator during this first week of the activity schedule: (The term facilitator will be used for the rehabilitation worker during the remainder of this schedule.) This final preliminary action will require that the facilitator set up a one-hour meeting of all participants (this follows the individual conferences). The purpose of this meeting is to teach clients what group counseling is: to review the schedule, to give an explanation of what is expected by participants, and what role or roles the facilitator will play. If video or audio equipment is being considered for use in the groups, it will be wise for the facilitator to receive a group consensus on this as well as any other technical concerns.

In this initial meeting, the group members are receiving instruction from the facilitator, and the climate should resemble an "open classroom" type of session. If honesty and openness is to come later, it is extremely important that the facilitator be honest about the purpose: "It's to help you adjust to work," for example. Also, the facilitator should share with the group all the "secret and mysterious things" about group dynamics which he or she has learned (dependent in degree, of course, on the ability of the clients to understand). Every effort should be made to avoid burdening the group members with the facilitator's problem of "wearing two hats—teacher and facilitator." The facilitator is encouraged to say that "sometimes I will be there as your counselor, and I will do most of the listening in order for you to speak and listen to each other about the way you feel. Later I will be a more active participant as we begin to work on specific problems regarding your plans for employment or training." And, of course, the facilitator should inform the clients of his own pledge of confidentiality. This informal meeting of the group should provide the facilitator with additional background information about the group members in order to plan for a ten-week schedule that will be uniquely suitable. And last, it is important for the facilitator to avoid during these first meetings a manipulative approach—be honest. For example, if direction is needed in your judgement, give it, but, watch for and avoid the more subtle "guarded and hidden" manipulative stance.

II. Small Group Activity—Phase I

(First four weeks of encounter approach—one hour per session)

An opportunity is provided for clients to follow the basic encounter approach in group work—for each client to develop interpersonal skills with other members, with the facilitator encouraging clients to be sensitive to feelings and to speak openly about them (if they so desire!).

Certain exercises from books on encounter work, cassette tapes and other programmed instruction in interpersonal behavior may be helpful to "new" practitioners (especially in working with people who are retarded). These aids are intended as *temporary* devices to assist the facilitator in establishing early a climate of trust and openness in this particular phase of the plan. Coulson cautions us to be wary of these "gimmicks"—and who can be *for* gimmicks? A *gimmick* is defined as an "ingenious or novel device, scheme, deception or hidden disadvantage" (Random House Dictionary, 1968). However, the first part of the definition parallels the definition for *gadget*: "a mechanical contrivance or device; any ingenious article" (Random House Dictionary, 1968). Gadgets appear to be justified *only* when they are used on a temporary basis and *only* when they are carefully selected to avoid what Coulson calls "making things happen that the group itself can achieve." In this phase of the small group activity, clients are encouraged to stay with the "here and now" attitude within the group. The facilitator can assist the group in looking at strengths rather than weaknesses. Successful group counseling in this first four-week period would mean that each client experiences:

> greater acceptance of his total being—emotional, intellectual and physical—as it *is*, including its potential . . . [appreciates that] individuals can hear each other, can learn from each other to a greater extent; [the value of] feedback from one person to another, such that each individual learns how he appears to others and what impact he has in interpersonal relationships . . . [that] the learnings in the group experience tend to carry over, temporarily or more permanently in relationships with [others in different settings] (Rogers, 1970).

II. Individual Counseling Sessions—Phase II

(One week for personal interviews between the facilitator and individual clients—thirty minutes to one hour)

This week of individual conferences can be viewed as a bridge between the more "affective" area of group work which was experienced in the four week encounter sessions and the more "cognitive" area of group work which will be emphasized in the three problem solving sessions to follow. There are two major purposes for these interviews which "interrupt" the group counseling process:

1. The client has an opportunity to share privately any feelings and concerns about his experience in the earlier group sessions— he may feel uncomfortable or embarrassed about his "openness" or that of others.

2. The client has the opportunity to share privately any new ideas he may have about himself or his plans for adjustment to work.

Also, the facilitator at this point can briefly review plans for the more structured, problem solving group sessions, and in some cases he may assign a task for the client to work out prior to or during the group counseling.

III. Small Group Activity—Phase III

(For the next three weeks—one hour per session in group counseling)

The purpose of Phase III in this activity schedule for use of group counseling in rehabilitation is to begin to focus on general work skills that are common to all jobs. The tasks to be assigned to the group will relate to learning ways of becoming effective workers in the real world of work. Some of the assignments made by the facilitator in these three or more cognitive or task-oriented sessions will include:

First Assignment

Each group member will share with the group the problems that he is experiencing in whatever work situation in which he has been involved, either in prevocational or work evaluation settings or job-tryouts, etc. These problems may have to do with attitudes toward employers, fellow employees, work habits and other basic problems involved with the work setting. "Feedback" from others will be the key in these sessions.

Second Assignment

Each client will share with the group his own self-evaluation. A form can be devised by the facilitator to ask for a listing of strengths and weaknesses, including a statement at the end such as "What can I do to build on my strengths and find ways to eliminate or accept my weaknesses in order to become a free person with productive work?"

Third Assignment

Each client will share with the group *A Plan* he has set up by himself (at times, with the help of the facilitator, if required). The plan will indicate how he plans to assume responsibility for getting a job, a job-tryout, an on-the-job experience, or some kind of vocational training. In addition, each client will be asked to share his evaluation of the group experience and to share his thoughts and feelings about himself and his future.

(these three assignments are set up to provide for a "main topic" for each of the three task-oriented group counseling sessions as scheduled above)

IV. Individual Counseling Sessions—Phase IV

(One week for personal interviews between the facilitator and individual clients—thirty minutes to one hour each)

In an attempt to integrate the group counseling method into the total mental health and rehabilitation process, this last week of the activity schedule is designed to provide an opportunity for the facilitator to have an individual conference with each member of the group. The results of this interview will constitute a "joint communiqué" type of progress report in which the client and the facilitator sit down together and work out a report to be distributed to staff members and others who might be concerned with the client's adjustment to work or other activities. This report can be made in the form of a recommendation, e.g., "It is recommended that this person participate in additional work adjustment programs or enter an activity type program not involved with competitive employment or take vocational training or become employed."

This completes the pattern of organization. Activities that are involved with the feelings of clients and those that are emphasizing thoughts that will lead to action are viewed as a blending of these two areas (affective and cognitive) which will provide an opportunity for the mentally handicapped person to learn better how to adjust to the job.

> Group therapy has had a succession of attractive wrappings: it was, during World War II, the economical answer to a shortage of trained therapists; later it became a logical treatment arena of the interpersonal theory of psychology; and currently it is a medium for alleviating individual and social alienation. At present groups, self-disclosure, interpersonal closeness, touching are "in." Yet the medium is *not* the message. Group [counseling] is not primarily a vehicle for closeness and human contact. It is a method for effecting therapeutic

change in individuals. All other goals are metaphenomena and secondary to the primary function of the group.

IRWIN D. YALOM

GUIDELINES IN THE USE OF GROUP COUNSELING WITH MENTALLY RETARDED PEOPLE

As Rick Heber points out in the book he edited, *Special Problems in Vocational Rehabilitation of the Mentally Retarded,*

> The counseling process for mentally retarded clients is *essentially the same* as for all disabled persons. As with all developmental disabilities, lifelong experiences of failure and rejection often create particularly difficult rehabilitation problems which can only be resolved through personal counseling. The intellectual limitations of the retarded client, and particularly his deficit in verbal communication, do necessitate modifications in usual counseling techniques and require the utilization of a wider range of approaches (Heber, 1965).

In addition to these problems that mentally retarded people experience, other difficulties are experienced when a group counseling method is used by the rehabilitation worker. For example, in a study of techniques for predicting vocational success of mentally retarded adults conducted by the Human Resources Center in Albertson, New York, the work of the project director and his research associates show the special problems and also the promises of the use of the group approach:

> The relative importance of personal-social factors and specific skill factors depends on the nature of the job as well as the level of skill required in the job. It has been suggested that the lower the skill level required in the job, the more important become the personal-social factors. In other words, if little or no skill is required for a job, the only criterion for continued employability is the personal-social factor (Manus, Kovacs, Roberts and Levy, 1970).

As Henry Vicsardi writes in the foreword of this research study, "although the findings must be preliminary, they do suggest directions in the rehabilitation of the mentally retarded client that have been previously neglected or ignored . . ." (Manus, Kovacs, Roberts and Levy, 1970). And because of the special problems encountered in the field of mental retardation there has been a reluctance to provide a rehabilitation group counseling setting for people who are mentally retarded. Yet we know that mentally retarded people have been able to meet certain personal, social and vocational needs through counseling. George Baroff, a leader in the rehabilitation field of mental retardation, states: "Retarded individuals, like the rest of us, share needs for survival, structure, self-esteem, and self-expression. While the disability of mental retardation does not affect basic needs, qualitatively, it does influence their relative intensity and the likelihood of their being met" (Hardy and Cull, 1973). Most sheltered workshop and facility programs appear to have accepted these basic needs as expressed by Baroff or at least have given emphasis to similar models of "what" the retarded person needs; special projects in this field almost always report on the efforts to effect change in personal and social behaviors. But rarely have reports of these projects or observation of facilities shown the exploration into the area of group counseling as a formal procedure useful to the rehabilitation of persons who are retarded.

One research and demonstration project that does report on its use of the small group approach is the project mentioned earlier which was carried out at Viscardi's Human Resources Center and Abilities Inc. program on Long Island.

The following impressions were derived from utilization of group counseling techniques as a component of the total rehabilitation project:

1. Great reluctance on the part of the clients to talk about topics with emotional content, reflecting a general mistrust initially of the group leader.

2. Once the initial reluctance was overcome for many, it was noted that several members continued to remain silent: a factor attributed to anxiety over handling "excessive input," as seen in one member's question: "What do I do if everybody answers me at once?"

3. It appeared to the researchers that some members who remained silent had experienced more negative reactions to their attempts at verbalization in the past; under such circumstances, their reluctant verbal behaviors might be as much a reflection of continuing negative expectations of others as any inherent lack of ability to communicate.

4. Through serendipity, they found that the reduction in group size in one group experience overcame the problems experienced earlier relative to verbalization: "With the reduction of the group to four

members and a leader, the remaining counselees embarked on lengthy discussions of feelings previously avoided . . . The smaller group size seemed to lessen the fear of 'excessive input' and eliminated the 'classroom' feeling. As one of the trainees put it: 'The meetings were sort of like a family get-together.' "

5. Early in the group counseling sessions, it became apparent that coping with the label "retardation" and the loneliness prominent in many of the clients' daily lives were deterrents in the acceptance of realistic vocational goals (Manus, Kovacs, Roberts and Levy, 1970).

Since the findings of this study are in general agreement with other project reports related to the use of group counseling for persons who are retarded, and experience and observation would indicate that some reliable inference can be obtained from its logic, much of the modified activity schedule which follows reflects the impressions derived from this and similar observations.

As can be noted, the changes made in the outline of the schedule are mostly quantitative which also provides for greater emphasis in certain areas, e.g. orientation and instruction. It would not be accurate to assume that the changes are due entirely to the need for "slow" learners to have more time nor that there is more time available to the rehabilitation worker because of fewer group members; however, consideration has been given to these areas. The major reason for the changes center around the fact that most mentally retarded people will be employed in jobs that will require less technical skills but *more* interpersonal skills. This concept of group work for retarded people also encompasses the more specific problems demonstrated in the Human Resources Center's study: greater reluctance to speak openly of emotions; initially, a general mistrust of the group facilitator; anxiety on the part of clients caused by a feeling of "excessive input"; minimum verbal behavior reflecting the continuing negative expectation of others of what the retarded person says; the unrealistic goals of retarded people in regard to employment, etc. Reduction of the size of the group from eight to ten members to only four with the group approach for mentally retarded people—the major change—appears to be indicated in order to minimize or eliminate the problems listed above. In reviewing the more detailed pattern of organization recommended for group counseling with emotionally disturbed or mentally handicapped people, all other activities appear to be compatible with the needs of persons who are retarded, with one exception: it is anticipated that the rehablitation worker will be required to become more directive in assisting the client in developing the *PLAN*, with greater attention paid to external evaluative processes.

The schedule developed earlier in this chapter to offer a general guideline to follow in rehabilitation group counseling remains substantially intact; however, a few alterations are required to meet the more special needs of people who are mentally retarded. Five steps were outlined to convey the series of events occurring in the ten-week schedule:

(Changes or modifications of the original plan are *in italics*)

I.
1. During the first week, *four mentally retarded people* are selected for the group counseling experience.
2. The rehabilitation worker meets with the client in an individual counseling session for orientation *and instruction.*

One Week
3. A copy of the total plan is distributed to all members of the staff, including the administrative personnel.
4. The first meeting of the group is called and the *counselor assumes the role of a teacher—to instruct* the *four* member groups in goals of group counseling.

II.
Four Weeks
Four encounter-type small group sessions will be held— *two hours* per week for the four-week period. (Two hours may be divided into shorter segments during the week.)

III.
Individual conferences with clients for *feedback and additional orientation—one to two hours* for each client during the one-week period.

IV.
Three Weeks
Three task-oriented or problem solving group sessions— *two hours* per week for the three-week period. (Two hours may be divided into shorter segments during the week.)

V.
One Week
Progress report and plan prepared by the client and the rehabilitation worker through individual counseling sessions—*one to two* hours each for the one-week period.

SUMMARY

This chapter focuses on three major areas of concern as perceived by rehabilitation practitioners in accepting responsibility for leading or facilitating small groups whose members are mentally handicapped. These concerns include the lack of solid evidence that group counseling does produce satisfactory work adjustment for people with serious mental problems, the rehabilitation worker's anxiety and apprehension in regard to his new role as a group leader, and the lack of general guidelines that can offer a model or pattern to the rehabilitation staff. An attempt is made to provide a review of the literature demonstrating positive results of research and concepts developed by the various leaders in the group movement. This review also contains notes of caution and constructive criticisms from leaders in the field. Following the survey, an effort is made to offer a rationale for the rehabilitation worker's role in group counseling with mentally handicapped people. A pattern is formulated for use by the practitioner in the establishment of an activity schedule for beginning group work. In a final special section of the chapter, guidelines are suggested for adapting the activity schedule of rehabilitation group counseling methods to the needs of people who are mentally retarded.

REFERENCES

Arbuckle, Dugald S.: *Counseling: Philosophy, Theory and Practice*. Boston, Allyn, 1970.

Berzon, Betty, and Solomon, Lawrence N.: *The Use of Small Groups in Rehabilitation*. La Jolla, Western Behavioral Sciences Institute, 1968.

Brown, George Issac: *Human Teaching for Human Learning, An Introduction to Confluent Education*. New York, Viking Press, 1971.

Coulson, William R.: *Groups, Gimmicks and Instant Gurus*. New York, Har-Row, 1972.

Fullmer, Daniel W.: *Counseling—Group Theory and System*. Scranton, International, 1971.

Gardner, John W.: *No Easy Victories*. New York, Har-Row, 1968.

Glasser, William: *Reality Therapy*. New York, Har-Row, 1965.

Gust, Tim: Group counseling with rehabilitation clients. *Rehabilitation Record*, January-February, 1970.

Hardy, Richard E., and Cull, John G.: *Vocational Evaluation for Rehabilitation Services*. Springfield, Thomas, 1973.

Heber, Rick: *Vocational Rehabilitation of the Mentally Retarded*. Rehabilitation Services Series, No. 65-16, U.S. Department of Health, Education and Welfare, 1965.

Kramer, Elmer E., and Hawkes, F. James: *Reality Coping and Employment Adjustment: A Handbook for Post-Hospital Group Counseling*. Colorado State University, Fort Collins, Colorado, 1968.

Manus, Gerald I., Kovacs, Marika, Roberts, Norman, and Levy, Barbara: *Skill Analysis as a Technique for Predicting Vocational Success of the Mentally Retarded.* Albertson, Human Resources Center, 1970.

May, Rollo: Contributions of existential psychotherapy. In *Existence.* New York, 1958.

Neff, Walter S.: *Work and Human Behavior.* New York, Atherton, 1968.

Ohlsen, Merle M.: *Group Counseling.* New York, HR&W, 1970.

Rogers, Carl R.: *Carl Rogers on Encounter Groups.* New York, Har-Row, 1970.

Rogers, Carl R.: *Human Behavior.* Volume I, No. 6, November-December, 1972.

Rudd, Jacob L., and Margolin, Reuben J.: *Rehabilitation Medicine—Psychiatric,* West Medford, R.M.D. Publishers, 1969.

Sullivan, Harry Stack: *Conceptions of Modern Psychiatry.* New York, Norton, 1940.

The Random House Dictionary of the English Language. New York, Random, 1968.

CHAPTER V

SERVICES AND ORGANIZATIONS OF THE REHABILITATION UNIT IN A COMPREHENSIVE MENTAL HEALTH FACILITY

Thomas C. Dickinson

~~~~~~

- The Hospital Milieu
- Vocational Rehabilitation Team
- Personal-Vocational Counseling
- Occupational Therapy Experiences
- Continuing Rehabilitation Contacts
- A Workable Philosophy
- References

~~~~~~

IN DESCRIBING a rehabilitation program which effectively provides vocational counseling, employment assistance and continuing emotional support for psychiatric patients, one must, at best, work out a compromise between ideal and practical considerations. This chapter investigates a variety of factors essential to the conduct of an extensive vocational rehabilitation program, beginning with the initial stages of admission to a mental health facility, the ward routine, primary therapist planning, and contributions from allied staff. The emphasis upon re-introduction of the patient into the on-going community brings with it attendant responsibilities of adequate planning and assistance to equip him with more saleable job skills, motivation to put forth consistent effort toward realistic goals, and stability to withstand continuing personal and social burdens.

To further delimit our area of concern, Roberts (1970) has defined rehabilitation evaluation as "the total assessment of the client's assets and limitations to function from the medical/physical, psycho/social, and vocational/educational points of view." Risch (1971) states, "Here we can find the practical social testing ground to discover the kind of industrial assignment that best suits the unconscious needs of the emotionally beset patient." Our focus will be on evaluating patient needs and attributes, developing appropriate vocationally-oriented programs, and providing counseling services during hospitalization.

THE HOSPITAL MILIEU

In years past, mental health facilities oriented programs toward long-term custodial patients, offering diversional, recreational and therapeutic programs geared to lengthy hospital stay. Often these institutions were geographically removed from the employment and educational community. All too often, the patient was ill-equipped to fend for himself when discharged, leading to high re-admission rates. In recent years, more attention has been devoted to discharge planning, prevention of readmission, and provision of extensive services soon after admission to lessen hospital stay. In many instances, service availability when the patient first appears makes actual hospitalization unnecessary.

Inherent in such a shift of emphasis is a belief that lengthy hospitalization offers little in the way of benefits and, indeed, may serve to further isolate the person from family, friends, work and society. For a person marginally equipped to function independently in society, the hospital stay compounds his difficulties to leave him even less capable of picking up the pieces of his life upon discharge. Though the mental health facility serves a "protective" function, its program must bring reality to bear upon the individual in a manner in which he can begin to work out pressing problems. Therefore, the hospital milieu must be one of expectation that the patient will, as soon as possible, both return to the community and return better equipped than formerly to handle problems and challenges in an independent, realistic and satisfying way. Colton (1971) describes the "conversion" of the patient to a rehabilitative frame of mind, writing that "The patient must be helped to understand that he is no longer sick in a way that requires total dependence on the institution. He must be shown that the 'patient role' is no longer as rewarding or productive as it has been in the past." A modified therapeutic team approach has superseded traditional methods with chronic hospital inpatients. For example, Williams, Dudley and Guinn (1969) applied a "day treatment" approach to chronic inpatients with a mix of occupational therapy, educational therapy, recreational therapy, social therapy, and psychotherapy. Walker and Asci (1971) used a paid work program to find better social adjustment even though their long-term schizophrenic patients continued to function with considerable impairment.

Gradients of Reality Challenge

Though one cannot detail the numerous reasons for admission at a mental health facility, a number of concerns or beliefs stand out as a basic to such a decision. First and foremost, the patient no longer feels capable of handling the burdens of decision-making. Whether he seeks assistance independently, whether other family members have encouraged him to seek help, or whether his behavior and actions have led members of the community to recommend hospitalization (such as hallucinations or delusions which bring him into contact with legal authorities), the patient needs emotional support and guidance in handling life problems. He frequently comes with an emotional plea for help from others with whom he vests the authority and responsibility for his life. Expecting quick and specific treatment from hospital personnel, the patient searches for "specific facts" and "answers" to complicated and often long-lasting concerns and interpersonal difficulties. The first goal of hospital personnel is to accurately understand the circumstances surrounding his plea for help, his personal make-up, and his underlying ability to deal with these concerns at this point in time. This is a situation where little pressure or challenge is placed upon the patient—rather he is allowed an opportunity to ventilate his feelings and problems in an emphathetic atmosphere.

A typical mental health facility operates with a flexible professional therapeutic framework of psychiatrist, psychologist, social worker, rehabilitation counselor, occupational therapist and mental health technician. In initial interviews, the stage is set for differential decisions regarding professional staff members the patients will see and tentative programs to enter. These run the gamut from immediate admission to the inpatient facility, provision of outpatient psychotherapeutic sessions, provision of psychotropic medications, referral to another agency, and so on. This chapter deals with social and vocational adjustment difficulties which surface at time of admission, focusing upon various treatment modalities and services appropriate for individuals with varying personality characteristics, abilities and potential.

A Limited-pressure Setting

The traumatic experiences which abound when the patient enters a mental health facility can be almost as terrifying and depressing as the life problems which confront him. In part, the decision to enter the hospital is a chance to obtain help; nevertheless, it is a realization that one cannot solve problems and conduct one's affairs without assistance. This concrete personal failure is often the most upsetting element beyond the embarrassment, fear and isolation one experiences.

Hospital admission procedures are all too often designed for the benefit of orderly administration. A multitude of forms and questions confront the patient, making for a bewildering array of brief encounters and swirling faces which ultimately end in the confines of a small room with bed and cabinet. The first night is one of edgy awakening with half-asleep recollections of faces, people talking, occasional cries and shouts, and cutting recriminations over one's decision to "come here in the first place." The patient may perceive his situation as a helpless one where others around him are unaware of his specific predicament. Even though the patient may view the staff as brusque and indifferent, they have already begun to develop an impression of him and to tentatively marshal programs for a care plan.

Psychotherapeutic Confrontation

With "hearsay" information from other patients and brief meetings with certain members of the treatment team, the patient finds himself "scheduled" for a number of "therapies" and interviews. He may be assigned a "primary therapist" with any of a number of professional backgrounds. The therapist provides the majority of the face-to-face personal discussion and decision making help. Though the individual may meet members of many other professions, he maintains a stable and continuing relationship with his therapist. This relationship is developed during a number of psychotherapy sessions and continues through a variety of "programs" and "experiences" as the patient progresses toward discharge.

The patient himself typically speaks about his "restlessness" in the hospital and desire to "work out" a number of major concerns. This sense of wishing to come to grips with problems can be utilized in counseling sessions and carried over to therapeutic assignments in various daytime hospital programs. Each therapy program has two immediate goals: first, to develop an impression of the patient and his personal abilities and limitations; second, to introduce him to a pattern of gradually increasing challenges and pressures whereby he can successfully cope with demands and build self-confidence. Gellman (1971) has described hospital adjustment programs with a view of work as an agent of behavior modification, remarking that, "one innovative development during the last two decades attempts to implement work therapy by treating the work situation as an experimental setting in which psychosocial work variables can be altered to facilitate or modify work adjustment."

VOCATIONAL REHABILITATION TEAM

Guided by the therapist, new ideas and suggestions are made regarding a somewhat different "program" which has more than a "personal therapeutic" goal—one of greater reality stress and awareness to reveal both personal strengths and weaknesses. Counseling, through an analysis of information about what the patient can and cannot do, involves constructive self-evaluation of one's interests, feelings, interpersonal relationships and work tolerance.

The vocational counseling program also means a shift in perceptions by meeting new people and moving to a somewhat different "work area." The patient finds greater demands placed upon him to describe himself, make decisions and participate actively and independently with varying amounts of encouragement and emotional support. In contrast to personal counseling and group therapy discussions about personal feelings and social relationships, a new concept of "work adjustment" is introduced.

The vocational rehabilitation team may encompass primary therapist, rehabilitation counselor, psychologist, vocational evaluator, vocational placement specialist and other professional titles which frequently cause considerable apprehension and consternation when first mentioned to the patient. The considerable overlap of duties and responsibilities among these vocational specialists requires definition of the various steps in the patient's reentry into the community.

Coordination of Service Roles

The traditional functions of the rehabilitation counselor or psychologist as a "coordinator" of services and as a "facilitator" for the psychiatric inpatient require a workable program with a sharing of certain functions along with the gathering of recommendations from other professions. Conceptualization of "service roles" as somewhat distinct from and independent of "professional identities" is needed. For example, the "counselor" for the specific patient could well be a rehabilitation counselor, a social worker, a clinical psychologist, a mental health techncian, or so on. The "therapist" essentially is the person who has formed a close and trusting relationship over a period of time in contrast to the flow of other allied persons with specific responsibilities and goals. In the eyes of the patient, each staff member assumes a therapeutic role. Indeed, Parker (1970) studied perceptions of rehabilitation services on the part of psychiatric hospital staff to conclude that the staff endorsed a "counselor" rather than a "coordinator" orientation.

The therapist and patient bear major responsibility for decisions at program choice-points. Elaboration of these in greater detail is often the responsibility of the counselor in early sessions with the patient discussing and offering alternative routes toward work, education or job training. An extensive vocational therapy program involves personal-vocational counseling, psychological appraisal, prevocational evaluation and occupational therapy, vocational evaluation, work adjustment experiences, and work placement. The key to successful counseling is the accurate blend of services to match the patient's particular needs and abilities.

PERSONAL-VOCATIONAL COUNSELING

Inherent in successful vocational planning is accurate assessment of patient strengths and weaknesses to provide ameliorative and rehabilitative services of sufficient strength and degree to develop the skills necessary to solve life problems independently. A variety of levels is possible in personal counseling, the therapist judging appropriateness for various therapeutic regimens. Three questions stand out as having major importance in rehabilitation planning: Does the patient manifest circumscribed life and vocational adjustment problems rather than presenting a picture of chronic and extensive maladjustment in interpersonal, personal and vocational realms? Does the patient have the motivation to change his situation rather than depend upon secondary gains from disability? Can a time-limited program of counseling make a serious change in the person's psychological situation?

In developing guidelines for evaluating client "readiness" for rehabilitation, Richman (1964) included aspects of premorbid social history, precipitating causes of breakdown, results of treatment to date, verbalized interests in vocational rehabilitation, realistic views of a vocational plan, home and community supports, and current functioning assessed through psychological or psychiatric consultation. Peffer (1953), on the other hand, listed three general criteria for patient selection, citing stabilization of psychiatric condition to the extent that the patient does not show acute behavior disturbance or symptoms; ability to conduct himself without difficulties on weekend passes and ground privileges; and no recent evidence of aggressive, suicidal or anti-social behavior.

Answers to these questions are formulated from a number of sources within the first few counseling sessions. Background information often indicates the relative length and degree of maladjustment (for example, a series of hospitalizations or long-term family and social instability). Similarly, the patient who has left other "rehabilitation" programs in the general community would present a more serious and lengthy counseling task. Another consideration is diagnostic formulations developed through prior hospitalizations or during this admission. Patients with "adolescent adjustment" or "reactive depression" diagnoses, on the whole, have better prognoses for rehabilitation success than patients manifesting severe thought or behavior disorders. Richman (1964) details significant attitudes and behaviors, both positive and negative, which serve as guides to counseling and understanding the patient. For example, positive aspects include ability to verbalize hospital treatment experiences, to concentrate on plans for recovery through actual participation, and to willingly accept realistic appraisal of abilities. Negative aspects include poor interpersonal relationships, current overt disturbed behavior, poor concentration, preoccupation with illness or total denial of illness, and resistance to movement or change.

In developing a rehabilitation plan, counselor judgement of expressed motivation similarly involves a continuum for indifference and apathy to sincere interest and commitment to personal-vocational concerns. Within this continuum is the majority of clients who enter rehabilitation programs because "it was suggested to them" or "because they saw others helped by it." In addition to past history information and client comments, an estimate of motivation can be made from concrete behavioral factors (for example, coming on time for appointments versus coming late, keeping appointments rather than "forgetting" or "having other things to do", contributing thoughts freely in counseling sessions versus repetitious statements of an "I don't know" type). Experience has shown that successful clients look forward to counseling and rehabilitation programs with a certain "interest" or "zest," anticipating that problems can be solved by learning more about themselves. Sessions may take on a free back-and-forth discussion of thoughts and ideas where the patient assumes the responsibility to grapple with concerns. In this situation the counselor serves as an "information source" or "experience mirror" to help in analyzing questions and problems. At the other end of the continuum is the patient who must be remotivated in each counseling hour to think about problems and solutions or who manifests chronic dependency and surrender to external pressures.

Psychological Appraisal

In addition to historical data, admission information, counseling discussions, and behavioral patterns in the hospital setting, psychological measures play an important part. In a sense, standardized psychological testing integrates intra-agency observation with characteristics of the community at large. Impressions of the patient in the hospital are colored by the social context of other patients and the specific agency. The patient viewed as successful in a hospital program where the majority of patients manifest severe depression or faulty reality contact may yet be well below the level of ability needed for competitive employment and independent living. Psychological testing meaningfully relates a number of life dimensions of the patient to both hospital programs and to potential rehabilitative experiences beyond the agency doors. This appraisal surveys dimensions of intelligence, personality, educational and vocational aptitudes and interests, and current motivation for rehabilitation experiences. Sacks (1957) describes psychological evaluation of patients to specify such areas as patient reaction to tests and noted anxiety, anger, or withdrawal; reaction to the examiner as an authority figure; patient's perception of himself; the level of intellectual functioning; his attitudes toward others; general outlook; defenses against anxiety; general clinical state and stability; and possible indications of work area or work environment to meet the patient's specific needs.

To discuss psychological appraisal in any depth is beyond our scope, but certain considerations should be mentioned to portray the variety of recommendations testing can make. The psychologist is conceptualized as a resource for information of a special type of information regarding personal characteristics and potentials unavailable through counseling sessions or behavioral observation. Psychological evaluation should answer specific questions at decision-points in personal counseling sessions. For example, patient and counselor may be weighing entrance into a vocational evaluation program versus immediate job-finding experiences, where further information regarding job skills is desired. The client may voice good intentions regarding vocational decision-making, but lacks clear-cut vocational interests or preferences. Questions phrased in the manner of "Can the patient successfully handle college-level educational programs?" or "Does the patient have the motivation and stability for a vocational evaluation program?" delimit and focus the concerns of the therapist. This gives the psychologist essential leeway in selecting measures to provide recommendations.

Psychological evaluation can determine movement into more intellectually and educationally challenging programs and experiences and indeed determine the type and level of personal counseling (deciding whether the client can successfully work with more abstract personal concerns and pull together disparate thoughts to make decisions or be the recipient of suggestions and concrete guidance from the therapist). They can be helpful in predicting future performance in hospital therapy programs, recommending the level of task complexity within the patient's grasp, and developing community goals following hospitalization (such as sheltered workshop placement, supervised living arrangements, and continuing outpatient therapy).

Personality measures yield an impression of current and stable personality characteristics which both describe the person as a unique individual and which relate him to people in general. The patient having difficulty in relating to authority figures could profit from an O.T. program stressing experience in dealing with persons in authority or supervisory positions. The patient with a profound sense of inferiority requires a lengthy program of building self-confidence with concretely graded tasks to develop initiative and stability. Severe interpersonal difficulties often necessitate group therapeutic sessions to develop new and more effective ways of interacting. Faulty reality contact noted upon projective tests may be a basis for a special "reality therapy" program to develop a firmly-based understanding of events around him and perceptions of others. Each alternative may be implemented by a specialized program or experience made available within the confines of the institution. Gurel and Lorei (1972) concluded that "low motivation" was the most potent work predictor in symptom ratings made prior to hospital release. Similarly, Dragow and Dreher (1965) have predicted client readiness for training and placement in vocational rehabilitation with a combination of Rorschach, MMPI, and Kuder Neuropsychiatric Key measures.

In general, testing information serves a two-fold purpose: first, to develop recommendations regarding the most appropriate therapeutic goals and avenues, and second, to provide feedback to the patient himself regarding special areas of concern or potential skills.

Information is not gathered in a vacuum but becomes an integral part of the therapeutic process. This is often most dramatically seen with measures of vocational and educational skills, providing material for counseling sessions. Occupational interest inventories stimulate thinking regarding return to the general community and specific areas of endeavor or employment.

In summary, psychological evaluation provides information valuable in a number of contexts: diagnostic formulations to recommend placement at a specific stage or type of hospital rehabilitation program; insights into personality dynamics which can be dealt with in further counseling; and recommendations regarding vocational skills and interests which can be utilized in developing community-oriented goals.

OCCUPATIONAL THERAPY EXPERIENCES

Therapeutic programs must often begin with elementary tasks and requirements, selecting a level at which the patient can experience success and competency. Past onslaughts and debilitating experiences have reduced his tolerance and confidence to such a low level that basic skills such as dressing, shaving, taking care of personal needs, and social interaction are poorly carried out or ignored. Again, the crux of planning is to begin at a level the patient views as meaningful to him—tasks he perceives as somewhat challenging yet reasonably within his grasp. They must not be too simple or easy to make him feel that the staff lacks confidence in his ability and must not merely be "busywork" that "anybody can do." The timing of entrance into theraupetic programs is important, with the prevailing philosophy being one of "the sooner the better." Walker, Allenson and Johnson (1971) contrasted immediate versus delayed entrance into a rehabilitation program to conclude that "early exposure to meaningful work in an O.T. Clinic leads to a measurably higher level of inhospital adjustment" measured through a sheltered work situation.

Terms covering O.T. and pre-vocational adjustment programs often lack clear distinctions but should be viewed as offering varying degrees of reality stress. Roberts (1970) distinguished vocational exploration involving work samples or miniature job tasks from "pre-vocational evaluation" historically occurring in medical settings under the supervision of an occupational therapist. The O.T. can, indeed, develop a variety of experiences graded from quite simple and basic tasks through those of average complexity and difficulty to those involving considerable skill, talent and work. The patient can progress at his own pace, moving on to more challenging tasks as he feels more comfortable and willing to take on additional work. Similarly, the type of task is selected through a consideration of presenting personality, education and work history, and expressed interest. Certain tasks are primarily of a psycho-therapeutic nature to give a feeling of "pure accomplishment" through expression in a concrete medium (painting, ceramics, woodworking, weaving, and so on). Other tasks have an "evaluative" or "pre-vocational" component (containing elements of assessment of personality traits such as steady motivation, impulsivity, or intrinsic interest in skill areas).

The patient moves from one task to another or one level to another with careful attention to his personal reactions. Frustration, irritability, boredom or disinterest, aloofness or isolation, and so on would signal the need for change to a different experience more meaningful to him or within his judged ability. Prevocational tasks offer an opportunity to simply "explore" work areas to concretely give the patient information about interests. For example, a patient unable to verbalize any vocational interests or work plans could engage in a number of job-related areas to learn which appeal to him. Continuing observations of work quality and output and relationships with other patients and staff members allow the therapist to chart the patient's progress, with counseling sessions delving into the patient's view of therapeutic tasks as well as dealing with his perceptions of problems in the "outside world."

One can ideally set up a hospital-based social interaction to duplicate the stress areas for which the patient seeks help. For example, he can participate in hospital situations with graded contacts with "authority figures" to learn better methods of interacting with others which hopefully carries over to community and employment settings. Ratings of rehabilitation were used by Perkins and Miller (1969) to predict vocational outcome. Results indicated the patient's knowledge of why he entered the hospital, and his promptness and attendance at interviews correlated highly with ultimate employment success.

Interrelationships of evaluation and therapeutic goals have been described by Leshner (1970), who observes that "Grading task difficulty on such continue as simple to complex, or concrete to abstract, under conditions that range from congenial and permissive to highly structured and disciplined, yields clues to how the client can improve while at the same time nurturing competency and tolerance for coping with these kinds of conditions . . . as functioning becomes more complex and stressful, a higher degree of personality integration is required." As the patient progresses in personal stability and moves in counseling to a greater appreciation of himself and more accurate understanding of his feelings and behaviors, the overall emphasis toward discharge brings community decision-making forcefully to him. Sessions begin to reveal thoughts regarding living arrangements, financial considerations and future relationships with friends or relatives. For the patient with limited knowledge of the world of work, with limited understanding of his own abilities and job interests, and with various apprehensions and fears regarding seeking a job, further vocational evaluation may be valuable.

Pre-vocational Experiences

Therapy can be conceptualized as beginning with the initial contact between patient and primary therapist. Counseling stages begin with supportive sessions; move through encouragement for greater independence and decision-making; stress concrete actions in programs; and actualize eventual community return. In assessing referral possibilities to various rehabilitation services, psychological testing and counseling sessions offer two classes of information. But, as Patterson has observed (1962), "the fact that vocational adjustment takes place in a social situation makes situational observation desirable. The fact that many patients have had little or no occupational experience or have been out of the labor market for a long period gives situational observation an advantage over standard tests." Using a time-sequence approach, the patient moves from contact with the primary therapist to meetings with other team members through group therapy, psychological testing, social service contact, and participation in hospital therapy programs. As the patient moves from stage to stage with expanding hospital contacts, the therapist remains his primary support.

Frequently a disordered personal and family life is associated with

occupational dysfunction (in terms of poor work incentive or motivation, poor work habits, few intrinsic work interests, periods of unemployment, and marginal performance on the job). Mayfield and
Fowler (1969) found that a majority of their subjects experienced
occupational dysfunction, substantially exceeding the incidence of
dysfunction in family, community, and interpersonal areas. Beginning with a therapeutic O.T. program with major emphasis upon
re-motivation, concrete reality reinforcement, and emotional support, the patient moves to a level with greater independent action
where activities take on an evaluative light. Tasks are engaged in for
psychotherapeutic reasons and additionally involve analysis of skills,
abilities and interests related more directly to employment criteria.
The patient may be expected to come to therapy at specified times
and go about tasks with little overt direction and encouragement. Relationships with patients and staff members are evaluated with an
eye toward development of smooth work relationships, going beyond simple involvement in social activities. As Barton (1970) has
concluded, the rehabilitation facility must supply vocational development experiences essential for an adequate work personality. Differential use of work situations in treating maladjustment is especially
valuable for patients who do not respond readily to a verbal relationship. Lustig (1970) specified such dimensions as time devoted to a
particular task, work location, speed requirements, type of interpersonal work relationship with supervisors, nature of co-worker relationships, and so on as variables for manipulation.

In many respects, pre-vocational experiences have a "teaching"
component where important qualities or characteristics of independent living and employment are covered. Basic vocational skills may
be taught, involving attendance and punctuality, ability to follow
directions, correct ways of relating to employees and supervisors,
procedures for asking questions, taking of "coffee breaks", and so
on. Other skills may be assessed through concrete activities such as
ability to count, to read, to write in a logical and grammatically correct fashion, to follow written directions, to carry out repetitive
manual or assembly tasks, and to use common tools. Williams (1963)
utilized group therapy sessions to develop a general orientation to
the world of work, with sessions covering completion of job appli-
cations, appropriate behavior during job interviews, resolution of

typical problems encountered on a job, and financial management. Zimmerman (1969) arranged work reinforcements through several different jobs, specifying isolation-avoidance procedures to focus the client's attention on doing a good job without separating him from his work. As in other therapeutic encounters, the impressions of staff members through the prevocational program can be filtered to the client in personal counseling sessions to give him an accurate picture of his performance.

Vocational Evaluation

With suitable progress or sufficient initial ability upon admission, the patient is helped to formulate thoughts regarding return to the community. As he begins to work through these many problems and obstacles he frequently experiences renewed surges of dependency upon staff. After growing accustomed to hospital routine and content with therapy activities, considerable anxiety is engendered when the therapist speaks of movement back into the community to practice new concepts and tools he has acquired. Formerly ill-equipped to handle life decisions, the patient finds possible resolutions to future problems through individual and group therapy sessions which offer alternatives for vexing discharge problems. Another avenue is a vocational evaluation program which seeks to provide a more secure, rewarding and financially stable work arrangement. Risch (1971) viewed rehabilitation workshops as most valuable toward the end of hospitalization, observing that therapeutic team members often dread the period in recovery when the patient is too well to remain longer in the hospital but cannot yet be accepted either by his family or by industry.

Vocational evaluation assesses current vocational skills and potentials. Whereas O.T. and pre-vocational programs have a major supportive and therapeutic aspect, vocational evaluation *per se* is a reality experience designed to measure skill levels and personal tolerance through work samples. Though some agencies have all three programs in one physical space and gradually shift patients from one program or track to another, the more effective route is to have distinct workshop areas which ensure a stable and well-defined work atmosphere. Olshansky (1969) discussed nonverbal communication channels in behavioral change, noting that the physical plant, its location, the attitudes of supervisors, the kind of work offered, and the shop organization communicate messages regarding the "silent power of the possible."

The rationale in vocational evaluation is that samples of work in a specific skill are the best predictors of success in that job. Work samples selected to cover a range of occupational experiences provide impressions of potential ability in many employment situations. Vocational evaluation programs differ mainly in number and type of job samples, just as different localities differ in the types of labor and industry they possess. Most workshops have a variety of areas such as clerical-secretarial work; drafting; art; woodworking; metal working; janitorial work; plumbing; small appliance repair; assembly work; auto collision repair; and mechanical, electrical, and radio-television repair. Barton (1970) wrote "from inside the client's skin vocational evaluation activities may look like, feel like, and perhaps even smell like real work. Pay for work produced heightens this realistic work flavor even more. Clients in such vocational evaluation settings may thus see themselves more readily as 'workers' than as 'evaluees.' " Each vocational area should be selected according to criteria such as relevance to actual employment opportunities in that geographical area; appropriateness for objective measurement of ability or potential; capacity to distinguish job characteristics into levels from simple untrained activities to more complex, sophisticated and technically demanding ones; and ability to not only predict capacity for a specific job, but for related jobs through basic work dimensions or traits.

Under the guidance of a vocational "evaluator" or "supervisor," the patient moves from one work area to another in a "work atmosphere." The patient initially is interviewed by the evaluator who gathers information regarding education, work history, vocational interests and tentative work goals. At this time, the patient may complete a "job application" covering employment history and skills. This interview provides his first in-depth experience with "job interviewing" as well as providing a first-hand outline of the vocational evaluation program and its broad limits for completion. In general, some patients can complete the various work samples in a few weeks or may proceed swiftly to more challenging and sophisticated tasks in a matter of days with a five-day-per-week schedule. Other clients of lesser ability or stability may spend relatively longer time in each work sample so that six or seven weeks are necessary. The client progresses through each work sample at his own pace and receives as much personal attention and supervision as required until he manifests maximum proficiency. Movement through work samples which may not be viewed as interesting can provide a chart of vacillating motivation and attentiveness patterns. Leshner (1970) wrote of a progression of success experiences as a "developmental, learning-by-doing activity operating on the broad principle of building confidence or tolerance, general work competency, and particular coping behaviors. How the strains and stresses are applied is determined by the individual's responsiveness." Progress is matched by counseling sessions with the therapist and feedback sessions with work supervisors. The most effective procedure is one of realistic and straightforward discussions with the work supervisor which can be reviewed in sessions with the therapist in a more analytical and nondirective light.

Work Adjustment Experiences

A vocational workshop program can include only a limited number of work samples dependent upon space, staffing and local job demands. Again, only a small number of clients can be extensively supervised in workshop tasks. A major tool in vocational evaluation is the agency itself through its many parameters of employment which offer diversified and extended job experiences. In this way, the typical hospital-based rehabilitation program can offer potential work experiences in areas such as nurse's aide or orderly, office clerk, typist, carpenter helper, electrician helper, central supply packager, and mail clerk. The extent of such experiences is limited only by the size and diversity of the hospital, staff creativity, and patient abilities. Vocational evaluation helps to crystalize a number of appealing jobs or work areas which can be explored to a greater degree in counseling and work supervision discussions. A mutual decision may be reached to explore these areas more fully by actual work experiences in the agency where the patient is treated as a "regular employee" under the direction of the regular work supervisor. For example, a patient interested in nurse's aide work could work as a nurse's aide under the direction of the head nurse of a hospital service. Similarly, an expressed interest in carpentry could lead to experiences in the hospital carpentry shop assisting with actual repair and construction projects.

Supervisory comments and recommendations are again discussed in counseling sessions with awareness of critical vocational behaviors essential for employment. Krantz (1971) provided job-getting behaviors and job-keeping behaviors, concluding that work adjustment is most needed when the issue is the client's ability to be employed at all.

A number of vocational programs include salary for production tasks. McCourt (1964) concluded that such programs enable all but the most seriously regressed patients to work for pay at tasks ranging from simple production operations to technically demanding assignments. Transitional, paid-employment programs can develop self-reliance, strengthen work habits and skills, and assist in interpersonal and independent adjustment. Such programs have an intrinsic motivation of financial remuneration and freedom to use money independently, as noted in the Community Hospital Industrial Rehabilitation Placement (CHIRP) program described by Walker (1969) for in-patients bussed to community industrial firms for work contracts.

Again, this experience is viewed as time-limited, usually consisting of two or three weeks or more of "work" under continuing supervision. It can be extended or changed according to the patient's reactions and progress. Various rehabilitation programs omit this actual work experience while others find it valuable for their patients to receive extensive experience for a number of months. Again, the guiding criteria are the patient's needs and limitations and the range of possibilities at the specific agency. A strong sense of identity emerges as the patient moves from one work area to another or one phase of rehabilitation to another. He perceives the staff and program as intimately involved with his special problems and progress. Other clients may react more negatively to such a program. They may view it as disinteresting, unrelated to their specific concerns, or voice severe frustration with workshop tasks or experiences. Increased counseling contacts, brief program interruption, or change to another phase more in line with capabilities may offer possible answers. A shift to a less challenging situation is couched in terms of "current ability and tolerance" to avoid damaging an already fragile sense of personal ability. On the other hand, considerable attention is devoted to stimulating and challenging the patient to prevent complacency which might impede therapeutic progress. Such a result has been observed by Barbee (1969) where patients in a work therapy program maintained their associations with the hospital through outpatient and low-intensity services for a significantly longer period of time. The staff must strenuously avoid fostering institutional dependency through repeated concrete experiences designed to move the patient toward the community life. Valuable at such points are patient-team conferences where the therapist, team members and patient discuss his progress and problems to date to develop a better understanding of his situation and plans. Such conferences "clear the air" by providing a mix of impressions and opinions to help the patient make realistic choices. They help him put into words his vague and uncrystallized thoughts about himself through objective and realistic feedback from others.

Community and Work Placement Assistance

As the patient moves successfully from one phase to another, gradually adjusting to greater and greater responsibility for decision-making and self-guidance, he is encouraged to make more frequent, lengthy, and more personally demanding contacts with the community. For many inpatient rehabilitation programs, this entails weekends at home with family and friends, attendance at social and cultural events around the city, greater and greater time away from the hospital during daytime or evening hours, and greater attention to job-finding efforts.

Feeling more secure in his decision to leave the hospital, the patient nevertheless continues to receive support and guidance from hospital staff. Again, a continuum of care is involved with choices dependent upon the patient's current emotional state and anticipated capability in future months. Possibilities range from less demanding to those requiring more complete personal independence and competence, bringing into focus a number of community programs and agencies. For example, the patient who has progressed slowly, with difficulty, may well require a lengthy outpatient therapeutic program with "daycare" or "nightcare" possibilities. Here the separation from the hospital is more gradual, providing lengthy security and support. Another patient may be able to function in a more autonomous way with occasional outpatient individual or group therapy sessions. Considering employment possibilities, patients may be referred for job interviews while in the vocational evaluation and counseling programs to gain experience in job application. Role playing and videotaped interviews can condition and refine the patient for actual job interviews. The therapist or workshop supervisor may arrange and accompany him to interviews and contact employers in the patient's interest. Referral to community helping agencies such as the State Employment Service, Office of Vocational Rehabilitation, and other rehabilitation facilities or social service agencies can be completed before the patient leaves the hospital. Hoffman (1971) specified social development, work personality, work methods, work habits, physical tolerance, and basic academic skills as areas of consideration. It may be beneficial for community agencies to have liaison personnel attached to the hospital. In this way they are integrated with the therapeutic program at a stage where the client is most receptive to referral. Such arrangements also lessen the "time lag" as agencies compile records, check eligibility and gather information early in the program.

CONTINUING REHABILITATION CONTACTS

Implicit in rehabilitation is the gradual movement from one stage of ability to another. As the patient progresses in handling reality problems and personal concerns on his own, therapeutic contacts decrease in frequency until he functions in a completely autonomous manner. Readiness to assist in the future is communicated throughout the program and is especially reinforced in terminating sessions. A realistic approach to rehabilitation entails awareness of the frequent difficulties and stresses which, expected or unanticipated, spell defeat for the patient. This is portrayed by follow-up investigations such as that of Olshansky (1973) who found only 21 percent of patients employed in regular industry, 5 percent in job training or sheltered workshops, 44 percent unemployed, and 10 percent in the hospital. In similar fashion, Schaefer, Bartholow and Niewoehner's (1972) two-year study found 34 percent of patients returning to the hospital to demonstrate the high frequency of disruptions in rehabilitation processes and point out the value of extending follow-up support. Kunce (1970) concluded that rehabilitation techniques and strategies often make the most difference for the marginal patient, enhancing his ultimate vocational adjustment but not necessarily ensuring complete and sustained social independence.

A WORKABLE PHILOSOPHY
Successful rehabilitation involves genuine interest in the patient, flexible programs to focus on inherent patient strengths and hopes, and flexible relationships among staff members. A rehabilitation program cannot expect success with all individuals but must build upon the guiding philosophy of developing each person's capabilities and strengths to the fullest while minimizing the detrimental effects of personal, vocational and social limitations. Inpatient programs must adapt to the patient's unique characteristics and concerns, at all times reinforcing the belief in potential for growth. Some programs will succeed and some will fail—just as some patients will profit while some will abandon their efforts. In the final analysis, the ultimate success of rehabilitation must be defined in personal and human terms by each patient and professional.

REFERENCES
Barbee, Margaret S., Berry, K.I., and Micek, L.A.: Relationship of work therapy to psychiatric length of stay and readmission. *Journal of Consulting and Clinical Psychology, 33*:735-738, 1969.

Barton, E.H.: Vocational evaluation and work adjustment: Vocational development companions. *Journal of Rehabilitation, 36*:35-37, 1970.

Colten, S.I.: Institutional psychiatric rehabilitation. *Rehabilitation Research and Practice Review, 2*:1-6, 1971.

Denholm, D.H.: The design and layout of a rehabilitation workshop. *Rehabilitation Literature, 33*:166-169, 1972.

Drasgow, J., and Dreher, R.G.: Predicting client readiness for training and placement in vocational rehabilitation. *Rehabilitation Counseling Bulletin*, 94-98, March, 1965.

Gellman, W.: The future development of vocational adjustment programs and workshops. *Rehabilitation Literature, 32*:108-113, 1971.

Gurel, L., and Lorei, T.W.: Hospital and community ratings of psychopathology as predictors of employment and readmission. *Journal of Consulting and Clinical Psychology, 39*:286-291, 1972.

Kotin, J., and Schur, J.M.: Attitudes of discharged mental patients toward their hospital experiences. *Journal of Nervous and Mental Disease, 149*: 408-414, 1969.

Krantz, G.: Critical vocational behaviors. *Journal of Rehabilitation, 37*:15-16, 1971.

Kunce, J.T.: Is work therapy really therapeutic? *Rehabilitation Literature, 31*:297-299, 1970.

Leshner, S.S.: The relationship of work evaluation to work adjustment training. *Journal of Rehabilitation, 36*:32-34, 1970.

Lustig, P.: Differential use of the work situation in a sheltered workshop. *Rehabilitation Literature, 31*:39-42, 1970.

Mayfield, D.G., and Fowler, D.R.: Occupational class, occupational adequacy, and occupational dysfunction in psychiatric patients. *Diseases of the Nervous System, 30*:379-384, 1969.

McCourt, J.F.: What's worthwhile about paid patient programs? *Rehabilitation Record*, 37-40, May-June, 1964.

Olshansky, S.: Behavior modification in a workshop. *Rehabilitation Literature, 30*:263-268, 1969.

Olshansky, S.: A five-year follow-up of psychiatrically disabled clients. *Rehabilitation Literature, 34*:15-16, 1973.

Parker, R.M., Thoreson, R.W., Laugen, J.L., and Pfeifer, E.: Vocational Rehabilitation service needs of mental patients: Perceptions of psychiatric hospital staff. *Rehabiltation Counseling Bulletin, 13*:271-279, 1970.

Patterson, C.H.: Evaluation of the rehabilitation potential of the mentally ill patient. *Rehabilitation Literature, 23*:162-172, 1962.

Peffer, P.A.: Money: A rehabilitation incentive for mental patients. *American Journal of Psychiatry, 110*:84-92, 1953.

Perkins, D.E., and Miller, L.A.: Using a modified NMZ scale to predict the vocational outcomes of psychiatric patients. *Personnel and Guidance Journal, 47*:456-460, 1969.

Richman, S.: The vocational rehabilitation of the emotionally handicapped in the community. *Rehabilitation Literature, 25*:194-209, 1964.

Risch, F.: Gainful employment: A psychiatric prescription. *Journal of Rehabilitation, 37*:22-25, 1971.

Roberts, C.L.: Definitions, objectives, and goals in work evaluation. *Journal of Rehabilitation, 36*:12-15, 1970.

Sacks, J.M.: Psychological examination and evaluation of member-employee candidates. In Peffer, P.A. (Ed.): *Member-Employee Program: A New Approach to the Rehabilitation of the Chronic Mental Patient.* Brockton, Mass., V.A. Hospital, 1957, pp. 136-141.

Schaefer, I.J., Bartholow, G.W., and Niewoehner, G.J.: A follow-up study of 73 psychiatric rehabilitation clients. *Rehabilitation Research and Practice Review, 3*:35-39, 1972.

Walker, R., Allenson, Elizabeth A., and Johnson, Mary E.: O.T. CHIRP: A method of early assignment of hospital psychiatric patients to paid work. *Rehabilitation Literature, 32*:360-364, 1971.

Walker, R., and Asci, Marguerite: Evaluation of an experimental rehabilitation ward for chronic mental patients. *Rehabilitation Literature, 32*:40-41, 50, 1971.

Walker, R., Winick, W., Frost, E.S., and Lieberman, J.M.: Social restoration of hospitalized psychiatric patients through a program of special employment in industry. *Rehabilitation Literature, 30*:297-303, 1969.

Williams, J.D., Dudley, H.K., and Guinn, T.J.: Use of day treatment center concepts with state hospital inpatients. *American Journal of Orthopsychiatry, 39*:748-752, 1969.

Williams, P.M.: Pre-employment adjustment program developed for mental patients. *Journal of Rehabilitation, 29*:21-22, 1963.

Zimmerman, J., Overbeck, Carole, Eisenberg, Heidi, and Garlick, Betsy: Operant conditioning in a sheltered workshop. *Rehabilitation Literature, 30*:326-334, 1969.

CHAPTER VI

REHABILITATION SERVICES AND ORGANIZATIONS IN THE COMMUNITY

DONALD B. DEROZIER

- A PLACE FOR THE MENTALLY ILL
- EMOTIONAL PROBLEMS AND THE COMMUNITY PRACTITIONER
- COMMUNITY AGENCIES
- MAKING A GOOD REFERRAL
- RECEIVING A REFERRAL
- PERSONAL COMMUNITY ACTION
- BIBLIOGRAPHY

COMMUNITY ATTITUDES and beliefs define the limits and kinds of citizen involvement in rehabilitation. To be seen as "different" contributes to the presence of specific services and organizations. The approach to the problem of rehabilitation services for the mentally ill, the emotionally disturbed, and the socially deviant client is necessarily grafted to the essential community attitudes as they are communicated to these exceptional citizens. Community attitudes set the stage for expected actions to be performed. As a playwright changes scenes to effect a shift in audience participation, so community attitudes determine the types of organizations the client is presented for his participation. Several basic principles regarding the mentally ill are held at the attitudinal level and these may be expressed in both the orientation of the rehabilitation worker and the available community structures.

A PLACE FOR THE MENTALLY ILL

A fundamental question is whether these disturbed persons are to be considered as disabled or handicapped (Wright, 1960). Within a community, to be disabled implies that the person once had an ability which was lost through no fault of his own. This implication leads to the belief that the disability is fairly circumscribed and does not involve the total personality of the individual. To be disabled then connotes that the individual can be rehabilitated by means of calling upon other personal resources to substitute for the lost function. The community may hold that the mentally ill individual suffers such a disability and, is so well publicized within the area of vocational and physical rehabilitation, all the client has to do is muster up other personality strengths to cope with his loss of mental faculty. This attitude has a disadvantage in that it leads to simplistic formulations for the emotionally disturbed and indeed can contribute toward further emotional stress by supporting "locker room" services.

The locker room rehabilitation worker will impress upon the client that if he would "give 100 percent," or believe that "when the going gets tough, the tough get going," then he would be happier, more successful, and accepted by the community. There is an advantage to this attitude in that the mentally ill are not discriminated against because of the "mental" nature of their problem. If this attitude is combined with a belief in the essential worth of the individual, then some good will be derived from the support entailed in deemphasizing the exclusiveness of their condition.

To be handicapped implies that the client experiences total involvement of personality and behavior in the illness. The handicapped person is wrapped up in his disability and is exclusive of self-help. He is seen as dependent upon the community for satisfaction of his basic needs. This dependency can lead to a range of stereotyped reactions. The community may assume a paternal role and protect the individual from stress, or it can assume an autocratic role and deprive the client of his rights "for his own good." At either extreme, the client is treated as an umbilical yo-yo which is attended to first centrally, then peripherally, and later forgotten for some other game.

Community attitudes do not often seem to encompass the fact that the disabled mentally ill or disabled deviant person experiences conflicts much the same way as the non-disabled. Rather than seeing the need for specific services and the need for specific goals, the community often assumes that rehabilitation for the mentally ill means rehabilitation of the total person in all his adjustments. Consequently, it is more prevalent to find communities united in their efforts to create or expand institutions than to establish facilitators of de-centralized service-oriented programs.

To provide for funding of rehabilitation efforts, many communities seem to demand the presence of a building, an agency or a hospital which should provide for rehabilitation of the whole individual. As a result of this demand, there exists in most communities structures for total care. State institutions, county hospitals, municipal clinics, departments of social services, training schools, live-in centers, and a variety of workshops all seem related to the need of the community to have a "place" to send those who are "different" (Kittrie, 1972).

EMOTIONAL PROBLEMS AND THE COMMUNITY PRACTITIONER

Attitudes not only lead to the establishment of structures but also to professional functions in the community. Individual professional persons in the community oftentimes exert their personal preferences into existing and proposed structures. It is true that most of us cannot work with the myriad of idiosyncracies in human nature, and consequently we are selective about the kinds of individuals and kinds of problems for our attention. For the rehabilitation worker, it is necessary to fathom the particular preferences of the professionals in the community in order to become a more effective provider of services for the client.

Physicians, psychologists, the clergy, lawyers and a host of professional and subprofessional citizens are available in the community for the rehabilitation of the emotionally disturbed individual. Whether in a public or private capacity, members of these groups are likely to establish preferences in certain problem areas. A few of these preferences are presented.

Pediatricians become involved in behavior problems, hyperkinesis, problems associated with epilepsy, and discrepancies in growth and development. Because these psychosocial problems are presented to him, the pediatrician develops a rehabilitation sense for problems with children; he becomes a valuable resource to the rehabilitation worker. The pediatrician also shares common medical interests with the gerontologist because of the physiological similarities between the old and the young. He may also provide meaningful consultation concerning older disturbed individuals.

Obstetricians and gynecologists see many emotional problems associated with their specialties. Sexual, marital and family problems are brought into their offices along with the physical complaints. Similarly, the emotionally disturbed individual frequently experiences distress in psychosexual areas, especially as these are manifested in marital or dating relationships. Because of the expertise of these physicians, the counselor can establish reciprocal relationships with him to provide for maximum support, information giving and professional advice in these matters. Lastly, surgeons can provide consultation concerning the physical aspects of body image, self-concept problems associated with physical integrity, and a host of physical dimensions.

The clergy is another tremendous resource in the community. Oftentimes clergymen are the first persons contacted by the family concerning a mentally ill individual. The clergy frequently initiates referrals and provides follow-up care after psychological intervention. The role of personal morality and ethical behavior in building a unifying philosophy of life and in providing motivation essential to goal-directed efforts cannot be underestimated in planning a rehabilitation program.

Attorneys provide legal services for the emotionally disturbed or mentally ill person. Whether he is involved in establishing estates and wills, designating insurance beneficiaries, or advising the client concerning contracts and obligations, the attorney is becoming more and more involved in the overall behavioral picture. He is involved in marriage or family squabbles, criminal and juvenile delinquency difficulties, and in the legal affairs of professionals. The attorney is a resource to the rehabilitation counselor with reference to these socio-legal problems.

Psychologists in community practice are either agency-affiliated or are engaged in private practice. These individuals, along with the above-named professional groups, can provide meaningful service in the area of diagnostic and treatment planning for the mentally ill. Specific psychological functions are mentioned elsewhere in this book, but it is safe to say that professional psychologists only recently have become concerned with rehabilitation problems. Because of their university- and hospital-bound history and because of the absence of supported rehabilitation training experiences in graduate programs, psychologists continue to contribute minimally to community rehabilitation efforts. Whereas psychology has been lax in its efforts, social work has become more aggressive; often social services personnel will be found engaged in essentially psychological functions with the mentally ill. Still, if he is willing, the psychologist can provide for behavioral assessment and psychotherapy for mentally ill persons with vocational, occupational and personal adjustment problems. He also can relate these services to schools and employers in such a fashion as to assist in modifying subjective attitudes and in producing objective evaluative criteria.

Particular interests and preferences should be known for appropriate use of these professional people. It is unlikely that any one of these can or wants to attempt to provide services for all emotional disturbances. The attitudes toward the mentally ill that are vested in the community are oftentimes demonstrated in the work of these professionals and paraprofessional groups. These attitudes and preferences must be known for effective rehabilitation counseling. In an attempt to provide for a silent integration of the mentally ill or emotionally disturbed individual into the community and into the mainstream of society, the rehabilitation counselor or professional working in this area must familiarize himself with the community's preferences for a quiet slipping-into its structures. Drop-in clinics, free clinics, crisis-intervention centers, telephone services, and a myriad of volunteer agencies are available to the community practitioner to assist this process. They will not be described in depth at this point. Suffice it to say that in all of these programs there is a concern for the rehabilitation of the mentally ill person, and it evolves from the community's basic attitudes.

COMMUNITY AGENCIES

There are community structures emerging from the shifting of attitudes along the continuum of segregation to integration of people with problems. Many communities provide hospital services, public school programs, guidance centers, sheltered industries, crisis-intervention agencies, and legal-police programs which can be afforded to the mentally disturbed client. Community hospitals provide psychiatric services, rehabilitation services, extended care services, and emergency services which can be brought to bear upon many presenting problems. The advantage to hospital programs is the accessibility of the program on an emergency basis. There are limitations, however, as in most cases a physician is required for admission and for treatment planning while in the hospital. Also, the programs available in the community-based hospital are relatively expensive and seldom fully covered by existing insurance plans. When the individual is confronted with or is unable to meet the criteria for acceptance in these hospital-based programs, a public program may be needed.

Many counties provide guidance centers or mental health centers which are available to the emotionally disturbed individual. In most of these, the focus is upon the child and on the parent-child relationships. Some, however, provide follow-up services or post-hospital care and psychotherapy and medical supervision for adults. In many cases, demands on these public agencies exceeds the capacity or power of the agency to provide the needed services. Thus in many centers, emergency and long-term programs may be minimized or deleted. Diagnostic evaluations are in constant demand from schools and medical people, and these may take precedence over treatment. Where this is the case, treatment needs have to be filled elsewhere.

The expenses to the client who is involved in the county center are usually less than those provided in hospital-based centers. Criteria for fees is based upon the ability to pay, with the wealthier client often referred to private agencies. One advantage to the use of a county mental health center for rehabilitation efforts is the center's connection to the various community services for complementary planning. The juvenile court, the department of social services, private social service agencies, and many private professionals have a working relationship with the mental health center; these relationships can provide for effective patient flow and for the matching of clients to programs.

In most communities, the public schools provide some services for the mentally ill or emotionally disturbed child and his family. Counseling, group therapy, social case work supervision, psychological assessments, curriculum planning, and behavioral modification programs may be provided for by school personnel. In these cases, the fees are insignificant. However, because of tremendous demands for service and the expense of these services to the school system, there is often reticence to provide these services to the more seriously disturbed individual.

Communities may provide sheltered work experiences for the mentally ill. Work skill orientation, preferences for work adjustment goals, and socialization via occupational stability are often the key goals in the sheltered industry. This is particularly true for the physically handicapped individual who may be emotionally disturbed as well. The mentally retarded and the medically supervised psychotic patient could find these services in the sheltered industry beneficial to vocational and social adjustment. The criteria for acceptance of a client vary from agency to agency and from area to area, and this requires that the professional working in rehabilitation must familiarize himself with these criteria.

"Hotlines," drop-in clinics, free clinics, etc. are designed to keep solutions to problems close to the source of the problem. The intervention nature of their services can be a real asset to the mentally disturbed individual who experiences crises from time to time. It is likely that more service is provided by these sorts of agencies than is publicly known because of the privacy policy involved in their dispensing of service. The rehabilitation worker who is in communication with these kinds of service groups will find himself at an advantage when confronted with off-hour calls from clients concerning emotional upheavals.

Lastly, every community has access to a law enforcement agency such as the police or sheriff. These professionals are becoming more and more involved in the intervention of emotional problems, in the screening of serious disturbances from the not-too-serious disturbances, and in providing "on the spot" treatment. The police are most likely to respond to someone who may be considered dangerous to himself or to other people and as such, can be an adjunct to the rehabilitation worker who is confronted with these life and death situations. As emphasis in crisis management becomes more characteristic in advanced training for policemen, it is likely that they will become more rehabilitation-oriented in their reactions to emotional and behavioral disturbances. Much as teachers have evolved into diagnosticians of learning and behavioral problems in school, so will the police become diagnosticians of personal and social adjustment problems in the community.

MAKING A GOOD REFERRAL

In community functioning, most often the client is referred to an existing service structure by someone who was involved early in treatment. Making a good referral is critical to the rehabilitation process. In order to make a reasonable referral, it is necessary to know the needs of the client, the positive and negative aspects of available resources, the possibility for a complementary "match," and to provide for an easy movement of the client into the particular program.

In order to assess the needs of the client, emphasis should be placed on desired behavioral objectives as well as on estimates of the change potential in the client. The availability of supportive services and their ability to effect those objectives have to be considered. For example, it makes little sense to refer a mentally disturbed individual to a county guidance center which is several miles from the home if no personal or public transportation is available, if no child care is available, or if the guidance center has a waiting list which is too long. It is possible that many of the "spontaneous cures" cited in the therapeutic literature, as associated with a failure of the individual to appear for treatment, are a function of no transportation as well as a function of self-reintegration. Once the individual's practical situation is assessed and the needs are delineated, the choice of referral source comes into focus.

In assessing the positive and negative aspects of available resources, the staff composition and staff quality must be considered. Also, consideration should be given to the individual or agency orientation with reference to its philosophy and methods of reaching treatment goals. For example, to send a brain damaged and retarded person to a psychoanalytic institute which specializes in talking therapies is not a good idea; or to refer a suicidal patient to a sheltered industry is not good judgment. Furthermore, in assessing the positive and negative characteristics of a referral resource, the cost to the client has to be considered if the client is to follow through with the referral. When it is feasible in terms of costs and availability, the client will be treated in an efficient, respectful and goal-oriented manner.

When the needs of the individual and the characteristics of the referral resource have been assessed, it is necessary to "make a match." Here the rehabilitation worker must recommend to the client the referral possibilities and involve the client in his own treatment planning. This is especially important early in the decision-making process, just as it is in the early steps of a counseling relationship. It is not adequate merely to list and mention the referral possibilities and tell the client to "take your pick." In many cases, the emotionally disturbed individual will require considerable moral support in separating himself from one agency or professional person to another. It may be necessary to have pre-placement visits and to review available literature concerning the source. Sometimes it helps to meet with significant others in the client's life in order to provide for a smooth, supportive transition. At times it makes sense to accompany the individual to the first contact as an overt declaration of your support for his decision. Similarly, following through with the individual and with the referral person after the first contact can help the client realize that he is not being abandoned nor being pushed from pillar to post but, rather, is being guided towards goals that he has for himself.

Once the decision has been made and a match has been effected, there are certain "helps" which can be beneficial to the client. Although it may seem to be a lot of bother, establishing a personal contact is of prime importance. The sharing of information up to the limits of professional ethics will be beneficial to the client. Later follow-up, even if it involves no more than a question as to how the client is doing, will strengthen the commitment to the recepient of the client and provide for more effective community professional relationships. Lastly, it is beneficial for the rehabilitation worker to make himself available for reciprocal consultation once the client has been referred. Oftentimes the recipient agency or person requires subsequent information or wishes other consultative services from the rehabilitation specialist. If this can be provided, it is likely that referrals will be accepted more willingly because the agency will recognize that the client is not being "dumped" upon them.

RECEIVING A REFERRAL

It goes without saying that the recipient of a rehabilitation client must accept the client's basic "right to treatment." He should not accept a client unless he is prepared to provide a service. Once the referral is accepted, the rehabilitation worker will implement maximum involvement with that individual over the course of their relationship and within the limits of his commitment. In order to maintain perspective in this agreement, it is necessary to be familiar with the problems associated with the particular disturbance of the client. Acceptance of referrals via telephone or letter may lead to a mismatch and to an inadequate commitment on the part of the recipient following the initiation of treatment. Along this same line, the rehabilitation worker must have a critical understanding of his own limits, as well as the limits of the client. Grandiosity is destructive to rehabilitation efforts. To assume that a few hours of counseling, a few inventories and preference schedules, and the rehash of the social history will provide for the overall adjustmental needs of the mentally ill individual is to assume a degree of credulity in rehabilitation efforts which may be enthusiastic but unrealistic.

Once the client appears, it is necessary to arrive at a goal or objective-oriented contract with him. At this point, the rehabilitation worker provides mental health housewife functions. By this is meant various maintenance functions, mixing the day's ingredients to enhance rehabilitation efforts, and ironing out difficulties in communications. This is especially true in those areas which hold problems or residuals of prior care efforts. Other housewife functions include providing an atmosphere for psychological growth, emphasizing acceptance and understanding, as well as a willingness to use common sense, and dusting off those social graces and manners which may have been ignored in the face of more dynamic issues. The last housewife function is to provide patient, sustaining efforts, knowing all along that these efforts, if successful, are likely to be appreciated by others as they see the results in day-to-day living and as others perceive the client's psychological well-being. As with the good housewife and mother who raises her children to the best of her ability, knowing that as adults, the children will move away from her to experience their own self-expression and not primarily the expression of her, the rehabilitation worker must be willing to work with the mentally ill, expecting to stand criticized for the positive or negative behavior of the client under his care, even after termination of service. Tolerance for a degree of ambiguity in the results and tolerance for the lack of feedback from successes are essential factors in maintaining the proper rehabilitation posture.

PERSONAL COMMUNITY ACTION

This article began with a concern for questions related to community attitude formation and change. It is fitting to complete the circle by commenting on the obligations of the rehabilitation specialist to make a personal contribution to positive community action for the rehabilitation of the mentally ill. By means of providing direct or consultative services to volunteer agencies, the rehabilitation worker can influence and upgrade the standard of care. Similarly, active participation in professional and civic groups can contribute directly to a change in community attitudes which, as seen before, directly influences the services available. Mental health associations; associations for retarded children; Recovery, Inc.; and other public and private groups are eager for participation by professional as well as lay members. The rehabilitation worker can contribute significantly to the goals and methods established by these organizations.

Public education for rehabilitation of mentally ill individuals continues to lag behind technical and theoretical advances. The rehabilitation counselor or psychologist working in this area can contribute to community education by means of public appearances, speeches and active involvement in community-based efforts. This need not be limited to profession-related efforts. As a citizen, the worker in this field can become involved in local government, in city, county, or state legislative bodies in such a way as to effect positive changes in mental health facilities and to attract public attention to the needs of these clients.

BIBLIOGRAPHY

Kittrie, N.N.: *The Right to Be Different.* Baltimore, Johns Hopkins, c1972.
Wright, B.A.: *Physical Disability—A Psychological Approach.* New York, Har-Row, 1960

CHAPTER VII

TRANSITIONAL AND ONGOING SUPPORTIVE SERVICES FOR THE MENTALLY DISABLED

THOMAS-ROBERT H. AMES *and* JOEL MARTIN LEVY

- SERVICES IN TRANSITION TO INDEPENDENCE
- ONGOING SUPPORT FOR MAXIMUM INDEPENDENCE
- STAFFING FOR TRANSITION AND ONGOING SUPPORT
- CONCLUSION
- REFERENCES

THE PROCESS of total rehabilitation for the mentally disabled is, after all, concerned with human beings who have individual rates of growth, unique levels of potential, and differing strengths and weaknesses. Not everyone may be capable of handling competitive employment and/or living on his own within the community. But each mentally disabled person is able to utilize, to some degree, a variety of therapeutic, transitional and supportive services that will promote change, growth and self-determination.

American society prides itself on providing opportunities for individual achievement; however, this has historically been more possible for those physically and mentally well equipped for the struggle. The list of casualties in this struggle has been long, although our society is now sufficiently sophisticated that we recognize a number of divergent groups of individuals requiring some special assistance or circumstance in order to realize their full potential. The mentally disabled form such a group, and transitional and ongoing supportive services provide realizable opportunities for assistance (Kissin and Carmichael, 1960; Ames, 1968).

Many of those having incurred a mental disability can develop the inner resources to maintain themselves in the larger community when provided with appropriate and adequate rehabilitation training requisite in solving the personal, social and vocational problems facing them. They may need only limited after-care as a transition to full independent functioning. Bear in mind that the mentally disabled person has developed a well-learned pattern of not facing up to anxiety, and that new anxiety-producing situations may tempt him to return to old habits to escape the intolerable stress. The transitional phase must be flexible enough to give the necessary support needed (Kris, 1960; Stewart, 1964; Carson, 1969).

There is also a significant group of the mentally disabled which can be identified as having potential for development, but for whom the prognosis and feasibility for rehabilitation services is more guarded. Several variables may markedly affect the probability of ultimate rehabilitation success: the severity of the disability; the chronicity of the handicap; and various serious socio-economic and environmental factors such as extreme poverty, deprivation, adverse familial interaction, or isolation from adequate services which could help sustain their functioning once they are ready to reenter the community. These factors truly make this a disability of the total individual and for this group, long-range provision must be made for after-care and supportive programming on an indefinite or permanent basis (Ames, 1969; Patterson, 1967).

It should be remembered that each individual's needs will be uniquely his own and will possibly change with time. The selection of services to be provided should take into account the indivdual's right to continue growing and to be as independent as possible. No service should be provided in such a way as to encourage or maintain an unhealthy or unnecessary dependency. On the contrary, the focus must be to encourage self-reliance and self-confidence.

The range of services ought to allow for breadth and scope in a variety of life-styles and for the special needs of clients at different times of life. (Ames, 1968; Reiff and Scribner, 1970; Grimberg, 1970).

Whatever services are developed and made available should function within the context of the principle of normalization which is "the utilization of means which are as culturally normative as possible, in order to elicit and/or maintain behaviors which are as culturally normative as possible" (Fritz, Wolfensberger and Knowlton, 1970). All such transitional and supportive services should be integral to the comprehensive programming provided by Community Mental Health Centers (Ferebee, 1965). As Dorothy Miller (1966) has pointed out:

> . . . what is needed to keep the great majority of them out (from rehospitalization) are things so simple that most of us take them for granted: adequate livelihoods; indications from doctors, employers and other professionals that they are well, competent, respected; a life partner to extend affection, share burdens, lend support; a consistent, structured, reassuring self-image and world. Yet our findings show that most released patients do not have these things. Their outside careers are fragmented, marginal, depressing, disillusioning. . . . The community must offer these patients and their families much more to help them build the new worlds they require.

Roe (1970) went so far as to suggest "community resource centers" routinely available to everyone in dealing with normal life problems as a preventive mental hygiene measure.

SERVICES IN TRANSITION TO INDEPENDENCE

For those mentally disabled leaving institutional settings and those, during childhood and adolescence, who have been in residential, private and public school special education programs, a period of transitional adjustment may be beneficial or even essential in helping smooth the way into full independent functioning in the community. The transitional phase is meant to form a bridge between the familiar protective environment and the stress inherent in adjusting to the world of adult responsibility. (Joint Conference on Childhood Mental Illness, 1968; MacLeech, 1969).

Transitional adjustment training should be designed to enhance the client's developing self-concept by: providing an environment conducive to the learning process and reinforcement for what is learned, facilitating his motivation for further learning, and providing whatever is needed in training and support to help him achieve and sustain maximum independent functioning. Such training necessarily utilizes and adapts principles and techniques of rehabilitation counseling, special education, psychology, social work, and other mental health and rehabilitation disciplines in a process designed to minimize anxiety, change and modify behavior, and develop new skills or behaviors for living. The training should be available to the client while still living in the hospital and continue concurrently with vocational training, sheltered employment, and even the early phase of competitive employment (Moseley, 1961; Brooks and Deane, 1962; Paul, 1963; Campbell and O'Toole, 1971).

Most adjustment services can be provided in small homogeneous groups of four to seven which lend themselves well to a curriculum, giving attention to individual needs in a specific, intensive treatment plan. The essential elements for such a plan are:

1. *Personal adjustment counseling* for the development of insight and the resources to handle problem-solving and change. Both individual and group techniques are useful in facilitating change in the client's feelings about himself as a dependent, inadequate person.

2. *Social adjustment training* to enhance interpersonal relations. An effort should be made to extend the client's social and recreational experiences to all those normal for his age-group peers in ways that insure the occasions will be self-reinforcing and build self-confidence in more complex interpersonal relations. Sex education is often an important element of such training in helping the client accept himself and others as sexual beings and develop those behavior patterns in dating and relating that can promote a greater sense of fulfillment. This is, all too often, a neglected or inadequately attended aspect of social adjustment because of the ambivalent attitudes and conflicting moral standards within society. Without attention to this need, there is little hope for the client's attaining an optimum adjustment and maximum independence. Without focusing on the client's particular needs and allowing for alternative adjustment patterns, not traditionally or universally condoned, additional burdens are heaped upon the shoulders of an already over-burdened person with every right to express his sexuality.

3. *Communication skills training* to increase the client's ability to relate and receive information productively. Many will need special attention to problems such as adequate feedback and monitoring of what is said, comprehending and remembering what is seen and heard, as well as other aspects of spoken and written communication. Frequently, very basic behaviors such as concentration and listening must be relearned or strengthened.

4. *Employment adjustment training* to develop an understanding of work; the complex role of being a worker; and the sense of dignity, fulfillment and independence it imparts. The client's behavior may be inappropriate for the training or work setting. His awareness can be heightened by the use of visual aids. Discussions with others of his peers, who are successfully training or working, can help his motivation for this experience. Where appropriate, this aspect of training should be coordinated with selective job placement and the routine follow-up efforts to develop the employer's acceptance of the client through assistance provided the client and employer in resolving work adjustment problems.

5. Other elements of training that may be valuable in enhancing the client's capacity to function more independently are: remediation in reading, arithmetic, budgeting, and, in large urban communities especially, travel by public conveyances.

6. A final element of programming often crucial in the successful transition to independent living is family counseling. Again, the use of individual and group experiences are helpful in encouraging a change in familial attitudes and responses to the client. If the counselor is successful in effecting a change or breakthrough in negative attitudinal and behavioral patterns, the family can often be an effective part of the rehabilitation team and help smooth the client's transition.

It should be noted that at least one other feature of aftercare is very important during the transitional phase. This is medical supervision and regulation of whatever chemotherapy that may be found beneficial for the client (Avedon, Arje and Berryman, 1962; Williams, 1963; Ames, 1973; and Sankovsky, 1971).

A number of specific techniques which hold promise for work with clients in a transitional adjustment program should, at this point, be discussed:

1. *Assertive behavior training* involves training in behaviors "which enable a person to act in his own best interests, to stand up for himself without undue anxiety, and to exercise his rights without denying the rights of others." The technique is based on the concept of "reciprocal inhibition of anxiety. That the two conditions are mutually exclusive in the human organism. When assertiveness increases, anxiety decreases." The procedures in assertive behavior training are derived from the principles of behavior modification primarily and use both role-playing of anxiety producing situations for the client and reinforcement for successful responses in graduated experiences that previously induced the anxiety reaction. The technique is useful in a variety of individual group sessions and has shown itself effective with both the withdrawn, passive person and the aggressive, acting out client. (Alberti and Emmons, 1972).

2. *Other behavior modification techniques*—Frequently, attempts at providing adjustment services are vaguely conceived, haphazardly structured, and poorly integrated. There is a basic need for a systematic approach to determining the client's adjustment needs, implementing training, and evaluating the results. There is considerable evidence of success in using various behavior modification techniques with the mentally disabled to effect desired changes in personal, social and employment behaviors. The systematic development of behavioral contingencies and the related usage of token reinforcers which can be exchanged for a variety of primary and secondary reinforcers such as extra food, merchandise or passes is an innovative approach to many of the problems presented in transitional programming. The additional elements of feedback in the system and evaluation of the achievement of behavioral objectives in a flow chart model such as Sawyer suggests may give integration and purpose to the overall adjustment program. (Atthowe and Krasner, 1965; Henderson, 1968; Scoles and Henderson, 1968; Sawyer, 1972; Mink, 1971; Campbell, 1971; and Cushing, 1969).

3. *The use of videotape* as a training device is valuable in clarifying for the client how he behaves in various situations and how others see him. It can very quickly present the client with the full impact of a situation that might otherwise take many hours of discussion and interpretation. Short, taped sessions can be played back

at will for review and comment and are useful in conjunction with other techniques such as psychodrama and assertive behavior and in various types of training groups. (Video article, 1967; Hollander and Moore, 1972).

4. *The counseling contract* is a technique for helping the client to see himself "as the dynamic force in his rehabilitation process." It involves delineating both the client's wishes and the counselor's conditions for the realization of those desires. Between sessions the conditions of the contract are to be carried out by the client and counselor. Future sessions can be used to review, revise and add to the contract. Within group sessions, the counselor may utilize the experience of other clients in helping the client who is working on his contract, but the structure of the session would discourage extraneous verbal interchange among the group members. The client is encouraged to think and act for himself in the process of developing greater self-assertiveness while changing his behavior and solving his problems. (Nickerson, 1972).

5. *Volunteer work* as a transitional work-conditioning technique is useful with many clients who have never worked before or who have not worked for a long period of time. It can be used in conjunction with other techniques to build positive attitudes, appropriate behavior, and self-confidence. As Freud stated in 1939 " . . . work has a greater effect than any other technique of living in the direction of binding the individual more closely to reality; in his work at least, he is securely attached to a part of reality, the human community" (Michelson, 1964).

In 1957 the Young Adult Institute and Workshop, Inc. in New York City pioneered a transitional adjustment program such as is discussed above. In 1966 a longitudinal study was completed which examined the overall adjustment of the first 100 clients served in the agency's Adjustment Center between 1957 and 1963. For the most part, these clients had been determined unfeasible for services by the New York State Division of Vocational Rehabilitation using then existing criteria for acceptance. Some of the findings were:

Range of Achievement Attained	Time Spent in the Adjustment Center (One term equals five months)
1. Achieved success in independent functioning, productive employment and appropriate social relationships 39%	3.8 terms
2. Achieved significant gains in enhanced vocational readiness, socialization and independence....39%	4.0 terms
3. Achieved limited gains—improvement to a degree but not sufficient to have affected status materially 20%	1.9 terms
4. Achieved no appreciable gains—remaining at the level at which he was upon entrance into the program 2%	1.0 terms

Most of those clients in groups 2 and 3 were transferred to the agency's ongoing supportive service program (The Alumni Club) when it was initiated in 1965. (Ames, 1969).

The function of the halfway house and the problems related to developing community acceptance and involving community resources in the transitional phase will be covered later in the chapter in the discussion centering on the hostel or permanent residence.

Transitional Adjustment services are in reality a segment in a continuum of total Life Adjustment programming beginning prior to vocational training in the hospital or special classroom and continuing on, in some cases, indefinitely in the form of ongoing supportive services. (Ames, 1968).

ONGOING SUPPORT FOR MAXIMUM INDEPENDENCE

"The ex-patient must have more than psychotherapy; he must have a place to stay, someone to care for him, money enough to live on, and a chance to both work and love" (Miller, D.H., 1966).

The person who has a life history of chronic mental disability may well seek to retreat again and again into the maladaptive pattern but with decreasing intensity and for decreasing periods of time providing appropriate supportive services are given. Such episodes are not failures or major setbacks, but merely a temporary return to old behavior patterns not yet relinquished. For still other disabled clients, a plateau may be reached in developing independent functioning; or there may be a marked slowing down in acquiring additional appropriate behaviors needed for full independence. While a tremendous amount of growth may have been accomplished and further learning can be expected, the client may have reached a developmental level allowing for relatively independent functioning providing certain supportive services are available to lend assistance. It would be foolish indeed to deny the opportunity for the degree of self-assertion and self-regulation that exists merely because there is yet room for improvement. Conversely, it would be unwise to abandon the client as he makes his way in a complex and bewildering world. (Stewart, 1964; Joint Conference On Childhood Mental Illness, 1968).

One such supportive service is the hostel or residence, "A supervised residential facility for mentally disabled persons on a long-term or indefinite basis." (Mental Hygiene, 1970). The hostel is not a treatment facility although the staff must consider each resident's needs and evaluate his continuing ability to handle self-care needs, personal problems and ancillary problems related to work and group-living. Some remediation in deficient areas may be necessary from time to time in order that the client can continue to function at his optimum level.

A moderate number of residents, perhaps ten to thirty would seem ideal in order to facilitate a home-like atmosphere and group-spirit. In choosing an area for the hostel, one must take into consideration the accessibility of: public transportation and recreation facilities, as well as dental and medical services, shopping centers, and the residents' places of employment. Time and cost factors must also be considered.

In order to build a more adequate self-concept and improve the resident's awareness of himself as a separate, responsible adult, he should have the opportunity to pay his own way. Even if supplementary funding from outside sources is necessary; direct family subsidies are unwise as they continue the psychological dependence of the resident. (Ames and Levy, 1973).

The halfway house, mentioned in the section on transitional adjustment services, provides the same function as the hostel but for a limited period of time during the transitional phase. Its use is most important for those for whom a return to the family would not be recommended and for those who have no families. (Kissin and Carmichael, 1960; Mikels and Gumrukcu, 1963).

Some residents may grow beyond the need for so closely supervised a home environment and be able to function quite well in satellite apartments scattered throughout the community and shared with others at a similar level of readiness. Such an opportunity allows for even greater responsibility in meeting personal needs and sharing the tasks inherent in the experience. Periodic evaluation of the situation and how the residents are meeting their individual and mutual responsibilities could be made by a staff member or advocate who might also be available for consultation on particular problems the residents wish to bring up. (Ames and Levy, 1973).

In a few cases the severity of the disability may warrant placement in a sheltered village such as Camphill Village in Copake, New York. In such an environment, preferably in rural areas, a homelike cottage setting can be provided with opportunities for sheltered work in garden and farm activities as well as shop tasks such as ceramics, weaving, baking and printing. With the added features of educational, social and recreational programming, severely chronically disturbed and withdrawn people can gain a measure of achievement and a sense of belonging and security with dignity. (Joint Conference on Childhood Mental Illness, 1968).

Other services for those living marginally independent lives within the community might include:

1. A social-recreation club designed and organized to allow members the opportunity to plan and conduct their own activities with the aid of staff as necesary. The club's activities might encompass: monthly business meetings; evening socials; special events such as a theater party, discotheque or out-of-town tour; and various hobbies. These affairs would supplement the small group activities and dates the clients arrange themselves.

2. A continuing educational program that might focus on: helping prepare clients to pass an appropriate civil service examination, take the high school equivalency examination, or perhaps a current events discussion group. Such a program could facilitate the clients' growing awareness and interest in the world around them, help

them to form opinions on important matters, upgrade their vocational opportunities, and participate more effectively as citizens.

3. Weekly or bi-weekly group-counseling sessions may be beneficial for certain of the clients in helping resolve new problems arising from the stresses inherent in our complex society.

4. The client advocate who can be available to clients for occasional or periodic assistance, advice or counseling for particular problems or in developing new plans such as moving to another community or changing jobs. Most of us are accustomed to seeking assistance when faced with questions or problems in which we lack expertise or familiarity. For mentally disabled clients, the range of perplexing situations is frequently broader so that special opportunities for assistance are needed (Ames, 1968).

5. Alerting various public and community services to the needs of the mentally disabled may uncover interesting facilities and opportunities they can utilize. Certainly the clergy should be involved as valued allied health professionals. Often the clergy are an important link both in interpreting to the community the presence, needs and potential of the mentally disabled and in facilitating their reintegration into the fabric of community life. (Gregg and Aitken, 1970; Ames, 1971).

STAFFING FOR TRANSITION AND ONGOING SUPPORT

More than fifteen years ago the mental health professions became concerned with the developing shortages of personnel needed to work with the mentally disabled in minimizing the probability of their eventual rehospitalization. Additionally, there has long been the problem of under-utilization or mis-use of the talents, skills and expertise of various professional personnel in dispensing necessary services.

"There is evidence, in fact, to indicate that some of the tasks which professionals attempt to perform might be done better by those with less or different kinds of education and experience." (New Careers in Rehabilitation Project of N.R.A., 1969). Programs of transitional and supportive service can be more meaningful if ways are developed to bridge the gap between agency and community. A variety of groups such as community volunteers, para-professional indigenous aides, as well as associate and baccalaureate degreed technicians can and should be structured into the delivery of the various types of services at all stages of the rehabilitation process. (MacLennan, Klein, Pearl and Fishman, 1966; Holzberg, Whiting and Lowy, 1964; Hallowitz and Riessman, 1967; Ames, 1970; Ames, 1971; Ames, 1972; Ames and Levy, 1973; and Savino, 1968).

There is considerable concern among some in the helping profession that these volunteers and "new careerists" may water down or pollute the quality of professional care and service. This has not been the authors' experience. When given adequate professional supervision and when the non-professionals' roles have been appropriately structured to utilize their particular capabilities, the services rendered have, in our experience, met the needs of the clients.

One particular instance where associate degreed community mental health technicians have been hired to serve as residence counselors is in a hostel for multiply-disabled adults. These counselors share apartment living quarters and rotate responsibilities in working with the residents under professional supervisors. Because the staff is nearer the age of the residents, they have been able to develop good rapport; lessen the residents' feelings of being mothered; and enhanced their opportunities to help the residents handle, on an adult level, their vocational, housekeeping, sexual, recreational and other social needs. The residents perceive the staff as friends and neighbors, not merely supervisors.

It is our experience that a youthful, energetic and highly motivated staff, properly trained and supervised, can cope with the sustained periods of stress and pressure manifested in helping multiproblemed, mentally disabled clients and still provide the latitude for independence and growth. (Ames and Levy, 1973).

CONCLUSION

Adjustment is a daily effort even for so-called normal people and requires their best to meet life's challenges in a world fraught with problems, anxiety, pain and indifference. How much more difficult can the struggle be for a person seeking to make his way back after a breakdown and period of hospitalization or a person chronically disabled and capable of only minimal functioning? Unless transitional adjustment services and more long-range supportive services are made available to help sustain them in their fight for a greater sense of dignity and a fuller measure of integrity, many may be unequal to the challenge. As has been pointed out by Kissin and Carmichael thirteen years ago, all the kinds of services and in the numbers needed are not available to a great portion of the mentally disabled population requiring them. They go on to say, "No matter how good a plan has been evolved, nothing has been accomplished unless it can be implemented" (Kissin and Carmichael, 1960).

One may well ask, how far do we go in providing supportive services? We go all the way. The criteria rest in the real needs of mentally disabled people at different stages in life. What other function is there for society than to provide services for its members which they cannot provide themselves and which they need in order to live reasonably meaningful and productive lives? "Balzac once wrote that most of us are ordinary mortals seeking extraordinary destinies. Truly then, are not these patients extraordinary mortals seeking ordinary destinies?" (Heilman, 1964).

We have made a beginning; we know much more about what can facilitate and sustain optimal functioning. We, who are concerned with their rehabilitation, can continue to develop and fight for imaginative programming and seek to educate the citizenry and government to our mutual responsibility for the mental health of all our people.

REFERENCES

Alberti, Robert E., and Emmons, Michael L.: *Your Perfect Right*. Impact, San Luis Obispo, California, 1972.

Ames, T.R.: Intensive life adjustment training for multiply-disabled young adults. *Journal of Rehabilitation*, Publication in progress, 1973.

Ames, T.R.: The associate in rehabilitation counseling. An unpublished manuscript presented in the session, "The Impact of Associate and Bacheloriate Degree Programs on Rehabilitation Counseling." Second Annual Northeast Regional Conference, National Rehabilitation Association (Kerhankson, N.Y.) June 7, 8, 9, 1972.

Ames, T.R.: Ministering to the mentally handicapped and their families in the community. *The Journal of Pastoral Counseling*, 5:51-55, Winter, 1970-1971.

Ames, T.R.: Training program for new professionals, paraprofessionals and volunteers part of a Kit—*Showcase of Innovative Manpower Programs in Mental Health* prepared by the National Association for Mental Health, Inc., New York, 1970.

Ames, T.R.: Independent living for the mentally handicapped: A program for young adults. *Mental Hygiene, 53*:641-642, Oct., 1969.

Ames, T.R.: Training and supportive services for the mentally handicapped adult. Unpublished manuscript presented before the California Chapter of the American Schizophrenia Foundation, Oakland, California, Nov., 1968.

Ames, T.R.: and Levy, J.M.: The hostel: Plans and Purposes. *Journal of Rehabilitation 39*:28-30, May-June, 1973.

Atthowe, John, and Krasner, Leonard: The systematic application of contingent reinforcement procedures in a large social setting: A psychiatric ward. A paper delivered at the A.P.A. Meeting, Chicago, Ill., 1965.

Avedon, Elliott M., Arje, Frances B., and Berryman, Doris: Work is not enough. *Journal of Rehabilitation, 28*:23-29, July-Aug., 1962.

Brooks, George W., and Deane, William N.: Rehabilitation of severely disabled hospitalized mental patients. *Journal of Rehabilitation, 28*:13-14, Sept.-Oct., 1962.

Campbell, Norma: Techniques of behavioral modification. *Journal of Rehabilitation, 37*:28-31, July-Aug., 1971.

Campbell, John L., and O'Toole, Richard: A situational approach. *Journal of Rehabilitation, 37*:11-13, July-Aug., 1971.

Carson, R.: *Interaction Concept of Personality*, Aldine, Chicago, 1969.

Cushing, Martha: When counseling fails—then what? *Journal of Rehabilitation, 35*:18-20, July-Aug., 1969.

Ferebee, E. Emory: The renaissance in mental health. *Journal of Rehabilitation, 31*:24-25, Nov.-Dec., 1965.

Fritz, Margaret, Wolfensberger, Wolf, and Knowlton, Mel: Position on an apartment living plan to promote integration and normalization of mentally retarded adults. Douglas County, Nebraska, 1970.

Gregg, Robert A., and Aitken, P. Wesley: The clergyman as an allied health professional. *Journal of Rehabilitation, 36*:37-39, July-Aug., 1970.

Grimberg, Moises: The Surrogate Society: A new approach to rehabilitation. *Journal of Rehabilitation, 36*:34-35, May-June, 1970.

Hallowitz, Emanuel, and Riessman, Frank: The role of the indigenous nonprofessional in a community mental health neighborhood service center program. *American Journal of Orthopsychiatry, 37*:766-778, 1967.

Heilman, Henrietta: In-hospital vocational training. *The Psychiatric Quarterly Supplement, 38*:280-289, 1964.

Henderson, John D.: Conditioning techniques in a community-based residential treatment facility for emotionally disturbed men. Unpublished manuscript, Philadelphia, Spruce House-Horizon House, Inc., 1968.

Hollander, Carl, and Moore, Charles: Rationale and guidelines for the combined use of psychodrama and videotape self-confrontation. *Group Psychotherapy and Psychodrama, 25*:75-83, 1972.

Holzberg, Jules D., Whiting, Harry S., and Lowy, David G.: Chronic patients and a college companion program. *Mental Hospital, 15*:152-158, 1964.

Kissin, Gerald, and Carmichael, Donald M.: Rehabilitation of psychiatric patients. *Journal of Rehabilitation, 26*:24-28, Sept.-Oct., 1960.

Kris, Else B.: When the mental patient returns to the community. *Journal of Rehabilitation, 26*:20; 44-47, Mar.-Apr., 1960.

MacLeech, Bert: A forward-looking concept in rehabilitation. In MacLeech, Bert, and Schroeder, Donald R. (Eds.): Seventh Annual Distinguished Lecture Series in Special Education and Rehabilitation. Los Angeles, U. of S. California, 1969, pp. 19-30.

MacLennan, Beryce W., Klein, William, Pearl, Arthur, and Fishman, Jacob: Training for new careers. *Community Mental Health Journal, 2*:135-141, 1966.

Michelson, Elaine: Volunteer work aids mental patients. *Journal of Rehabilitation, 30*:14-16, Jan.-Feb., 1964.

Mikels, Elaine, and Gumrukcu, Patricia: A therapeutic community hostel. *Journal of Rehabilitation, 29*:20-21, May-June, 1963.

Miller, Dorothy: Alternatives to mental patients rehospitalization. *Community Mental Health Journal, 2*:124-128, Summer, 1966.

Miller, D.H.: Worlds that fail. *Transaction, 4*:36-41, 1966.

Mink, Oscar G.: Learner-oriented instruction. *Journal of Rehabilitation, 37*:25-27, July-Aug., 1971.

Moseley, Lebaron: Returning the ex-patient to employment. *Journal of Rehabilitation, 17*:33-34, Sept.-Oct., 1961.

New careers in rehabilitation project of the National Rehabilitation Association: *Serving More Disabled People Better Through New Careers in Rehabilitation.* Office of the Manpower Administration, U.S. Department of Labor, 1969.

New York State Department of Mental Health: *Regulations For the Operation of Hostels For the Mentally Disabled.* Utica, State Hospitals Press, July, 1970.

Nickerson, Peter R.: Counseling contracts. *Journal of Rehabilitation, 38*:35, Mar.-Apr., 1972.

Patterson, C.H.: Counseling the emotionally disturbed person. *Journal of Rehabilitation, 33*:8-21; 45, Mar.-Apr., 1967.

Paul, Norman L.: Helping the mentally ill: Failure and progress. *Journal of Rehabilitation, 29*:43-44, Mar.-Apr., 1963.

Reiff, Robert, and Scribner, Sylvia: Rehabilitation and community mental health employability and disability issues. *Journal of Rehabilitation, 36*:11-15, May-June, 1970.

Roe, Ann: Community resources centers. *American Psychologist, 25*:1033-1040, 1970.

Sankovsky, Roy: Adjustment services in rehabilitation. *Journal of Rehabilitation, 37*:8-10, July-Aug., 1971.

Savino, Michael T., and Schlamp, Frederic T.: The use of non-professional rehabilitation aides in decreasing re-hospitalization. *Journal of Rehabilitation, 34*:28-31, May-June, 1968.

Sawyer, Horace W.: Adjustment: A systems approach. *Journal of Rehabilitation, 38*:33-36, July-Aug., 1972.

Scoles, Pascal E., and Henderson, John D.: Effects of token reinforcement on the social performance of psychotic men. Unpublished manuscript, Philadelphia Spruce House, Horizon House, Inc., 1968.

Stewart, Horace F.: A critical point in rehabilitation of the mentally ill patient. *Journal of Rehabilitation, 30*:19, March-Apr., 1964.

Video gives patients clearer view of themselves. *Journal of Rehabilitation, 33*:24-25, May-June, 1967. (a reprint from August 12, 1966, *Medical World News*).

Williams, Paul M.: Pre-employment adjustment program developed for mental patients. *Journal of Rehabilitation, 29*:21-22, Jan.-Feb., 1963.

Work Group Reports and Recommendations from the Joint Conference on Childhood Mental Illness, February 21-23, 1968. Sponsored by the National Association for Mental Health, Inc. and the Joint Commission on the Mental Health of Children, Inc. pp. I-7, 8, 9; IV-1-4; V-1.

CHAPTER VIII

THE USES AND ABUSES OF PSYCHOLOGICAL ASSESSMENT AND PSYCHOLOGISTS

ALAN FRANKEL *and* JOSEPH J. DUETSCH

WE ARE WRITING this on the assumption that it will be read primarily by rehabilitation counselors engaged in developing a rehabilitation plan with people who have been accused of being "mentally ill." As you can tell from our wording we are in agreement with Szasz, Sarbin, Laing and others that the label of "mental illness" is at worst a sociopolitical accusation and at best a dysfunctional label. It should be noted that others have different opinions, see particularly Meehl (1972) who adduces evidence that for certain psychiatric syndromes—namely manic-depressive psychosis, unipolar depression, and schizophrenia—there is behavioral genetic data to warrant that these are entities, and that there are reliable diagnoses of schizophrenia vs. nonschizophrenia. However, within the sociopolitical context, we would agree with the position that says that a mentally ill person is a person who has been labeled as such and taken to a societally sanctioned person for societally sanctioned treatment.

After reading this chapter, we hope that you will (1) gain a better understanding of what psychology can and cannot do, (2) be better able to evaluate reports given to you by a psychologist, (3) be able to discriminate when a call for psychological services is based on administrative concerns or counseling concerns, and (4) have a set of guidelines for evaluating the adequacy, usefulness and general sensibleness of what you receive from a psychologist.

SOME DETERMINERS OF BEHAVIOR

A profitable framework for viewing client behavior is: behavior is a function of the person, the situation, the particular response, and the philosophical background in which the whole business is embedded. Endler, Hunt and Rosenstein (1962) have shown in developing their Stimulus Response Inventory of Anxiety that individual differences between people account for very little of the overall variance in their anxiety questionnaire. What really counts is the situation and the interactions, in a statistical sense, between persons, situations and items. If you want to be able to predict behavior, then this is the question you have to answer: what person giving what response in what situation (Endler and Hunt, 1969). Look at this in contrast to trait theory, where people are presumed to be carrying around traits embedded in them, or typology theory of personality where, without really thinking it through, there is a tacit assumption that people labeled schizophrenic *act* schizophrenically 24 hours a day; people labeled retarded *act* retarded 24 hours a day, and that their behavior is always expected to be discrepant from the demands of the situation.

The assumptions of trait theory and typology theory do not fit the data. For example, it has been demonstrated that when a group of persons was admitted to a psychiatric service, significant levels of pathology were detected. When the same people were put into a treatment program which totally ignored pathology and concentrated solely upon social skills, the following happened: at follow-up, there was a vast improvement in social skills. People were functioning at highly improved skill levels and their pathology scores had not changed at all. What this obviously suggests is that sick people can act normally. If sick people can act normally, why bother assessing their "sickness?"

Braginsky, Braginsky and Ring (1969) in a series of studies have shown that people labeled schizophrenic, people admitted to a mental hospital, can engage in a process of *impression management* to meet their needs, e.g. whether to stay in the hospital or leave the hospital early and return to the community. The process of impression management involves presenting oneself so as to get maximum payoff from the environment.

From another point of view, Dembo, *et al.* (1956) have suggested, in the context of physical disability, that one of the reasons that persons with a physical disability see themselves as unfortunate is that others expect them to. If the person with the physical disability does not act as expected, he is devalued. This expectation on the part of the person without a disability is, in Dembo's frame of reference, the "requirements of mourning." The person without the disability *requires* the person with the disability to mourn. The concept is that the person without the disability engages in this kind of behavior to maintain his own value system. This phenomenon is exemplified by: a person accused of being schizophrenic does not get up in the morning to eat breakfast in the day room of the ward. The staff responds with, "We have to investigate this; this is probably symptomatic of his disease." (This is particularly true when the staff member that morning chose to skip breakfast at home.) The concept is: "What can you expect of him; he is a nut." There is another school of thought, however, which says: "You usually get what you expect; if you expect nutty behavior, you get nutty behavior." It has been shown repeatedly in the behavior modification literature that when a person is a patient on a psychiatric service and acts bizzarely, the consequence of this verbal or physical behavior is social attention. Therefore, deviant behavior is reinforced; acceptable behavior is nonreinforced. Ergo, there is a predominance of unacceptable behavior.

After this long, rambling, hopefully not too disjunctive, introduction, the essential point that we would like to make is that *behavior is multidetermined. And as a rehabilitation counselor your concern is: under what condition can this person act in a socially reasonable fashion?*

To answer this question, we suggest you need the following information. What are this person's *competences?** What are his *commitments?* And what goes on inside of him, his *personality?* By competences, we mean things like his biologically given equipment and limitations; in what behavior settings does he function, what social environments, what roles is he called to carry out, what are his problem solving skills, his self-regulation skills?

In terms of his personality, what does the mosaic of his self-concept look like? What does the mosaic of his people concepts look like? What does he see as the reason for his existence?

In terms of his commitments: what are his values, his responsibilities, his goals and reinforcers, his aversions and avoidances? What is his ethical system and how is it translated into behavior? What are his plans for the future?

It would be beneficial for rehabilitation counselors to ask the same questions of themselves, not only because of the intrinsic value of such an exercise, but to discover how the client's system differs from the counselor's system. At this point, if you are reading this chapter as part of a course requirement as opposed to intellectual curiosity, you may very well be asking, "What has all this got to do with psychological testing?" Our response is: it has to do with the conceptualization of a reasonable social, scientific, ethical, political framework in which this whole business goes on. It has to do with the initially different stance of the counselor and the counselee. The rehabilitation counselor is embedded in a federally funded (despite the reality of erratic budget cuts), nationwide system of providing services to people who are in need. For example, the system has become so elaborate that frequently counselors are not aware of all the facilities and rights in terms of helpful programs for counselees. Counselees can in no way be aware. Counselors come out of a background of knowledge of hypercomplex governmental systems; counselees, at a simpler level, are looking for a way out.

*We are indebted to Michael J. Ebner for this conceptual schema.

WORKING WITH A PSYCHOLOGIST

In our clinical experience, perceptive experienced counselors, using their own source of information and psychological skills, frequently arrive at a reasonable, direct, accurate assessment of the counselee with whom they are working. However, due to agency restrictions the counselor may not be allowed to attach a certain label or write down a clinical judgement because that is supposed to be the purview of the "expert." This might be viewed as duplication of skill or might be viewed simply as silly. However you choose to label this process, it is reality. Therefore a productive thing to do with reality, when you can't change it, is to accurately label it. We think it is appropriate for a rehabilitation counselor to come to a psychologist and say: This is what I think is going on with this person. However, I need you to say so, because the agency says so. Now that we can get this business out of the way, we can go on to work together to change agency policy. But first let us do what must be done so that the counselee can get his needs met.

Another instance in which the counselor needs the psychologist is when the counselor is stuck. A psychologist and counselor, depending upon how much freedom they have and how much freedom is allowed by the agency, can engage in a variety of activities. One is to do what the counselor asks, namely to respond to a question such as, "I think this person is too disturbed at this time to handle the job of gas station attendant; what do you think?" This is not asking for a label; it is asking for an opinion. Another question might be, "I don't think that this woman would profit from a four-year course in nurse's training because I do not think she can use it right now because of situation x, y, z. What do you think?" These are good questions, they are functional and not questions like "Do you think this person is schizophrenic?" This is a silly question which any counselor can answer with the same degree of accuracy that a psychologist can.

Psychologists answer this kind of question actuarially; that is, they administer an MMPI, compare the MMPI with the profiles of people who have been labeled schizophrenic in the past, and then make the judgement: Does this profile match what is called the "schizophrenic" profile? For this kind of matching procedure, you don't even need a person; you need a computer. Some of the computerized

MMPIs will print out the probability of this person being called mildly, moderately or severely disturbed, and thus answer the question, "Is he schizophrenic?" The literature has shown that machines always do at least as well as people if not better; so for decision making of the simple type, go to a machine. However, knowing that a person is schizophrenic is probably of little help in deciding whether this person will make a good gas station attendant. If there were actuarial data where you have schizophrenic profiles matched against good and bad gas station attendants, then I think you could use a computer. Unfortunately, that information is not available at this time. Similarly, the kinds of practical situations with which counselors come to psychologists demand extrapolations that sometimes are very hard for psychologists to make. As Walter Neff (1968) mentions quite frequently in his book, psychologists by and large are not interested in the world of work. They are interested in the world of intrapsychic dynamics and behavior. Therefore their concerns about work have to do with making statements like, "He is probably able to work; he is probably not able to work." And statements of that sort are not helpful to a counselor working with an individual.

THE TESTING SITUATION

A critical variable in the assessment of people is the situation. We have learned that the definition of a test is a sample of behavior in a standardized situation. This definition has limits and many implications. The testing situation is standardized in one sense in that you ask the same questions, but the interactions between people are different in that they elicit different responses from both parties. It would be useful to understand some of the parameters of the test situation from the viewpoint of the testor and the testee. In the following section, we will draw heavily on the work of Roy Schafer (1954) whose conceptualization of the testing situation can be found in greater detail in his *Psychoanalytic Theory of the Rorschach.*

Some of the roles adopted by testors are that of voyeur, saint, oracle and autocrat. In the testing situation the testor asks, probes, listens and looks at what is going on inside the testee from behind a cloak of objectivity. It may be that the testor enjoys the role of voyeur or that the testee enjoys the role of exhibitionist. If either party has conflicts over this situation, what comes through and is labeled "paranoid guardedness" is in reality a privacy issue. For example, the voyeur/testor is trying to get maximal amount of data out of the individual and the individual is responding with, "Keep your hands off. Keep out of my head." The testee could respond to this peeping tom as a sexual issue or as a control issue. (Nobody can tell me what to do. You can't force me into anything.)

The testor sees hidden meanings; he is an oracle. For instance, a person sees a Rorschach blot and sees a crab; a standard cookbook definition for a crab is a "rejecting mother." So in the Rorschach if you see a crab, you had a rejecting mother. None of us really like to be in a position where another person is reading our mind. We all have dirty laundry of which we are ashamed and we get angry with people when we think they see it. Similarly, the all-knowing person does not like to be thwarted in his all-knowingness, so the reluctant patient who gives minimal responses may elicit anger, ofttimes labeled as some perjorative psychiatric statement, i.e. passive aggressive, which can in some instances damn the testee.

Another role that a testor may take is the saintly role. He is operating in a helpful relationship, trying to ameliorate the problem situation. If the testor is hooked into this role, then he sees himself as the testee's salvation through Rorschach. If the testor is in conflict and embittered by the situation (a client not seeking salvation) then he can say, "Tough, it is not my problem." Each of these roles and expectations is coped with by most testors adequately and productively. They are not pathological dimensions of the testing situation. They are real dimensions of the testing situation. The important part of this discussion is: when you read a report from a psychologist, ask yourself this question—how does the writer of this report feel about the person of whom he is writing? What is the general tone? Is he talking about a maze of intricate dynamics that somehow leaves you with the feeling that you have just been through a labyrinth and you don't know where you are? Is he talking about a human being trying to cope, struggle and exist in his world? Is he talking about a beautiful person who has just been misunderstood totally by society? Is he talking about an angry, unhappy, frightened person full of loathsome and fearful impulses which could burst through at any moment?

When one of us is in the business of helping students learn how to assess persons, a device used would be to say to the student, "After you have done all your testing, write a letter to your mother that begins with, 'Hey, Mom, I just met this person. Let me tell you about him or her.'" If you get that kind of report from a psychologist, a report that accurately discriminates the person, the testor's reaction to the person, the person's reaction to the testor, with inferences accurately labeled, you have a report which will be productive to use in your counseling.

Let us look for a moment and focus on the dynamics of the testee. What the testee is being asked to do is engage in full self-disclosure in the absence of trust, a position nobody in his right mind would get into if he had a choice. Simply, the testee is out of control of the situation. Further, the testing situation allows, even demands, the testee to engage in a massive self-confrontation; an exercise in which most of us choose not to engage. (An analyst friend of ours, after four years in training, was asked to take a Rorschach and said that he was scared to death, as if there were a part of himself that was out of his self-knowledge.) When a person is given the opportunity to engage in self-confrontation, this is a tremendous freedom, a freedom for which many people clamor. Very few of us are equipped to deal with such freedom in a mature way, not because there is anything wrong with our character structure, but because we have had very little practice. Our society demands that we engage in the opposite of self-confrontation. Therefore, a useful question that a counselor can ask after reading the report from a psychologist is, "How did the counselee feel about the process of being tested?"

At this point we have concentrated on the behavioral interaction between the testor and the testee. Therefore a most important section of a report from a psychologist will be that section labeled "Behavior during the test situation." If this section of the report is minimally informative, we strongly suggest that you give feedback to your psychologist, that such and such is what you need. The best way to obtain full information from a psychologist is to ask direct questions. For example, when in practice, one of us was asked to see a seven-year-old child with cerebral palsy and the referral question was "IQ?" The strong temptation was to send back a report that said, "85." If the question had to do with the nature and type of school placement, then it should have been worded differently. Our guess is that the physician making the referral could have made just as good a rough estimate of intelligence as we could, based on his interaction with the child during the physical examination.

HOW PSYCHOLOGISTS FUNCTION

We would like to provide you with a nonexhaustive list of some of the things psychologists can and cannot do, particularly the sources of data from which psychologists make inferences. It should be underlined that these are *inferences*. The more these inferences are related to the original data base, the easier it is to check them out. For example, from the data base of an intelligence test such as the WAIS, one can get normative statements such as this person scored higher than X percent of the population. Further, one could say under what conditions this person could expect success, based on his intellectual competence. While the WAIS is used as a quantitative measure, it can also be used as a sample of many different behaviors. Psychologists see psychological testing as a task to be dealt with by the individual, and the primary question is *how* does he deal with this task? To answer this, you have to know the parameters of the task and the nature of the interaction.

The WAIS has been used, for example, to assess the ability to abstract, so that we can say, "This person's thinking is abstract rather than concrete." The WAIS, however, also assesses the person's ability to adopt an abstract *attitude*, which is the ability to go beyond the immediate givenness of a stimulus. It is more than the ability to say that a pen and pencil are both writing instruments. When Kurt Goldstein originally talked about brain injured soldiers adopting a concrete attitude, he was referring to the behavior of the soldier who returned to his room and found that his comb or brush had been moved from one corner to another corner on his dresser. The soldier with a concrete attitude panicked in such a situation, in Goldstein's words, had a "catastrophic reaction." That is what Goldstein originally meant by a concrete attitude.

The WAIS can also be used to assess performance as a function of attitudes towards authority. Some of the tasks in the WAIS demand that the person adopt a pupil role, such as the Arithmetic subtest. This can be used as a marker of how a person will respond in a teacher-pupil type relationship (situation). In the Comprehension sub-test of the WAIS where a person is given free rein to respond to such questions as "Why should people pay taxes?", one can obtain a measure of verbal social adjustment, that is, how well can this person verbalize what the rules of society are? If a person says, "I don't think anybody should pay taxes; the government is a rip-off," that technically would be scored as a zero. However, if you go on to ask the question, "O.K., but what do you think most people would say?" and get the response, "Well, what the hell. It is for the government," technically this is a contaminated answer, because of the previous zero response. It is important to know that the person *can* give the acceptable response, which implies that under some conditions he can role-play the socially acceptable person. To be able to role-play a socially acceptable person is an important fact for the counselor.

The attitude of "I have seen your response, now show me your maximal performance," is an important aspect of the process of testing of which counselors should be aware. For example, the Bender-Gestalt is frequently used as a test of perceptual motor dysfunction which is a marker variable for brain damage. One of us was asked to assess a person, a DVR candidate, who had a history of severe drinking. People with histories of severe drinking are frequently "organic." His Bender-Gestalt productions were rapid, impulsive, sloppy and of poor quality. This person had a life style that could be characterized as a stevedore life style: harsh, primitive, confrontative. After he had finished with the designs, the psychologist said, "Cut the crap. I want you to slow down and do the best job you can," whereupon he did slow down and produced excellent reproductions. Accordingly, if you do standardized testing and pick up aberrant responses, it is incumbent on the testor to push for maximal ability. If this has not been done, then the counselor, who is not aware of this facet of testing, lacks knowledge which may have dire consequences for the client.

The Block Design sub-test of the WAIS has been traditionally used as a nonverbal measure of abstract ability. There are, however, many reasons why a person doing a block design might perform poorly; one important reason may be how the person approaches the task of problem solving. Is he impulsive, does he rush, does he fiddle, does he correct, does he lose a great deal of credit because he is hypercompulsive? The WAIS is a sample of behavior of a human being who is asked to respond to different tasks along many different dimensions. What comes out of a person's performance on the WAIS should be a picture of a human being, not a set of interrelated traits and abilities. What we are after is a picture of a human being performing in a certain kind of situation so that we can make inferences and generalize to other situations.

We can also obtain from the WAIS a reasonable assessment of some of the questions we raised earlier: what are reinforcing events, what are the threatening events, what are the avoidances, the aversions in this person's life? For example, one of the questions that points toward an hysterical organization of the individual's personality is a deviant response to the question, "Why does the state require people to get a license in order to get married?" From the verbal content of the person's responses, you can obtain a content analysis of his statements and come up with some useful notions about how this person sees himself, the world, and the people in it. This is, of course, contingent upon the personality theory of the person being tested. It is also contingent upon the personality theory of the counselor.

Frequently psychologists will administer the MMPI, Rorschach and TAT in order to assess personality. These are multi-dimensional instruments making multi-dimensional demands on the person responding to them and the person interpreting the responses. The Rorschach and TAT are usually interpreted in the context of psychoanalytic and dynamic theory. One could, and in the old days psychological interns were frequently called upon, to write eight-page, single-spaced reports subsequent to a battery of tests, describing in exquisite terms the current dynamics of the individual. It may be helpful to understand that psychoanalysis concerns itself with fantasy and intrapersonal dynamics and is not particularly concerned with what people *do*. Psychoanalytic theory is concerned primarily with psychological forces inside the person, their strengths, their interactions, their contributions to and adjustment of conflictual states of affairs. The prevalent behavior that psychoanalytic theory deals with is behavior *inside* the psychoanalytic consultant's room.

To go from delineation of dynamics inside a person to prediction of behavior in the world is a very tenuous affair. The validity of psychological constructs leaves a lot of room for error. If indeed there is some demonstrated ability to show the forces, traits and dynamics of people, the relation of those dynamics to overt behavior is very tenuous and of equivocal validity except for a few isolated instances. Therefore, a good axiom is: the best predictor of behavior is behavior. But there is a hooker, and the hooker is that some clinicians are magicians. Some clinicians can look at a protocol and make statements about what the person will do down to the level of which sock he will put on first in the morning. Goldberg (1965) suggests studying such clinicians, to discover how they weight different pieces of data and combine them in a multiple regression fashion and achieve their high hit rate. Goldberg suggests generating actual regression functions from such clinicians and using these mathematical formulas as prediction devices. Unfortunately, for the practice of assessment, some of the decisions called for in assessment settings can be done by machines at least as well as people and frequently better; however, the diagnosing that machines can do better than people, e.g. neurotic vs. psychotic, is often thought to be trivial by practicing therapists and administrators. The clinician working with the Rorschach is prepared to supply data in response to such questions as "What things are aversive to this person; what things (stimuli) trigger conflictual responses; what characterizes his effective coping styles; under what conditions will this person act less effectively?" The Rorschach and other projective instruments can provide cues which need to be validated by overt behavior.

It would be useful to return to the question of how people behave. We have purposely said *how* rather than *why*. The why type of question can be thought of as a never-ending regress, Calvanistic, demanding, guilt-inducing type of question. *How* demands a description of conditions under which behavior occurs. *Why* demands a justification.

A clue to understanding how people behave can be obtained by data collection. For example, clues from the Rorschach come from a person's *response to ink blots*. What has to be answered and not simply taken as gospel is how much can a response to ink blots generalize to other situations such as being in an office? There are some gross guidelines in that some ink blots are more structured than others, and therefore you can make statements about the person responding to unstructured situations. When reading a psychological report, if you know how the testee behaved in the situation, how the testee and the testor felt about each other; if you know what the data bases are (this comes from Rorschach; this from WAIS; this from behavioral observations, verbal and nonverbal), then you are in a good position to test out some of the hypotheses generated by this report. Psychological reports are not sermons on the mount or from the mount. They are sets of well-calculated, highly educated guesses; and guesses can be wrong.

We are assuming that people reading this chapter have had at least one course in testing and know the basic questions and problems involved in validity. There is a study reported where ten of the top Rorschachers in the country tried to predict success in jet pilot training in the early 1950s. The experts were given twenty Rorschach protocols and sorted them into success and failure piles. Nine of the ten experts performed at chance and one expert performed significantly worse than chance. If they had done otherwise, it would have been a miracle. In the early days of jet pilot training, if you wanted to know who was going to succeed as a pilot, you should have asked people working at military aircraft fields; and they would have probably said, "The craziest guy in the group." The frequency of crashes was so great that you had to be some kind of nut to engage in this kind of behavior at all. Rorschach experts were people who sat in their private offices and constructed their vision of a successful jet pilot. It seems very difficult for a person sitting on Park Avenue or in Beverly Hills to know what it is to be a jet pilot in the early 1950s, i.e. going up in an airplane, knowing that the probability is fairly high that you will crash. The moral of this story is that psychologists can articulate a picture of what is going on inside an individual; but how these kinds of predispositions, tendencies and feelings are related to job performance is an empirical question.

What evidence do we have that people with difficulties in controlling impulses make poor hamburger flippers or good car washers, or good bank vice-presidents or poor bank vice-presidents? Probably the most useful kinds of information that we can have about people as related to jobs has to do with actuarial variables, e.g. age, sex, educational background. We suspect that counselors are far superior in their knowledge of these variables than are testors. Let us consider a person who has been in a state hospital for three years, comes out, and goes to work in a car wash. Whether or not that person succeeds depends on situational factors such as his home environment, his boss, his boss' experience, and the person's ability and willingness to play the role of worker instead of the role of patient.

Psychologists cannot tell you if a person will succeed in a job or course of training. They can only guess based on certain sources of information. If the psychologist's construction of the job does not match that of the employee, the supervisor, or the counselor, there is a very good reason why the psychologist cannot give you a useful recommendation: he does not have all the information. A psychologist cannot tell you whether or not a person will succeed in a course of training for the same reason. A course of training can be advertised as "learning to be a butcher," but as all psychologists, rehabilitation counselors, and persons who have gone through a college curriculum know, what is advertised in the catalogue is not necessarily what happens in the course. Counselors know that if they are working with a client towards an on-the-job training experience, the supervisor in that setting will have to be carefully chosen. The counselor will probably know how a particular supervisor reacts to the unique sets of problems brought to the job by the trainee. Therefore, what would be most helpful to the psychologist would be the following type of referral question. Given two kinds of supervisors, which setting would be best for the trainee?

Counselors, and frequently psychologists themselves, get trapped into believing that psychologists have a crystal ball, can read people's minds, can predict the future, and do all kinds of magical things. There are one or two magical clinicians who have powers that seem truly extraterrestrial. The rest of us balance, evaluate, interrelate and test out data; in the absence of data we cannot do very much.

We have been harping on data throughout this discussion because we think that professionals in the mental health field get all caught up in the dilemma of *reputation vs. data*. Once a person has a reputation of being a good (bad) patient, a good (bad) counselor, a good (bad) psychologist, we interpret everything he does within that context. It is very hard to shake a reputation and respond to the data.

Let us consider a person who has been labeled chronically schizo-phrenic, works successfully for four months on a job, has a psychotic episode, and sees imaginery people. He becomes irritated and upset; he upsets the people around him, is fired, and goes to jail. Another unsuccessful work experience is entered on his record. We would suggest that this is responding to the reputation and not the data. It could just as easily have been interpreted as "This was the most suc-cessful work experience this person has had."

It is useful to look for the data before you make judgement. If you do, you may end up in a different decision-making framework and a more productive, more authentic framework. Many people have an implicit theory of personality, based on "assumed intention-ality," i.e. you take what people do, assume why they did it, and then react to that assumption without checking it out. This can be-come character assassination which is one of the favorite pastimes of staff meetings (often mislabeled as "case conferences").

DISCOVERING THE CLIENT

When the psychologist and the counselor are working with an in-dividual, it would be helpful to discover the self-assessment procedure that the client has done and why he thinks his treatment plan has failed. When a person comes to a physical or mental health practi-tioner for help, it is a very good bet that the client (or significant others) has observed his behavior, made a diagnostic statement about it, formulated a treatment plan, tried the treatment, and experienced failure. Then the client generates an alternative diagnosis and treat-ment plan and it too fails. The client is now coming to a professional for yet another diagnostic statement and treatment plan. We do exactly what the client has done: observe behavior and formulate a diagnostic impression and treatment plan. This process is probably old hat to the client. Therefore in helping graduate students to learn about assessment, one of us has proposed that the client seeking help be asked to write a psychological report about himself. An excellent format for doing this is provided by Kanfer and Saslow in a 1965 article. What we have done is given the Kanfer and Saslow outline to people and asked them to respond to it.

George Kelly has promulgated the notion that just as scientists have a construction of what the physical world is like, all people have a construction of what they and their interpersonal world are like. This position is close to Rogers' theory of Self: People generate concepts of themselves, filter in confirming evidence, and deny or distort disconfirming evidence. Given that people do have a construction of themselves, a useful technique is to ask them to write it down.

WORKING TOGETHER
Productive Use of Psychologist's Time

There are at least two states, Oregon and Florida, whose DVR systems have each hired a chief psychologist at the same administrative level as the chief medical examiner. The chief psychologist is responsible for the utilization of psychologists and psychological services. His job is to work with the agency to develop the most rational plan for obtaining the services of psychologists. For example, in some states, psychologists are called upon to administer interest tests. It seems economically extravagant to ask a psychologist to be paid at his hourly rate to administer a test which could easily be administered by a clerk. Many tests given by psychologists, e.g. the MMPI, could be administered by almost anybody with a minimum amount of training and a reasonable amount of responsibility. In some states counselors are giving and interpreting intelligence tests as well as giving and interpreting the MMPI under varying degrees of supervision. Given the limited number of psychologists, the large case loads that counselors carry, and the even larger number of decisions that counselors are called upon to make—we urge that rather than argue on the basis of credentials, argue on the basis of function and competence. Identify where psychologists, counselors and clerks overlap; identify the special expertise of each of these persons and maximize the functioning of the total system. We think that the plan of adopting a chief psychologist for each state DVR is an excellent one, facilitating the most functional use of psychological services.

At a local level, as psychologists, one of the more frustrating events is, after writing a report and telephoning the counselor for feedback, receiving nothing but platitudes. Just as counselors need feedback, so do psychologists. We do not want to put the onus only on the counselor; it belongs on the counselor and the psychologist and the agency structure. What we are sharing with you is our view as psychologists; that when we do get feedback, we receive it as useful information, not as a personal attack.

Given the state of current psychological technology, certain tests used with a very high frequency may not in fact be maximally helpful to the counselor and the client. We strongly urge counselors to use psychologists as assessment consultants in the development of new instruments. Some psychologists have expertise in test development and research strategy which can be used to assist counselors in their high frequency decisions. Consultation in the medical field is traditionally thought of as physician A working with a patient and is presented with problems beyond his skill. He then asks physician B, say a cardiologist, for an opinion and a recommendation. The patient then returns to physician A. This is certainly one model of consultation. Caplan (1964) talks about different modes of consultation. One strategy utilized occurs when the consultant's goal is not to directly problem solve with a client but to work primarily with the counselor to increase the skills of the counselor and thus enable the counselor to problem solve. As psychologists we think this is one of the more productive methods of psychological consultation. Another way that psychologists can be used is as program consultants. For example, the agency may have a testing program that they feel is not particularly helpful. Psychologists can be helpful in evaluating and redesigning the testing program.

The message we have been trying to get across is that psychologists can do some things and cannot do other things. You should be aware of how and when to use them. Psychologists are fallible people with fallible instruments. The more that counselors know about what and how psychologists do assessment, the more likely that psychologists and counselors can work productively for the good of the client.

REFERENCES

Braginsky, B. M., Braginsky, D.D., and Ring, K.: *Methods of Madness.* New York, Holt, Rinehart & Winston, 1969.

Caplan, G.: *Principles of Preventive Psychiatry.* New York, Basic, 1964.

Dembo, T., Leviton, G.L., and Wright, B.A.: Adjustment to misfortune—a problem of social psychological rehabilitation. *Artificial Limbs, 8*:4-62, 1956.

Endler, N.S., and Hunt, J. McV.: Generalizability of contributions from sources of variance in the S-R Inventories of Anxiousness. *Journal of Personality, 37*:1-24, 1969.

Endler, N.S., Hunt, J. McV., and Rosenstein, A.J.: An S-R Inventory of Anxiousness. *Psychological Monographs,* 76: 1962.

Goldberg, L.R.: Diagnosticians vs. diagnostic signs: The diagnosis of psychosis vs. neurosis from the MMPI. *Psychological Monographs,* 79: 1965.

Kanfer, F.H., and Saslow, G.: Behavioral analysis; an alternative to diagnostic classification. *Archives of General Psychiatry,* 12:529-538, 1965.

Meehl, P.E.: Reactions, reflections and projections. In *Objective Personality Assessment.* New York, Academic, 1972.

Neff, W.S.: *Work and Human Behavior.* New York, Atherton, 1968.

Schafer, R.: *Psychoanalytic Interpretation in Rorschach Testing.* New York, Grune, 1954.

CHAPTER IX

DEVELOPING PSYCHOLOGICAL SERVICES IN VOCATIONAL REHABILITATION WORK

John G. Cull *and* Richard E. Hardy

~~~~~~

~~~~~~

DEVELOPING AND USING PSYCHOLOGICAL AND RELATED SERVICES WITH THE MENTALLY ILL AND OTHERS

THIS CHAPTER will purposely broaden from mental illness to include various concepts concerning the development of psychological services in state vocational rehabilitation settings. The num-

151

ber of mentally ill persons being rehabilitated at present through state vocational rehabilitation efforts has skyrocketed. Psychological services in rehabilitation must be expanded and improved, and this is a priority consideration in serving the mentally ill and other rehabilitation clients.

The rehabilitation counselor has been called the key to effective rehabilitation work and rightly so since he is the center of activity—the coordinator and often the developer of services to his clients. The responsibility for the success of various steps in the rehabilitation process rests upon the counselor's shoulders—psychological and related services are no exception.

Psychologists are engaged in a wide variety of activities, many of which relate directly to the goals of the vocational rehabilitation program. The rehabilitation counselor must develop professional psychological resources in much the same way that he develops community resources. Of the wide array of services offered by psychologists, three in which the rehabilitation counselor will be particularly interested include the following:

1. General psychological evaluations—relatively superficial but broad spectrum screening evaluation.

2. Speciality psychological evaluations—narrow in-depth evaluations (diagnosis of learning disabilities; determination of abilities, aptitudes and interests; and description of personality patterns of handicapped clients).

3. Individual and group adjustment counseling.

Rehabilitation counselors are becoming increasingly aware of the need for making the most effective use of psychological services during the counseling process. Therefore, the new rehabilitation counselor should acquaint himself thoroughly with the services provided by the psychologist and the role each of these services plays in the rehabilitation process. He can then provide the most needed services to his client at the appropriate time in the professionally appropriate manner.

INDICATIONS FOR PSYCHOLOGICAL EVALUATIONS

Quite often the new rehabilitation counselor is in a quandary concerning when he should obtain additional psychological data. He feels, as a counselor, it is his responsibility to evaluate his client in order to counsel him. While he can agree on the necessity for psychological evaluation in the rehabilitation process, he needs some rather specific guidelines relative to securing such evaluation. The most obvious response to this question is, "The counselor should secure a psychological evaluation when he has a specific question regarding his client's personality or personal attributes." More specifically, the counselor should obtain a psychological evaluation when he is developing a rehabilitation plan which will be long-term. If a long-term plan is developed, some basic assumptions are made relative to mental ability, interests, aptitudes and emotional stability. These assumptions should be checked out early in order to help insure the ultimate success of the plan. If the assumptions are not verified by means of a psychological evaluation but are found erroneous, a great deal of the client's time and energies can be wasted. Similarly, if an expensive rehabilitation plan is being developed, a psychological evaluation should be obtained for almost the same reasons.

Many psychological evaluations are obtained at the beginning of the rehabilitation process during the diagnostic phase when the individual's eligibility is being established. A psychological evaluation should be made in cases in which eligibility is based upon mental retardation, functional retardation and behavioral disorders.

In developing the rehabilitation plan, the counselor needs to have a fairly complete understanding of the client's functional educational level, mental ability, aptitudes and interests. If this needed information is missing, it should be obtained. If part of the information the counselor has is unclear, ambiguous or contradictory, the counselor should clear up the confusion with a psychological evaluation. For example, if the client has a reported educational achievement level or reported level of intellectual ability substantially lower than that required on a job the client performed successfully, the counselor should clarify the obvious contradictions by psychological testing.

If the counselor suspects important talents, capacities, abilities or disabilities which are unreported but have a bearing on the probable vocational objective, a psychological evaluation should be purchased to delineate these attributes. Also an evaluation should be obtained if the client has certain disabilities which later on materially affect his capacities, abilities, skills or personality. For example, a client who is experiencing mild anaesthesia in his hands and fingers should be tested for manual dexterity prior to settling on a vocational objective calling for a manipulative ability. A client interested in electronics assembly work should be tested for color blindness.

Lastly, a psychological evaluation should be obtained if the client is exhibiting or has exhibited behavior the counselor does not understand. If the client's current behavior patterns are not predictable and are difficult to understand, the counselor should enlist the aid of the psychologist to explain the client's personality structure. If the client's past history is filled with events or actions the counselor cannot reconcile, such as unexplained job changes, frequent moves from one community to another, a lack of organization to the client's vocational history and so forth, a psychological evaluation is in order to describe the client's personality structure in an effort to explain his behavior patterns.

Contraindication for Psychological Evaluation

Perhaps looking at cases when psychological evaluation is unnecessary would be meaningful. An obvious case in which a psychological evaluation is unnecessary occurs when the client recently has been successfully employed and intends to return to his particular vocation following the physical restoration and other rehabilitation services he will receive.

If the client has been successfully employed but is now unable to find similar work because of employer prejudice toward the handicapped, it is necessary for the counselor to use his counseling and vocational placement skills to convince the employers of the client's ability. In this case it would not be appropriate to obtain a psychological evaluation in an effort to change the client's vocational objective.

Psychological testing is not needed when a client has been successfully employed and the new vocational objective constitutes only a minor shift or the new job is directly related to his prior work. There is no need for testing when the client has developed a long and rich background of information regarding a particular industry or job family; and his new vocational objective, though not previously performed by him, is sufficiently related for the counselor and client to be safe in assuming he can meet the demands of the job. A separate but related case concerns the client having a long and rich background of educational information and experience, and the client plans to study or work in areas related to his background. Evaluation is not needed in this case.

In essence, a psychological evaluation is needed when the client's behavior is to be predicted over a long period or his behavior is difficult to predict over a short period of time. An evaluation is not needed when the client's behavior is understandable and predictable or if he has established a related pattern of vocational growth over an extended period of time.

At times, counselors will threaten to deny rehabilitation services if a client refuses to submit to the testing and interviewing of a psychologist. In many instances if the client continues to refuse, the case is closed—"The client is not motivated." Even though this occurs much less frequently than it has in the past, it is appropriate to discuss. As rehabilitation counselors become more professional and more aware of the needs of clients, they will be more attuned to the motivating factors operating in the client. If the client refuses services which the counselor offers, the counselor should seek to understand and modify behavior through counseling rather than being threatened and defensive himself and reacting in a punitive manner toward the client.

REFERRAL FOR PSYCHOLOGICAL SERVICES

When securing psychological services, the counselor should ask himself some basic questions: What specific knowledge can be obtained from the psychologist which will be of value in the rehabilitation counseling process? What data can he (the counselor) obtain and what data should he request from the psychologist? When these questions have been asked and answered, the counselor is better prepared to make an intelligent referral to the psychologist. As mentioned above, there are numerous types of psychological evaluations; therefore, it is inadequate for a counselor to merely refer a client for a "psychological evaluation." If he is expecting highly specific definitive information from the psychologist, the rehabilitation counselor must set definite limits for the psychologist and provide him with the appropriate background information. Gandy's referral form, if used, will tend to increase materially the quality of psychological reports the counselor receives. This referral form should constitute the minimum information forwarded to the psychologist; however, generally little more than a request for an evaluation is sent.

REFERRAL FOR PSYCHOLOGICAL-VOCATIONAL EVALUATION

FROM:———————————————— DATE:————————

TO: ————————————————

IDENTIFICATION:

Name of Client————————————————————————

Social Security No.—————————————————————

Address——————————————————————————

Sex———— Age———— Race———————— Marital Status————————

No. Dependents————————

SOCIAL-VOCATIONAL-MEDICAL:

Economic Stratum—————————————————————

Family Environment————————————————————

Formal Education—————————————————————

Usual Occupation—————————————————————

Vocational Success—————————————————————

Leisure Activities——————————————————————

Physical or Mental Impairments————————————————

General Health——————————————————————

BEHAVIORAL OBSERVATIONS:

General Observations (appearance, mannerisms, communication, attitude, motivation):

————————————————————————————

————————————————————————————

————————————————————————————

REASON FOR REFERRAL:

Statement of Problem————————————————————

————————————————————————————

Specific Questions—————————————————————

————————————————————————————

————————————————————————————

Enclosures:————————————————————————

————————————————————————————

Note: This form was taken from Gandy, J.: The psychological-vocational referral in vocational rehabilitation. Unpublished Master's Thesis, University of South Carolina, 1968.

Much of the information called for on the form is already in the case folder so it is easily accessible to the counselor. In order to select the appropriate instruments and interpret them, the psychologist needs the social-vocational-medical background information. Therefore, to facilitate the work of the psychologist and relieve the client of having to answer the same questions repeatedly and to increase the effectiveness of the psychological interview, the counselor should make a concerted effort to supply the psychologist all pertinent information.

An individual's economic status, home situation, the degree of vocational success he has experienced, and the physical or mental impairments he has will have a direct and major bearing on his behavior and personality. Test responses and results have to be evaluated in comparison with the above factors. If this information is not provided to the psychologist, he will have to interview the client at some length. The more time he spends in this duplicative effort, the less time he has to evaluate the client.

The counselor generally has had several contacts with the client before the client is referred to the psychologist. Also, the counselor is a professional who is skilled in observations; therefore, it is of particular value to the psychologist to have access to the observations the counselor has made. These observations can be quite meaningful since the counselor sees the client under a variety of conditions and the psychologist sees the client only in the testing and interview situation on one occasion.

Perhaps the most important information the psychologist should receive is usually not given to him. This is a statement of the problem which prompted the counselor to refer the client to the psychologist. In order to specifically meet the needs of the counselor, the psychologist should have this statement since it will, in many cases, determine the particular instruments the psychologist will use. In conjunction with this statement of the problem, the counselor should outline the specific questions he wants answered by the psychologist. By considering these questions, the psychologist can further tailor his evaluation to the specific needs of the counselor.

Lastly, a good referral should include other reports, evaluations and examinations which have a direct bearing upon the psychological evaluation. These would include other psychological evaluations, social evaluations and reports, psychiatric data, the general medical examination report, and some medical examinations by specialists.

SELECTION OF A PSYCHOLOGIST

After deciding upon what information the counselor himself will obtain and what information will be expected from the psychologist, the counselor has to select a psychologist. The counselor can obtain psychological data himself or he may rely upon a psychometrist (an individual skilled in the administration and interpretation of psychological, vocational and educational tests; an individual trained at a lower level than that of a psychologist), a psychologist in private practice outside the agency, a staff psychologist, or a consulting psychologist (these latter two will be discussed later). Generally, if he selects either the psychometrist, the staff psychologist, or the consulting psychologist, the agency will describe the mechanics of referral in a policy manual or procedure manual. Therefore, here we will concern ourselves only with using the psychologist in private practice.

When the counselor is attempting to do part of the psychological study himself, it is very important for him to recognize his limitations in the field of evaluation. Certainly, few counselors are skilled in psychological evaluation to the degree that they are able to use a wide variety of instruments. All counselors, however, should be able to use skillfully a small number of tests comprising a specific battery. When the counselor is inexperienced in the type of testing which he feels should be done, he must be able to secure the services of a qualified psychologist.

When obtaining the services of a psychologist in private practice, the counselor should have at hand a list of psychologists who are well known for their competency and who are experienced in working with handicapped persons. It is generally felt that psychologists who belong to the division of clinical psychology, the division of counseling psychology, or the division of psychological aspects of disability of the American Psychological Association will be interested in the field of rehabilitation and will be most helpful to the counselor. However, the counselor must recognize that psychologists, like other professionals, have areas of special interest. A psychologist who is knowledgeable concerning the emotionally disturbed or the mentally retarded may be relatively inexperienced in testing the physically handicapped.

When the client is sent to the psychologist, he is referred on an individual basis just as he is for a general or specialty medical examination. The payment is made according to a fee schedule developed by the agency and usually the state or local psychological associations. As with a new physician, a psychologist in private practice who is being utilized for the first time should be contacted. The counselor should discuss the vocational rehabilitation program, its goal, its procedures for referral, reporting, payment, and the agency's fee schedule.

THE PSYCHOLOGIST'S REPORT

After the referral of the client, the counselor has every reason to expect and should demand speedy service for his client. This speedy service entails both a prompt appointment to see the client and a written report of the finding submitted. While the report should be received within ten days of the client's appointment, quite often it takes longer; however, if it routinely takes longer and at times exceeds three weeks, the counselor should discuss the problem with the psychologist so that he may receive better service or change psychologists. When the counselor receives the psychological report, it should cover five basic areas:

1. Clinical observations of the psychologist
2. Tests administered
3. Results and interpretation of results
4. Specific recommendations
5. Summary

The observations of the psychologist are important since they provide the flavor of the evaluation, and without them the evaluation would be quite sterile. These observations will comment on the client's emotional behavior, appearance, motivation, reaction to the testing, and so forth.

The tests which were administered should be spelled out for two reasons: first, most fee schedules are based upon the number and type of tests administered; but, more importantly, the counselor needs to know upon what data the psychologist is basing assumptions and making recommendations. In the reporting and interpreting of results, the counselor should find the results of all the tests given with an explanation of their importance. This section is highly technical; however, it should be very logical since this is where the psychologist builds his case. If some of the test results are not noteworthy or are not used in the diagnosis and recommendations, this fact should be mentioned and explained in the interpretation section. Essentially this is where the psychologist logically bridges the gap between his clinical observations, the test results, the diagnosis, and the recommendations he will make. Above all, the sections should be very sensible and understandable.

In the recommendations section, the psychologist should make a number of suggestions which are addressed to the specific referral problem and the questions the counselor asks on referral of the client. Recommendations should be stated clearly and concisely. If the counselor does not understand them, he should never hesitate to call the psychologist for clarification. The summary is a short, clear summation of the evaluation stated in nontechnical terms.

Use of Psychological Evaluation

After receiving the report, the counselor is confronted with how to use the evaluation. The use of the data will be easier if psychological evaluations are viewed as an integral part of counseling and closely related to all other rehabilitation services and not as an isolated event or service. The evaluation can be used in counseling sessions to aid the client in better understanding himself and in identifying his major problem areas. Additionally, the counselor can use the psychological evaluation as a counseling tool to aid the client in developing insights specifically related to his relative strengths and limitations and in helping him in making reasonable plans and decisions.

In interpreting the test results to the client, the counselor should develop short, clear, concise methods of describing to the client the purpose of the tests he took and the meaning of the results; but, by all means, the counselor should communicate only on the level at which the client is fully "with" the counselor. A most effective means of interpreting test results is relating test data in meaningful terms to the client's behavior. A trap to avoid is becoming overly identified with the client's test scores. They should be presented in a manner that will allow him to question, reject, accept or modify the presentation and interpretation without having to reject the counselor. The counselor should not project his own subjective feelings into the results he is using.

Cautions in Using Psychological Test Scores

While psychological testing plays a vital role in the rehabilitation process, there are some cautions which need to be exercised in their use. It should be remembered that test scores are just that—only test scores. The indications are a product of the interpretation of the scores. Tests are only an *aid* to the counselor; they should never become the prime reason for a program of action in a client's rehabilitation. They are too fallible. They are too susceptible to human error to be relied upon completely. While scores are valuable in indicating vocational areas which merit consideration, the counselor should remember that tests are rather weak in industrial validation. But most importantly, it should be remembered that the individual can adjust to several occupations. Inherent in testing philosophy is the concept that an individual is "predestined" to only one occupation.

DEVELOPING MODELS OF PSYCHOLOGICAL SERVICES FOR STATE REHABILITATION AGENCIES

As the scope and commitment of vocational rehabilitation has expanded to include services to the culturally disadvantaged and those with behavioral disorders, so has the reliance on and need for psychologists in rehabilitation work. Psychologists who are trained at the doctoral level and who are aware of rehabilitation objectives and procedures are needed urgently.

The number of psychologists employed in vocational rehabilitation is limited. In order to obtain psychological services on a statewide basis, many vocational rehabilitation departments have generally taken one of three approaches in developing models of psychological services. The approaches might be labeled as (1) the consultation model, (2) the strict panel model, and (3) the supervising psychologist model.

Description of Models

The *consultation model* is relatively simple in structure. The department of rehabilitation must develop cooperative relationships with psychologists who are employed by institutions or who are in private practice. Usually rehabilitation area office supervisors contact these individuals and ask that they serve as consultants in psychology to the vocational rehabilitation program.

There are some problems with this approach. Many rehabilitation workers are not knowledgeable about the selection of qualified psychologists, and many psychologists are unaware of the objectives of rehabilitation. Unless there is considerable effort on the part of rehabilitation personnel and psychologists to develop understanding, the relationship between the rehabilitation department and consulting psychologists can be strained. This type of working relationship results in complaints from rehabilitation personnel that they are not getting the type of information they really need from psychologists. In addition, psychologists may not become fully involved and committed to the objectives of the rehabilitation programs. In addition, there is often confusion about fees and the selection of psychologists for various types of work such as psychotherapy and psychological evaluation of clients with catastrophic disabilities.

The *strict panel model* is the second approach which is used by some departments of rehabilitation. In this model, a part-time state consultant in psychology is usually hired. The state consultant in psychology and the rehabilitation department, in cooperation with the state psychological association, selects a panel of psychologists who represent various phases of professional psychology. The panel rules on the qualifications of psychologists who apply to perform various service functions for the vocational rehabilitation department and specifies areas of competency of individual psychologists. The state psychological consultant for the vocational rehabilitation departments usually chairs the panel. Panel members develop a list of psychologists and describe services psychologists are qualified to offer to the vocational rehabilitation department.

This approach can be criticized as duplicated effort if the state has a certification or licensing board. Such boards examine the credentials of psychologists and determine areas of competency. The state licensing or certification board also is concerned with violations of ethical standards. The strict panel model can be very useful in states where no state board of examiners has been appointed.

The *supervising psychologist model* is a third approach which is used by departments of vocational rehabilitation. This model requires the employment of a full-time psychologist who serves as state supervisor of psychological services. The supervising psychologist has statewide responsibility for developing effective working relationships with other psychologists employed on either a full-time or part-time basis. He recommends psychologists for work with the rehabilitation department. He may also act as chairman of a panel of psychologists which meets to consider special psychological problems in vocational rehabilitation. The panel can also help in developing cooperative relationships between the rehabilitation department and consulting psychologists.

The supervising psychologist helps rehabilitation staff members develop understanding of concepts that will be of value to them in their work in vocational rehabilitation. He should participate actively in in-service training activities for professional rehabilitation staff members. He visits area offices and facilities in order to work with consulting psychologists and rehabilitation personnel.

In addition, the supervising psychologist assures that psychologists working for the rehabilitation department maintain standards of practice in accordance with the laws of the state and with standards established by the American Psychological Association. He may also plan training programs for them in order that they may develop improved understanding of the complexities of vocational rehabilitation work.

These models and general variations of them have been used by most state rehabilitation departments, although some departments have not yet developed psychological services on a statewide basis.

Of the three described models, the supervising psychologist approach seems most effective, mainly because it allows an individual who is a psychologist to devote a substantial portion of his time to psychological services within the department of rehabilitation. A supervising psychologist should hold a doctoral degree in psychology or a closely related field. He must be carefully selected. He has crucial responsibility for the effectiveness of psychological services in an important statewide social service program.

STATE REHABILITATION ADMINISTRATORS' VIEWS ON PSYCHOLOGICAL EVALUATION

The rehabilitation process relies, of course, upon a thorough understanding of the rehabilitated client. Counselors develop this understanding by careful evaluation and study of medical, social, psychological and vocational components.

The authors believe that the widening range of vocational rehabilitation services, along with the increasing complexity of disabilities with which rehabilitation has become involved, heightens the need for more comprehensive evaluation services in the rehabilitation process. Even though a high level of evaluation is essential to providing adequate services to the rehabilitation client, obtaining pertinent and topical psychological information has been a continued source of frustration to the rehabilitation counselor. Not only does obtaining psychological information present a problem to counselors who have difficulty locating psychologists to evaluate their clients, but the psychological evaluation of clients presents a challenge to the rehabilitation administrators who must plan budgetarily for the provision of psychological evaluation.

Considerations in Obtaining Psychological Evaluations

The dilemma of handling psychological evaluations is a topic of frequent discussion by counselors and administrators. A basic question seems to be how the rehabilitation counselor can obtain an adequate psychological evaluation of his client without paying prohibitively large amounts in psychological fees for the increasing numbers of clients who need this type of evaluation.

Rehabilitation counselors and administrators generally acknowledge that from their experience, psychological examinations are extremely important in overall planning in the rehabilitation process. A study by Sindberg, Roberts and Pfeifer has confirmed this acknowledgement by indicating that, in terms of the usage of recommendations of psychologists, reports are definitely useful in the rehabilitation process. More than half of the recommendations of psychologists were followed completely or were followed to a large extent by rehabilitation counselors involved with the cases in the rehabilitation process.

Administrators Sampled

This current study is concerned with reactions of state rehabilitation agency directors relative to satisfaction with psychological services obtained from psychologists in private practice and the use of rehabilitation counselors in obtaining psychological information. All state vocational rehabilitation agencies were surveyed during the summer of 1969; of the ninety-one questionnaires sent out, fifty-five or approximately 60 percent were returned. Thirty-two of the fifty-five questionnaires which were returned indicated that state agency administrators do not believe that rehabilitation counselors should be prepared to administer a basic battery of psychological tests. Of the administrators responding to the questionnaire, 49 percent (or twenty-seven) did believe that rehabilitation counselors should be trained to administer interest tests, 47 percent (or twenty-six) felt they should learn to give aptitude tests, and 44 percent (or twenty-four) believed that they could administer intelligence tests with training.

Results

All fifty-five administrators who participated in this study stated that private psychologists are their primary source of psychological evaluations. Almost half of those persons returning questionnaires indicated that their state agency had hired psychologists on a full-time basis. Forty-three of the fifty-five agency administrators indicated that they were generally satisfied with the adequacy of reporting and professional services offered by outside psychologists. The most often expressed reasons for dissatisfaction by the twelve agency administrators who were not satisfied with outside consulting psychologists were (1) reporting was not sufficient for rehabilitation purposes and (2) there was an unacceptable time lag in getting material from the psychologists. Agency administrators concerned with programs serving blind individuals stated that psychologists in private practice often were not trained to evaluate blind persons. This observation apparently supports the contention of the authors that an extremely small number of psychologists are trained and experienced in working with the physically handicapped.

A majority of the administrators (58%) indicated that rehabilitation counselors should not attempt to administer a basic battery of tests because counselors lack an understanding of the principles of testing and evaluation. Additionally, thirty stated that in their opinion counselors lacked the time necessary to achieve effective testing and evaluation.

In states that recommend that the counselor have a counselor's test kit for his personal use in evaluation of clients, the following tests were most often recommended:

1. *Tests of Intellectual Functioning*
   Peabody Picture Vocabulary Tests
   Wechsler Adult Intelligence Scale
2. *Tests of Academic Achievement*
   Wide Range Achievement Tests
3. *Tests of Vocational Interest*
   Kuder Performance Record-Vocational
4. *Tests of Motor Dexterity*
   Purdue Peg Board
5. *Tests of Vocational Aptitude*
   General Clerical Test
   Test of Mechanical Comprehension

In some states, the Otis Self-Administering Test of Mental Ability and the Revised Beta Examination are being used in lieu of the Wechsler Adult Intelligence Scale and the Wechsler Intelligence Scale for Children. The following comment from a state director on the eastern seaboard indicates the general thinking of state administrators concerning the use of a counselor test kit, "We feel very strongly that counselors should be able to administer basic pencil-and-paper tests requiring level B^2 competency and preparation. We strongly urge that they not become involved with projective techniques and complex personality inventories."

Results of this survey seem to indicate that about 42 percent of the state agencies are moving toward having counselors use tests to make initial screening judgements of their clients relative to some of his basic needs and toward gaining an understanding of the client. Also, it appears that these screening procedures being utilized by rehabilitation counselors are helpful to them in making decisions which concern whether the client should have further evaluation by psychologists or should be involved in extended evaluation. Since fees for psychological services represent a substantial portion of the case service budget in the state agencies' overall budget, it seems practical to screen many of these clients through the use of a counselor's testing kit along with evaluating other data from the social and medical areas which may be available in order to make basic decisions regarding the rehabilitation process for individual clients. After such screening, the number of clients referred to psychologists for in-depth psychological testing and evaluation can be substantially reduced. This procedure would seem to allow for improved services to all clients since much of the money expended for psychological evaluation could be spent on other case services; and comprehensive psychological testing could be completed only when, in the counselor's opinion, it would be necessary for the rehabilitation of the client. As a result of this study, it is the opinion of the authors that agency administrators have confidence in their counselors and generally believe that they can depend upon them to make the complex decisions which are required regarding the variety of types of psychological evaluation needed.

In summary, it was found that almost half of the state agency administrators felt counselors should be equipped to administer interest tests, aptitude tests and intelligence tests; however, a majority felt administration time requirements precluded counselors' routine administration of a basic battery of tests. While over half of the agencies have employed full-time psychologists, the major source of psychological evaluations in all cases was from psychologists in private practice. Although a large majority of state directors were satisfied with this arrangement, the main dissatisfaction concerned the relevancy of evaluations to vocational rehabilitation and the time lag in getting reports from psychologists.

Effective rehabilitation work requires comprehensive evaluation of clients. Psychologists offer invaluable information to the total vocational evaluation effort. The fullest and most effective use of their services by state rehabilitation departments is of high priority.

REFERENCES

American Psychological Association: *Ethical Standards of Psychologists.* Washington, 1953.

Cull, J.G., and Hardy, R.E.: State agency administrator's views of psychological testing. In *Rehabilitation Literature,* 1970.

Cull, J.G., and Wright, K.C.: Psychological testing in the rehabilitation setting, *Insight,* 1970.

DiMichael, G.: *Psychological Services in Vocational Rehabilitation.* Washington, D.C., U.S. Government Printing Office.

Hardy, R.E., and Cull, J.G.: Standards in evaluation. *Vocational Evaluation and Work Adjustment Bulletin.* 2: January, 1969.

Jerner, J.: The role of the psychologist in the disability evaluation of emotional and intellectual impairments under the Social Security Act. *American Psychologist, 18:* 1963.

Sindberg, R. M., Roberts, A., and Pfeifer, E.J.: The usefullness of psychological evaluations to vocational rehabilitation counselors. *Rehabilitation Literature, 29:* October 1968.

University of Arkansas: *Psychological Evaluation in the Vocational Process,* Fayetteville, Arkansas, In-service counselor training project for vocational rehabilitation counselors in Arkansas, 1957. Monograph 3.

CHAPTER X

ELIGIBILITY FOR STATE-FEDERAL VOCATIONAL REHABILITATION SERVICES

BARRY P. CRAIG*

- ■ THE COMMON RESPONSIBILITY OF MENTAL HEALTH AND VOCATIONAL REHABILITATION IN SERVING THE MENTALLY DISABLED
- ■ THE REHABILITATION POTENTIAL OF THE MENTALLY ILL CLIENT
- ■ VARIABLES IN SERVING THE MENTALLY ILL PERSON
- ■ BASIC CRITERIA OF ELIGIBILITY FOR VOCATIONAL REHABILITATION SERVICES
- ■ A CONCLUDING WORD
- ■ REFERENCES

IN THE FIELD of human services the *zeitgeist* of the 1970's is services integration and services coordination.[1] It has become evident

*The author would like to express his appreciation to his secretary, Mrs. Lenore H. Lohmann, for her invaluable aid in preparing this manuscript.
1. This is evidenced by the formation of human services umbrella agencies in many states in recent years and by the proposed "Allied Services Act of 1972," S. 3643, U.S. Senate. cf. *Rehabilitation Interagency Focus*, 5:1-12, June, 1972.

to many professionals in human services agencies that narrow categorical programs and services make it very difficult to bring together the array of services a troubled human being may need to help him solve his problems and resume or achieve a more normal life. A particular agency may be limited by the definition of its target population, by the limited array of services it may offer, or by the limited funding that it enjoys. Attempts by agencies to pool their resources and to work cooperatively have been marked by many difficulties. Because of limited funds and the all too-human unwillingness to assume responsibility, agencies have had a tendency to take a narrow and conservative view of their target populations, of their "traditional" services and functions, and of their service goals. The result has been gaps in services and a lack of continuity which is frustrating to the professional and disastrous for the client.

For there to be success in cooperatively deploying services to a particular target population, there must be substantial agreement on the definition of the target population and a recognition of a common responsibility to serve that group. There also must be agreement on what services are required, on the goals of those services, and on a division of labor in rendering services so that each agency will provide those services that it can render best and, more importantly, so that someone has clear responsibility for rendering each required service. If this agreement is not achieved there will be fuzziness in the role of each agency, and it is likely that there will be gaps in services and that role conflicts will occur which will be debilitating to combined efforts.

Two of the major human service programs which have attempted to work cooperatively to serve the mentally disabled are state mental health and state-federal vocational rehabilitation agencies. To the extent that they have been able to reach agreement about responsibility for serving the mentally disabled their cooperative efforts have been effective and successful. Unfortunately there has been more conflict and disagreement than one would expect in view of their histories and legal mandates. Historically and legally they have substantial overlap in responsibility, target population, traditional services, and service goals. This would seem to make cooperation easier. As a matter of fact, however, it is precisely this overlap that has caused such difficulty. Each agency looks at the other as a source of funding and resources for those clients it calls its own. There is often a fear in each agency that it will be seduced into providing a service that it thinks the other should be providing. Conversely, there is sometimes the fear that one agency will provide a service that the other agency thinks it has responsibility for. The underlying cause for such conflicts seems to be a lack of understanding of the historical and legal precedents which are the foundation for the cooperative efforts between these two agencies. Before we launch into the main subject of this chapter, the eligibility for state-federal vocational rehabilitation services, it may be useful to examine this foundation.

THE COMMON RESPONSIBILITY OF MENTAL HEALTH AND VOCATIONAL REHABILITATION IN SERVING THE MENTALLY DISABLED

For psychiatry and mental health, the mentally disabled are those people whose difficulties in living, body chemistry, brain function, or development produce in them clusters of behavioral symptoms and signs that can be labeled according to the categories of the *Diagnostic and Statistical Manual of Mental Disorders* published by the American Psychiatric Association (American Psychiatric Association, 1968.) Since, as we shall see later, vocational rehabilitation agencies use these same categories to document mental disability, we can assume that there is substantial agreement on the definition of the mentally disabled as a target population and that both agencies share a common concern for this group of people.

In an attempt to make a division of labor between the two agencies, it is often said that mental health is responsible for *treatment* and vocational rehabilitation is responsible for *rehabilitation,* or more narrowly, *vocational* rehabilitation. Harold R. Martin (Glasscote, 1971) has suggested that:

> ... *rehabilitation* be used when referring to activities which attempt to discover and develop the patient's assets, in contrast to *treatment* which is a direct attack on the patient's disability.

This conceptual distinction may be useful in some contexts, but as an approach to assigning responsibility to vocational rehabilitation and mental health it is problematic to say the least. Many activities which legitimately can be labeled rehabilitation, and even vocational rehabilitation, can be provided within the historical tradition and legal mandate of mental health. Conversely, many activities which legitimately are labeled treatment can be provided within the historical tradition and legal mandate of vocational rehabilitation. Even more confounding to those who would try to make this distinction is the fact that the same activity often can bear both labels. To elucidate this point, we shall now examine some of the historical and legal aspects of the development of these two human services which bear on this issue.

Historically, the state-federal vocational rehabilitation program is a relative newcomer to the field of psychiatric rehabilitation. If psychiatric rehabilitation refers to a process by which psychiatrically disabled people are helped to achieve the maximum functioning of which they are capable, then the historical roots of psychiatric rehabilitation in the United States can be traced back 150 years to the era of moral treatment in psychiatry.

In the early nineteenth century Phillipe Pinel in France and William Tuke in England instituted radical reforms in the treatment of the mentally ill. Pinel drew his inspiration from the liberal writings of the physician-philosopher John Locke; and Benjamin Rush, inspired by the same source, instituted less extensive reforms in America. Rush influenced other physicians, and by the time of his death in 1813 there was much interest in mental illness and wide acceptance of the principles of moral treatment. In 1817, four years after Rush's death, the first hospital in America founded expressly for the purpose of providing moral treatment was built by Pennsylvania Quakers and named Friend's Asylum. During the next thirty years, eighteen more state and private hospitals were built for moral treatment of the mentally ill in America (Bockoven, 1956, p. 173).

Bockoven traces the origins of moral treatment to the humanistic science of the eighteenth century which interpreted human behavior in humanitarian terms. He states that:

> Humanitarianism favored the view that lunatics had undergone stresses which robbed them of their reason. That such stress could result from disappointment as well as inflammation was a basic assumption. Stresses of a psychological nature were referred to as *moral causes*. Treatment was called *moral treatment*, which meant that the patient was made comfortable, his interest aroused, his friendship in-

vited, and discussion of his troubles encouraged. His time was managed and filled with purposeful activity.[2]

Patients were treated with kindness and civility. The staff of physicians and attendants dined with their patients, and patients had available to them a wide variety of social, educational, recreational and vocational activities.

> The very matrix of moral treatment was the communal life of patients and hospital personnel. Every aspect of daily living was utilized by the physician for its therapeutic effect in awakening of feelings of companionship in the patients. The chief modalities used in awakening such feelings were those endeavors which required the patient to invest interest in something outside himself in cooperation with others, namely, manual work, intellectual work, recreation, and religious worship.[3]

Manual work consisted primarily of farm work and various activities around the hospital such as the kitchen, laundry and repair shops. In 1847 Dr. Amariah Brigham found this inadequate and recommended that hospitals have a variety of workshops available to patients.

> In such rooms, dressmaking and tailoring, cabinet work, the manufacture of toys, basket-making, shoemaking, painting, printing, bookbinding, and various other employments may be carried on to the advantage of many patients, some of whom cannot be employed on the farm or in shops disconnected with the asylum.[4]

After 1850 the principles of moral treatment fell into disuse, and the long era of custodial care began. The many reasons for this decline are important issues in the history of psychiatry, but for the most part they do not concern us here. One issue, however, is how effective was moral treatment? Recovery rates were reported as high as 70 percent[5], and eventually skeptics like Dr. Pliny Earle charged that these figures were exaggerated.[6] Bockoven, in a recent review of the statistical studies done at the time, feels that the controversy then was engendered by methodological problems in han-

2.Bockoven, 1956, p. 172.
3.Bockoven, 1956, p. 302.
4.Bockoven, 1956, p. 302.
5.Bockoven, 1956, p. 174.
6.Bockoven, 1956, p. 292.

dling the data and in the definitions of "recovery."[7] He concludes that:

> The statistics of moral treatment reported here are at least presumptive evidence that efforts to meet the personal needs of patients are well worthwhile.[8]

Despite the fact that the lessons of moral treatment were ignored for nearly 100 years, moral treatment is the precedent for two ideas about work and mental illness. Work activity can be an important tool of psychiatric treatment (Osman, 1965), and psychiatric treatment is incomplete without due consideration to the vocational aspects of a patient's life. In the years between 1850 and World War II, psychiatry concerned itself with classifying mental disorders, with neurological and other organic etiology, with various physical methods of treatment, and with the dynamic formulations of psychopathology and treatment advanced by Freud and his followers. Although there was much less emphasis on work activity in the treatment of mental illness, these two ideas were not forgotten in the more enlightened and humane mental hospitals (Lewis, 1959).

World War II was a great stimulus to psychiatry, and it produced many changes in thinking about mental illness and treatment. New mental health disciplines, like clinical psychology, evolved. Many physicians returned from the war with increased awareness of emotional problems, and many of these men sought specialty training in psychiatry. The public too seemed more aware of emotional illness and the inadequate system of mental health care in the United States. This interest and movement finally culminated in the formation of the Joint Commission of Mental Illness and Health in 1955 whose charge was ". . . to analyze and evaluate the needs and resources of the mentally ill in the United States and make recommendations for a national mental health program (Joint Commission on Mental Illness and Health, 1959)."

The commission's report made sweeping recommendations for reorientation of mental health services and resources. The commission recommended that primary emphasis should be placed on community care of the mentally ill. Congress responded to this idea by

7. Bockoven, 1956, pp. 292-299.
8. Bockoven, 1956, p. 299.

enacting the Community Mental Health Centers Act of 1963 which made funds available to develop community-based service programs for the mentally retarded and mentally ill.

Since we are concerned here with psychiatric rehabilitation, it is interesting to note the commission's recommendation for this area. Because of its importance we shall be quoting it in full:

Aftercare, Intermediate Care, and Rehabilitation Services

The objective of modern treatment of persons with major mental illness is to enable the patient to maintain himself in the community in a normal manner. To do so, it is necessary (1) to save the patient from the debilitating effects of institutionalization as much as possible, (2) if the patient requires hospitalization, to return him to home and community life as soon as possible, and (3) thereafter to maintain him in the community as long as possible. Therefore, aftercare and rehabilitation are essential parts of all service to mental patients, and the various methods of achieving rehabilitation should be integrated in all forms of services, among them day hospitals, night hospitals, aftercare clinics, public health nursing services, foster family care, convalescent nursing homes, rehabilitation centers, work services, and expatient groups. We recommend that demonstration programs for day and night hospitals and the more flexible use of mental hospital facilities, in the treatment of both the acute and the chronic patient, be encouraged and augmented through institutional, program and project grants. [Italics in original.]

Aftercare services for the mentally ill are in a primitive stage of development almost everywhere. Where they do exist, services and agencies caring for the former patient tend to split off from mental patient services as a whole and further to approach the patient's problems piecemeal. Rehabilitation agencies should work closely with treatment agencies and preferably have representatives in the latters' institutional settings. It is important that rehabilitation be regarded as a part of a comprehensive program of patient services in which each and every member of the mental health team has a part to play.[9]

It is clear from this passage that the Joint Commission considered treatment and rehabilitation inseparable. The objective of *treatment* is ". . . to enable the patient to maintain himself in the community in a normal manner," and this obviously includes *work*. Mental health is being charged with responsibility for rehabilitation as part of its overall responsibility for treatment, and there is a clear call to both mental health and rehabilitation agencies to assume their

9. Joint Commission on Mental Illness and Health, 1959, p. xvii.

joint responsibility for serving the mentally disabled.

The Community Mental Health Centers Act of 1963 takes cognizance of this recommendation of the Joint Commission. In order for a mental health center to receive federal assistance it must provide a coordinated network of five essential services: inpatient care, outpatient care, partial hospitalization, emergency services, and consultation and education. These basic services may be expanded into a comprehensive program which includes, in addition, diagnostic and *rehabilitation* services, precare and aftercare services, training of personnel, and research and evaluation. Thus, comprehensive mental health services include rehabilitation.

From the discussion thus far it is evident that work activities can be treatment and that treatment and rehabilitation are inseparable. Mental health authorities have a clear legal mandate to provide rehabilitation services as a part of a comprehensive approach to the treatment of mental illness. *Moral treatment* has been resurrected. Karl Menninger notes in *The Vital Balance* that:

> The moral treatment of the mentally ill is used today in a more ambitious and extensive way than its proponents could have imagined. In good psychiatric hospitals today, there are assignments, there are exercises for the mind and the body, there are programs of activities and programs of inactivity. Instead of moral treatment, it is called milieu treatment or rehabilitation . . . the idea in back of it is the same, namely, to guide or lead or instruct the patient into a way of life and then gradually withdraw the instruction and the supports and permit him to take up an independent existence, once more using his own assets and his techniques. (Black and Benney, 1969, pg. 736.)

The state-federal vocational rehabilitation program was inaugurated by the Vocational Rehabilitation Act of 1920 (Public Law 236) whose purpose was to encourage states to organize vocational rehabilitation programs for disabled civilians comparable to programs provided under the Soldiers Rehabilitation Act of 1918. Public Law 236 provided grants to states which could be used to provide *physically* handicapped civilians with vocational guidance, training, occupation adjustment, prosthetics, and placement services. The objective of these services was gainful employment.

The mentally ill and mentally retarded became eligible for vocational rehabilitation services when Public Law 113 was passed in 1943. This law also made it possible to provide physical restoration services including hospitalization, surgery, and therapeutic *treatment*. From this point on it was legally possible for vocational rehabilitation agencies to provide treatment *and* rehabilitation services to the mentally ill and mentally retarded if these services were necessary to render mentally disabled individuals fit to engage in a gainful occupation. Implementation of services to those groups was not immediate, however.

The 1954 amendments (Public Law 565) gave impetus to the movement to provide vocational rehabilitation services to the mentally disabled through provision of grants for research and demonstration projects. Many of these projects demonstrated the rehabilitation potential of the mentally disabled through the use of a variety of modalities including day hospitals, ex-patient social clubs, halfway houses, special rehabilitation wards in mental hospitals, rehabilitation centers at state hospitals, sheltered workshops, etc. (Cubelli and Havens, 1969). This new law also authorized for the first time the use of federal funds for the establishment (through alteration or expansion) of rehabilitation facilities and workshops. These resources are very important in the vocational rehabilitation of the mentally disabled.

With the background of cooperative effort in various demonstration projects, state mental health agencies and state-federal vocational rehabilitation agencies were ready to initiate more ambitious cooperation; and the 1965 amendments (Public Law 333) made such cooperative programming possible. This law made possible the use of funds available to public agencies other than the state vocational rehabilitation agency as the "state-match" for federal vocational rehabilitation funds at the rate of three federal dollars for each state dollar. The use of third-party funds from mental health agencies made possible a tremendous expansion of cooperative programming between mental health and vocational rehabilitation. Many states were now able to implement the Joint Commission's recommendation for vocational rehabilitation units and facilities in state mental hospitals. There were also cooperative efforts and joint funding in day hospitals, halfway houses, rehabilitation-resocialization units, sheltered workshops, etc.

These cooperative efforts have resulted in an impressive array of services for the mentally disabled. Both agencies have a clear responsibility to provide rehabilitation services to the mentally disabled, and together they are providing those services in many states. Where then is the conflict?

Vocational rehabilitation agencies have certain restrictions imposed on them by federal regulations. The restrictions that are important to this discussion center in two areas: target population and services and their goals. It is in the interpretation and understanding of the restrictions in these areas that vocational rehabilitation and mental health have their opportunity for disagreement.

The target population of mental health is *all* of the mentally disabled, whereas the target population of vocational rehabilitation is that portion of the mentally disabled group which meets vocational rehabilitation's three criteria of eligibility. We shall be discussing eligibility in detail later. For now, it may be said that mental health sometimes wants vocational rehabilitation agencies to serve patients who do not meet these criteria. On the other hand, at times, vocational rehabilitation agencies seem to make a more restrictive interpretation of the criteria than is necessary. It readily can be seen that this kind of difference in understanding or interpretation can make cooperative efforts very difficult.

It should be clear by now that both vocational rehabilitation and mental health may provide treatment and rehabilitation services and that it is difficult to label many activities as clearly treatment or clearly rehabilitation. Vocational rehabilitation regulations stipulate that rehabilitation agencies may not provide services which another agency is legally obligated to provide, nor may rehabilitation agencies provide services for which a handicapped person would be entitled if he were not an applicant or client of the vocational rehabilitation agency. If mental health is legally obligated to provide a particular service or if it would provide that service to a patient who is not a vocational rehabilitation client, then vocational rehabilitation agencies may not duplicate that service and would look to mental health to provide that service to mutual clients. On the other hand, if mental health is authorized to provide a rehabilitation service, but is not doing so, that service, as a *new* service or as part of a *new pattern* of services, can be mounted through a cooperative program between the two agencies using the third-party funding mechanism. Decisions about legal obligation, duplication, whether a rehabilitation service is *new*, and whether a rehabilitation service has as its objective the gainful employment of clients are complicated at times.[10] It is in these decisions that mental health and vocational rehabilitation have another opportunity to disagree.

Despite the difficulties and complexities of working in cooperation, mental health and vocational rehabilitation have been willing to assume their joint responsibility to serve the mentally disabled. In many ways their cooperative efforts can serve as a model for services integration. The future success of this cooperation will depend on their continuing to understand their respective constraints and possibilities in serving mentally disabled people.

THE REHABILITATION POTENTIAL OF THE MENTALLY ILL CLIENT

Rehabilitation counselors who do not specialize in serving mentally ill clients are often victims of the same attitudes and prejudices that the general public has toward the mentally ill. Despite the growing effort to serve the mentally ill, there is still skepticism about their rehabilitation prospects. Table X-I shows the number of mentally ill persons rehabilitated by state vocational rehabilitation agencies from 1944, when they first became eligible, to 1970.

Inspection of this table reveals some interesting trends. From 1944 through 1956 the mentally ill never represent more than 4.0 percent of total rehabilitations. In the period from 1955 to 1965 this percentage gradually increases to 13.6 percent. However, with the additional resources and cooperative programming made possible by the 1965 amendments, the mentally ill come to represent almost 25 percent of all persons rehabilitated by state-federal agencies in 1970. There can be no question that, as a group, mentally ill people have, with appropriate resources and programming, as good a prognosis for rehabilitation as any other disabled group. A decision on the potential of a particular mentally ill person for rehabilitation is another and more difficult question which we shall deal with in a later section.

VARIABLES IN SERVING THE MENTALLY ILL PERSON

It is sometimes said that the vocational rehabilitation of the men-

10. For an excellent discussion of some of these issues see Crunk, William A.: Cooperative programming. In Cull, John G. and Hardy, Richard E. (Eds.): *Vocational Rehabilitation: Profession and Process*. Springfield, Thomas, 1972, pp. 274-291.

TABLE X-1

NUMBER OF PERSONS WITH MAJOR DISABLING CONDITIONS
OF MENTAL ILLNESS REHABILITATED BY STATE VOCATIONAL
REHABILITATION AGENCIES FISCAL YEARS 1944-1970, AND
PERCENTAGE OF TOTAL REHABILITATIONS *

Fiscal Year	No. of Persons **	Percent of Total Rehabilitated **
1970	63,267	24.7
1969	54,531	23.2
1968	40,156	19.6
1967	27,897	16.1
1966	21,991	14.2
1965	18,296	13.6
1964	13,863	11.6
1963	10,800 **	9.8 **
1962	8,800 **	8.6 **
1961	6,700 **	7.2 **
1960	5,703	6.5
1959	4,592	5.7
1958	3,745	5.0
1957	3,169	4.5
1956	2,516	3.8
1955	2,041	3.5
1954	1,829	3.3
1953	2,083	3.4
1952	2,081	3.3
1951	2,407	3.6
1950	2,038	3.4
1949	1,980	3.4
1948	1,750	3.3
1947	1,346	3.1
1946	1,082	3.0
1945	1,356	3.2
1944	511	1.2

Sources: U.S. Department of Health, Education and Welfare: *Statistical History, Federal-State Program of Vocational Rehabilitation, 1920-1969*. Washington, D.C., Social and Rehabilitation Service, Rehabilitation Services Administration, Division of Statistics and Studies, June, 1970.

U.S. Department of Health, Education and Welfare: *State Data Book, Federal-State Vocational Rehabilitation Program, Fiscal Year 1969*. Washington, D.C., Social and Rehabilitation Service, Rehabilitation Services Administration, Division of Statistics and Studies.

U.S. Department of Health, Education and Welfare: *State Data Book, Federal-State Vocational Rehabilitation Program, Fiscal Year 1970*. Washington, D.C., Social and Rehabilitation Service, Rehabilitation Services Administration, Division of Statistics and Studies.

**Beginning with fiscal year 1967, includes psychosis; psychoneurosis; personality, character and behavior disorders; alcoholism; and drug addiction. Prior to 1967, alcoholism and drug addiction were excluded. Fiscal year 1961-1963 figures include estimates for personality, character and behavior disorders.

tally ill is really no different than the vocational rehabilitation of the physically handicapped. This is a naive view of the situation, to say the least. There is no doubt that the basic concepts, methods and techniques are the same, but in their application to the mentally ill there are some distinct differences. Dr. Rives Chalmers, a psychiatrist, outlined some of the essential differences that he saw (Chalmers, 1961):

I. Differences for the client:
   A. Diagnostic evaluation of the client is not as precise.
   B. Prognosis is more difficult to evaluate because social variables have more crucial significance in the treatment process.
   C. The client's motivation and cooperation are more significant in determining outcome of treatment.
   D. The client has a major problem in interpersonal communication.
   E. Cost and time required for adequate treatment is greater than for the usual physical handicap.
   F. A major lack of adequate personnel and facilities for treatment.

II. Differences for the counselor:
   A. There is more personal involvement of feelings and attitudes in the counseling relationship.
   B. Personal psychodynamics of the counselor are a more important influence on the client with emotional disability.
   C. Relationships with other significant persons are more difficult and potentially more frustrating.
   D. Separation in closure of case is more difficult.
   E. Personal satisfaction with success is greater and more rewarding in personal and professional growth.

III. Differences for the community:
   A. Social concepts of mental illness, psychiatric treatment, bizarre thinking or behavior.
   B. Family dynamics oriented to promoting or increasing the client's disability, and resistance of the family to the client's personal growth.
   C. Employers caught between social and personal attitudes of the employees and the need for the client's services.

Each one of these differences is an important variable in serving the mentally ill person. Each one raises very complicated issues, and each could be the subject of an extended chapter by itself. We shall reconsider some of these differences as we discuss the eligibility of mentally ill clients for state-federal vocational rehabilitation services.

BASIC CRITERIA OF ELIGIBILITY FOR
VOCATIONAL REHABILITATION SERVICES

In discussing the eligibility of the mentally ill for vocational rehabilitation services we are dealing with the application of the three basic criteria of eligibility for vocational rehabilitaton services to the mentally ill. These three criteria are defined in Chapter 16, Section 1 of the *Vocational Rehabilitation Manual* (Department of Health, Education and Welfare, 1969), and it is important to our discussion to understand what this section says. We shall be quoting extensively from this document and will be referring to it as: *Manual*, 16-1-13, the last two digits referring to page numbers.

What then are the three basic criteria of eligibility? They are as follows (*Manual*, 16-1-3):

> The State agency is required to show that all the following conditions exist for each individual determined eligible for vocational rehabilitation services . . .:
> a. The presence of a physical or mental disability;
> b. The existence of a substantial handicap to employment; and
> c. A reasonable expectation that vocational rehabilitation services may render the individual fit to engage in a gainful occupation.

In the next three sections we shall be further defining these criteria, and we shall be discussing some of the problems involved in their application to the mentally ill client.

Is There a Disability?

The first criterion involves documenting a *physical* or *mental disability* which means:

> . . . a physical or mental condition which materially limits, contributes to limiting or, if not corrected, will probably result in limiting an individual's activities or functioning . . . (*Manual*, 16-1-3).
> The disability must be evaluated through diagnostic study which is adequate to provide the basis for establishing that a physical or mental disability is present. In all cases of mental illness, a psychiatric evaluation must be obtained; in all cases of mental retardation, a psy-

chological evaluation must be obtained . . . Examinations by other specialists must be obtained as needed.

Although additional diagnostic study may or may not be applicable for establishing the existence of a disability, it will include a complete general medical examination to provide an appraisal of the current medical status of the individual . . . and other necessary examinations, clinical tests and studies. (*Manual*, 16-1-4).

These requirements dictate that a *mental condition* must be shown to exist through a diagnostic study consisting of a general medical examination and a psychiatric evaluation in all cases of mental illness, or a psychological examination in all cases of mental retardation, and other specialty examinations as dictated by the findings in the particular case. There are several key words and concepts that need further discussion: mental condition, "limiting an individual's functioning," and diagnostic study.

Since *mental condition* is documented through examination by a psychiatrist or psychologist, vocational rehabilitation agencies accept the diagnostic categories of the *Diagnostic and Statistical Manual of Mental Disorders (DSM-II)* (American Psychiatric Association, 1968) as labels for *mental conditions. DSM-II* divides mental disorders into the following nine broad categories:

I. Mental Retardation

II. Organic Brain Syndromes (Psychotic and Non-Psychotic)

III. Psychoses (Not attributed to Physical Conditions Listed Previously)

IV. Neuroses

V. Personality Disorders (and Sexual Deviations, Alcoholism and Drug Dependence)

VI. Psychophysiologic Disorders

VII. Special Symptoms

VIII. Transient Situational Disturbances

IX. Behavior Disorders of Childhood and Adolescence

These categories encompass a very diverse group of problems. Some categories have as many as ten defined sub-groups of mental disorders. They cover mental disorders of intellectual functioning, brain functioning, emotional functioning and behavioral functioning. Some disorders are clearly caused by organic factors; some disorders are primarily psychological in origin. Some disorders seem to stem from an interaction of organic and psychological factors;

and there are other disorders for which the etiology is not clearly understood. *DSM-II* provides a scheme of diagnostic labels and descriptive definitions for those labels. Psychiatrists and clinical psychologists use these labels to designate various constellations of symptoms and signs. Once a constellation, or syndrome, is determined to exist in a particular person, there are often certain implications for treatment and prognosis. However, although this approach to classification may have its uses in psychiatry and clinical psychology, diagnostic labels have distinct limitations if we are trying to understand a particular person.

Sol Richman (1964, pp. 194-195), in writing about the vocational rehabilitation of the mentally ill, makes two observations which seem relevant here:

1. Mental illness does not stem from a single cause. It may derive from a combination and interaction of physical, psychological and sociological factors.
2. The outward manifestations of mental illness may be considered unique for each person in that they represent his reactions and subsequent adaptation to environmental demands. These reactions, however deviant, may be considered degrees of positive movement to adjust through interpersonal communication or by maintaining distance from others.

Thus, not only may mental disability be categorized into nearly 100 labeled groupings, but one person whose symptoms are correctly labeled may differ greatly in some aspects of his behavior from someone else who correctly bears the same label. Dr. William Eichman observes that (Eichman, 1961):

Patients are not alike any more than other people. My recent research shows that even within one diagnostic group—that of schizophrenia—patients differ more from each other than normal people. This fact was demonstrated most markedly by a measure of aggressive behavior. The acutely ill schizophrenic tends to be more aggressive than the normal person; the chronic or recovered schizophrenic, much less aggressive than normal people.

Thus, *mental condition* is a very vague term. Even when one speaks of a particular subgroup like *schizophrenics*, one is dealing with a diverse group of people. This diversity within diagnostic groupings creates difficulty in conveying information about a person by using diagnostic labels to describe him. As we shall see momentarily, the rehabilitation counselor requires much more information than the correct diagnostic label, although this may serve to document the presence of a *mental condition.*

For purposes of eligibility determination, it is important to recognize that a *mental condition* is a *mental disability* only if it "materially limits, contributes to limiting or, if not corrected, will probably result in limiting an individual's activities or functioning." This means that the rehabilitation counselor must document in what ways the mental condition limits or may limit a potential client's functioning. When one is dealing with a physical disability, this raises few difficulties; however, with a mental disability, this can be a very complicated problem. This is also a very important issue because the decision on whether a disability constitutes a substantial handicap to employment—which will be discussed in the next section—is a function of the relationship between these functional limitations and job related behavior requirements.

Leonard Oseas wrote a very interesting article in 1963 called: *Work Requirements and Ego Defects: Work Dilemmas for the Recovering Psychotic.* He relates work requirements to the ego defects of the psychotic. He says:

> In the broadest sense, the prerequisite psychological condition for the sustained successful performance of work is the capacity for integrative response to work's simultaneous physical, social and intra-individual demands. It is the impairment of precisely these integrative capacities which represent at once the main symptom or vestige of psychosis and the central handicap of the psychotic. Thus, in contrast to the physically disabled worker, whose handicap, as such, impedes only the mechanical performance of work, the psychotic's disadvantages are of a much more general and pervasive order. (Oseas, 1963, pp. 105-106.)

The "integrative capacities" Oseas refers to in this passage are *ego functions.* The term *ego* may be used to describe one of the parts or divisions of the personality. The other two parts are called the *id* and the *superego,* respectively. Each of these parts performs specific functions. Kolb (1968) says that:

> The *id* is a collective name for the primitive biological impulses. It represents the innate portion of the personality. . .

The *ego*, or reality-testing self, is that part or function of the personality which establishes a relationship with the world in which we live. The ego, of course, is a group of functions for which a metaphor is employed for ease of conceptualization. The ego deals with the environment through conscious perception, thought, feeling and action and is, therefore, the consciously controlling portion of the personality. It contains the evaluating, judging, compromising, solution-forming, and defense-creating aspects of the personality. The ego organization—concerned as it is with such important functions as perceptions, memory, evaluating and testing reality, synthesizing experience, and acting as intermediary between the inner and outer worlds—may be regarded as the integrative and executive agency. Its functions are to deal rationally with the requirements of reality, to adapt behavior to the environment, and to maintain harmony between the urges of the id and the demands and aspirations of the superego.

．　．　．　．　．　．　．　．　．　．　．　．　．　．　．　．

The third hypothetical segment of the personality structure is the *superego*, that segment conceptualized as an observer and evaluator of ego functioning, comparing it with an ideal standard—an ideal derived from standards of behavior perceived over time in parents, teachers, and others significant to the growing child.

．　．　．　．　．　．　．　．　．　．　．　．　．　．　．　．

In the well-adjusted person, behavior simultaneously and successfully meets the demands of the id, the ego and the superego. On the other hand, the behavior of the neurotic, the psychotic and the pathological personality with serious and repetitive social maladjustment may be considered to result from a disturbance in the dynamic checks and balances of the id, the ego and the superego.

Thus, to describe the way a *mental condition* is limiting to a potential client's functioning is to describe the deficiencies, defects and disturbances in his *ego functions* which arise from his mental condition. It is these disturbed ego functions which are his unique reactions and subsequent adaptation to stress, and it is with these that a rehabilitation counselor must contend in eligibility determination and in the subsequent rehabilitation process.

Table X-II is a table of normal ego functions and their disturbances found in the schizophrenias.

The limitations of any mental disorder can be described in terms of disturbances in one or more of these ego functions. This particular table (Table X-II) shows those ego functions that may be disturbed in one group of psychoses, the schizophrenias, but other psy-

TABLE X-ll

NORMAL AND DISTURBED EGO FUNCTIONS
[ADAPTED FROM BELLAK (1969), PP. 40-52]

1. REALITY TESTING

Function	*Disturbance*
For *Reality Testing* the major component factors are:	Perceptual distortions; projections; delusions; hallucinations; disorientation in time, place and person; déja vu; déja reconnu; perceptual vigilance; low awareness of inner psychological reactions.

A. *the distinction between inner and outer stimuli*
   1. accuracy of perception (includes orientation to time and place, and accuracy of perception and interpretation of external events)
   2. accuracy of inner reality testing (i.e., psychological mindedness and awareness of inner states)

B. *Judgment*

a. awareness of likely consequences of intended behavior (e.g. anticipating probable dangers, legal culpabilities and social censure, disapproval or inappropriateness)	Oblivious to severe dangers to life and limb, unrealistic appraisal of consequences of actions, fails to learn from previous experiences

   b. extent to which manifest behavior reflects the awareness of these likely consequences

2. SENSE OF REALITY

Function	*Disturbance*
For *Sense of Reality of the World and of the Self*, the component factors are:	Alienation, hypnagogic and hypnapompic stage fright, emotional isolation as a result of obsessive defenses, déja vu
a. the extent to which external events are experiences as real and as being embedded in a familiar context	Depersonalization, derealization, dream-like states, trances, fugues, major dissociations, world destruction fantasies, identity diffusion

b. the extent to which the body (or parts of it) and its functioning and one's behavior are experienced as familiar and unobtrusive and as belonging to (or emanating from) the individual

c. the degree to which the person has developed individuality, uniqueness, and a sense of self and self-esteem

d. the degree to which the person's self representations are separated from his object representations

3. DRIVE REGULATION AND CONTROL

Function	*Disturbance*
Drive Regulation and Control a. the directness of impulse expression (ranging from primitive acting out through neurotic acting out to relatively indirect forms of behavioral expression) b. the effectiveness of delay and control, the degree of frustration tolerance, and the extent to which drive derivatives are channeled through ideation, affective expression, and manifest behavior.	Temper outbursts, habit and conduct disorders, lack of frustration tolerance, acting out. Tendencies toward murder or suicide, impulsivity. Drive-dominated behavior, chronic irritability and rage, low frustration tolerance, catatonic excitement and rigidity, manic excitement, depressive psychomotor slow-up, accident proneness, parapraxes, lack of sphincter control, nailbiting, tics, excessive control of impulse.

4. OBJECT RELATIONS

Function	*Disturbance*
For *Object Relations,* the components are: a. the degree and kind of relatedness to others (taking account of withdrawal trends, narcissistic self-concern, narcissistic object choice or mutuality) b. the extent to which present relationships are adaptively or unadaptively influenced by or patterned upon older ones and serve present mature aims rather than past immature ones c. the degree to which he perceives others as separate entities rather than as extensions of himself d. the extent to which he can maintain "object constancy" (i.e., sustain relationships over long periods of time and tolerate both the physical absence of the object, and frustration, anxiety and hostility related to the object)	Withdrawal, detachment, narcissistic overinvestment of self, cannibalistic symbiotic-dependent attachments.

5. THOUGHT PROCESSES

Function	*Disturbance*
For *Thought Processes,* the components are: a. the adequacy of processes which adaptively guide and sustain thought (attention, concentration, anticipation, concept formation, memory, language) b. the relative primary-secondary process influences on thought (extent to which thinking is unrealistic, illogical, and/or loose)	Magical thinking; autistic logic; condensations; attention lapses; inability to concentrate; memory disturbances; concreteness; primary process manifestations and primitive thought processes as described by Freud, Piaget and others.

6. ADAPTIVE REGRESSION IN THE SERVICE OF THE EGO (ARISE)

Function	*Disturbance*
a. first phase of an oscillating process: relaxation of perceptual and conceptual acuity (and other ego controls) with a concomitant increase in awareness of previous preconscious and unconscious contents	Extreme rigidity in character structure and thinking where fantasy and play are difficult or impossible; unevenness in shifting from passivity to activity; regression of any ego function produces anxiety and disruption of functioning, lack of creativity, stereo-typed thinking, intolerance of ambiguity, prejudice and sterility. If first phase predominates, overideational thinking, pseudo-intellectuality, pseudo-artistic tendencies, eccentricity.
b. second phase of the oscillating process: the induction of new configurations which increase adaptive potentials as a result of creative integrations.	

ARISE refers to the ability of the ego to initiate a partial, temporary and controlled lowering of its own functions (keep in mind here the component factors of the other ten ego functions) in furtherance of its interests (i.e., promoting adaptation). Such regressions result from a relatively free but controlled play of the primary process and are called regressions in the service of the ego.

7. DEFENSIVE FUNCTIONS

Function	*Disturbance*
a. degree to which defensive components adaptively or maladaptively affect ideation and behavior	Parallel to loss of synthetic function, e.g.. repression fails and leads to primary process emergence and patient fails to "hold together"—secondary inability to concentrate, memory impaired, efficiency impaired. Probably because too much energy used at barrier function and not enough left for adaptation, e.g. with failure of defense have overstimulation by stimuli and mood liability. Failure of repression may lead to déja vu, parapraxes, lack of control of drives. An over-control of affect, ideation, and use of motor functions may be a last attempt to prevent breakthrough of drives.
b. extent to which these defenses have succeeded or failed (degree of emergence of anxiety, depression, and other dysphoric affects)	

Different defenses are important at different stages of development. The earlier the origin of a defense, the more pathological, e.g. projection and denial which affect relationship to reality.

Assessment needs to be not only of type of defense but also of liability or stability, (e.g., obsessive isolation or phobic withdrawal may lead to depersonalization and projection).

choses, (Engel, 1962) neuroses,[11] and personality disorders[12] also can be described in terms of disturbed ego functions. Even the limitations in functioning associated with mental retardation may be

11.Engel, 1962, pp. 346-350.
12.Engel, 1962, 350-355.

8. STIMULUS BARRIER

Function

The component factors for *Stimulus Barrier* are:

a. upper and lower threshold for, sensitivity to, or awareness of stimuli impinging upon various sensory modalities (externally, primarily, but including pain)

b. nature of response to various levels of sensory stimulation in terms of the extent of disorganization, avoidance, withdrawal, or active coping mechanisms employed to deal with them

Both thresholds and response to stimuli contribute to adaptation by the organism's potential for responding to high, average or low sensory input so that optimal homeostasis (as well as adaptation) is maintained: in the average expectable environment; as well as under conditions of unusual stress. Stimulus barrier determines, in part, how resilient a person is, or how he readapts after the stress and impingements are no longer present. Thesholds, as described for component (a) refer not only to reaction to external stimuli, but also to internal stimuli which provide proprioceptive cues, or those originating within the body but eventually impinging on sensory organs. Light, sound, temperature, pain, pressure, drugs and intoxicants are the stimuli to be considered relevant to assessing thresholds.

Responses, other than threshold variables, referred to in component (b) include motor responses, coping mechanisms, effects on sleep, and certain aspects of psychosomatic illness.

Together, the two components represent a way of scaling the degree to which the ego effectively and adaptively organizes and integrates sensory experience.

Disturbance

Easily upset by bright light, loud sounds, temperature extremes. Pain, resulting in withdrawal, physical symptoms, or irritability. Or, threshold overly high, where person is oblivious to nuances under-responsive to environmental stimuli, impoverishment of aesthetic sensibilities.

described in terms of deficiencies in thought processes, autonomous functions, and other ego functions (cf. Table X-II). This table, then, can serve as a scheme for the psychiatrist, the psychologist, and the rehabilitation counselor to assess and understand the functional limitations associated with mental conditions.

In this section, so far, we have discussed some of the issues and problems in labeling *mental conditions,* and we have proposed a

9. AUTONOMOUS FUNCTIONING

Function

For *Autonomous Functioning* the components are:
  a. degree of freedom from (or lack of freedom from) impairment of "apparatuses" of primary autonomy (e.g. functional disturbances of sight, hearing, intention, language, memory, learning, or motor function, intelligence)
  b. degree of, or freedom from, impairment of secondary autonomy (e.g. disturbances in habit patterns, learned complex skills, work routines, hobbies, and interests)

Disturbance

Functional blindness or deafness; catatonic postures; inability to feed, dress or care for oneself; disturbances of will skills; habits and automatized behavior are readily interfered with by drive-related stimuli; greater effort must be expended to carry out routine tasks.

10. SYNTHETIC FUNCTIONS

Function

For *Synthetic-Integrative Functioning*, we have the following components:
  a. the degree of reconciliation or integration of *discrepant* or potentially incongruent (contradictory) attitudes, values, affects, behavior, and self-representations (e.g. role conflicts)
  b. the degree of *active* relating together (i.e. integrating) of psychic and behavioral events, whether contradictory or not

Disturbance

Disorganized behavior; incongruity between thoughts, feelings and actions; absence of consistent life goal; poor planning, little effort to relate different areas of experience together.

Fluctuating emotional states without appropriate awareness of the change, as in hysterics. Minor and major forms of dissociation, from parapraxes to amnesia, fugues and multiple personalities.

Many other ego functions are called into play, sometimes very pathologically as in psychotic defences because of the basic feature of the integrative function.

scheme for describing the functional limitations associated with a *mental disability*. We shall now turn to a discussion of the requirements and issues relative to the "diagnostic study" in documenting mental disability.

As previously stated, a mental disability must be shown to exist through a diagnostic study consisting of a general medical examination and a psychiatric examination in all cases of mental illness, or a psychological examination in all cases of mental retardation, and other specialty examinations as dictated by the findings in the particular case. The documentation of the *mental disability*, however, is only *one* purpose of the diagnostic study.

The major purposes of the medical diagnostic study and evaluation in vocational rehabilitation are:

1. to establish, through competent medical judgement including psychiatric or psychological evaluation as appropriate, that a physical or mental impairment is present which materially limits the activities which the individual can perform, as one aspect of determining the individual's eligibility for services as a disabled person;
2. to appraise the current general health status of the individual, including the discovery of other impairments not previously recognized, with a view to determining his limitations and capacities;
3. to determine to what extent and by what means the disabling condition can be removed, corrected, or minimized by physical restoration services; and
4. to provide a realistic basis for selection of an employment objective commensurate with the disabled individual's capacities and limitations (McGowan and Porter, 1967).

We wish, then, to document and understand the mental condition and its limiting effects; to assess current general health status and other possible impairments and their limiting effects; to determine to what extent and by what means the mental condition or its limiting effects can be removed, corrected or minimized by treatment or other services; and we wish to have a realistic basis for selecting an employment objective. The examining physician(s) should be made aware of these purposes so that the counselor will receive the information he needs.

The importance of the general medical examination in cases of mental disability cannot be over-emphasized. Mentally disabled people often have multiple disabilities. Mental illness, as we have seen, also may have physical and organic causes at times. A medical assessment of all body systems is imperative.

A good psychiatric report will provide information in the following areas:

    I.   The Clinical History
    II. Mental Status
    III. The Physical, Neurological, X-Ray, Laboratory and Special Examinations
    IV. The Working Formulation of the Case
    V. The Diagnostic Impression

VI. The Outline of Treatment

VII. Prognosis

This much is usually suitable for the psychiatrist's own purposes, but a rehabilitation counselor would require, in addition, sections called:

VIII. Ego Functions and Deficiencies

IX. Implications for Work Behavior

If a psychiatrist can provide this kind of information the counselor is in a very good position to make tentative decisions about eligibility, services planning, and vocational difficulties.

A psychological examination is required by the regulations in cases of mental retardation, but a psychologist also can be very helpful in other mental disabilities. Many of the ego functions and disturbances can be evaluated best by the tools of psychology, e.g. intelligence, memory, accuracy of perception, concentration, abstracting ability. A psychologist can assess the limitations caused by brain damage and discern the presence of a learning disability. A psychologist can also provide information about aptitudes, educational achievement, and interests. Most importantly, a good psychologist can help the counselor, through his report and consultation, to translate data on ego deficiencies into statements about possible deficiencies in work behavior.[13] For these reasons, this writer feels that a psychologist should be consulted in all cases of mental disability.[14]

As with any other disability, the counselor should gather, in addition to medical and psychological data, information about the client's vocational background, his educational level, his social history and social adjustment, and his cultural and environmental background. These areas of client study are discussed in detail by McGowan and Porter.[15]

If the counselor has obtained and understands the information discussed in this section, he will be able to document a *mental condition;* he will be able to document how that mental condition constitutes a *mental disability* in terms of how it limits or may limit the potential client's functioning; he will know what possibilities there are for reducing the disability through treatment and other services;

13. Oseas, 1963

14. McGowan and Porter, 1967, p. 66.

15. McGowan and Porter, 1967, pp. 51-55, 70-77, and 78-85.

he will have some notion of how the mental disability has effected, or may effect, the client's work behavior; and he will have some idea of other factors that a client may be contending with such as educational deficiency, social maladjustment, or cultural background. The counselor is now ready to determine whether the client meets the second criteria of eligibility.

Does the Mentally Disabled Person Have a Substantial Handicap to Employment?

According to the *Vocational Rehabilitation Manual* (*Manual*, 16-1-5 to 16-1-6):

> Substantial handicap to employment means that a physical or mental disability (in the light of attendant medical, psychological, vocational, educational, cultural, social or environmental factors) impedes an individual's occupational performance by preventing his obtaining, retaining or preparing for a gainful occupation consistent with his capacities and abilities. . .
>
> A disability may constitute an employment handicap in either of two ways. In one, the employment handicap may be the direct result of the disability. In the other, the employment handicap may be related to the disability in the light of attendant medical, psychological, vocational, educational, cultural, social or other environmental factors. Examples of attendant factors are a lack of marketable skills; low educational level; community and employer prejudices and attitudes concerning disability; long-term unemployment; unstable work record; belonging to a disadvantaged group; residence in ghetto areas or pockets of poverty; long history of dependency; and poor attitudes toward work, family and community.
>
> A substantial employment handicap may also exist when a disabled person is employed but cannot obtain a gainful occupation consistent with his capacities and abilities. This provides the basis for state agencies to emphasize vocational rehabilitation services aimed at the problems of underemployment and the marginal and insecure employment of disabled people.

On the basis of all the data he has gathered in his client study, the counselor must judge whether the disability directly, or in the light of attendant factors, ". . . impedes . . . [the client's] occupational performance, by preventing his obtaining, retaining, or preparing for a gainful occupation consistent with his capacities and abilities. . . ." Mentally disabled clients will often qualify under more than one of these criteria, i.e. they will have a handicap which is directly the result of their disability; they will be victims of one or more attendant factors which cause difficulty in employment; and frequently, if they are already employed, they hold marginal and insecure employment.

In making this decision it may be useful for the counselor to address himself to questions like these posed by Richman (1964, p. 198):

1. Does the client possess the social-vocational ability to return to work with no need for vocational training, support, or placement? (Client may need other therapies or support but may not be vocationally handicapped.)
2. Is emotional stability aggravated by client's present occupation, which may result in job loss due to the fact that the job:
   a. Denies status to the extent of aggravating the vocational adjustment?
   b. Limits acceptance by family or community?
   c. Creates conflicts between aspiration and functional capacity?
3. Is client in need of a new occupation because he lacks one that would provide stable employment?
4. Does client's extended history of institutionalization or inaction indicate that he needs a refresher course for his old skill or training in new skill?
5. Does client need a special work environment due to the problems related to disabilities other than psychiatric illness?
6. Is the occupation suitable and does the job environment need adjustment to client needs?
7. Does client need special placement service beyond that of the State Employment Service?

If the counselor is satisfied that the client does in fact have a handicap to employment as defined above, he is ready to decide whether the client meets the third criterion of eligibility. This decision can be the most difficult decision in determining eligibility, and it is the most crucial for the client.

Is There a Reasonable Expectation That Vocational Rehabilitation Services Will Help the Mentally Disabled Person Obtain Gainful Occupation?

The third criterion of eligibility defines the services goal of vocational rehabilitation: *gainful employment*, and it asks the counselor to make a prediction, i.e. that there is "A reasonable expectation that vocational rehabilitation services may render the individual fit to engage in a gainful occupation" (*Manual*, 16-1-3). There are three phrases in this criterion which need further definition: "reasonable expectation," "fit to engage," and "gainful occupation."

> *Reasonable expectation* is a determination made by the State agency based upon adequate, sound and appropriate information about each individual . . . (*Manual*, 16-1-7).
>
> *Fit to engage* refers to an expected achievement level for a given individual to undertake a gainful occupation consistent with his capacities and abilities. It should be understood that this level will vary greatly from individual to individual, and that in some instances, this level may be quite low when compared to competitive standards. For this reason, the definition of "fit to engage" must be made relative to the definition of "gainful occupation" for the client in question (*Manual*, 16-1-8).
>
> *Gainful occupation* includes employment in the competitive labor market; practice of profession; self-employment; homemaking, farm or family work (including work for which payment is in kind rather than in cash); sheltered employment; and home industries or other gainful homebound work (*Manual*, 16-1-8).

In the previous two criteria the counselor is asked to look at negative factors: the applicant's disability and how it is handicapping. In the third criterion the counselor is asked to look at the client positively: with vocational rehabilitation services, can he work?

> This requires the state agency to evaluate and ascertain potential capacity of the individual for employment, taking into consideration the effect the agency's services may have on reducing or correcting the disability or on lessening his employment handicap and providing greater opportunity for employment. Consideration should be given to the probable effectiveness of the services that can be made available, rather than to anticipated length of services, extent of need for services, or nature of severity of the disability. Also, factors such as anticipated earnings or the period of work expectancy should not control the determination of individual's likelihood of engaging in a gainful occupation (*Manual*, 16-1-7).

The counselor is asked, therefore, to judge, on the basis of a thorough client study, what the probable effects of the agency's services will be in reducing or correcting the disability or on lessening the handicap, and whether these effects will be sufficient to render the client fit to engage in a gainful occupation. Counselors are instructed not to consider as controlling factors in eligibility determination:

the anticipated length of services, the extent of need for services, the severity of the disability, anticipated earnings, or the period of work expectancy.

Some counselors seem to believe that "gainful occupation" means only competitive employment. However, the definition of "gainful occupation," quoted earlier, permits a wide range of levels of work as possible employment objectives. In this regard, it is interesting to note that Chapter 24, Section 2 of the Federal *Vocational Rehabilitation Manual,* which outlines standards for terminating cases, even permits closing as rehabilitated clients who continue to reside in institutions and who only partially earn their maintenance through work activity which "reflects an adjustment of the individual under a vocational rehabilitation plan, as compared to therapy only." (*Manual,* 24-2-9 to 24-2-10). The chief factor to consider here and in the other "gainful occupations" that are not at the competitive employment level is whether the gainful employment is consistent with the client's capacities and abilities. This means that an applicant is eligible whose maximum potential is working in the institution in which he must live because of social problems or for therapeutic reasons, if ". . . wages or maintenance are earned, or fees for institutionalization are significantly reduced." (*Manual,* 24-2-9). No applicant, then, should be judged ineligible for vocational rehabilitation services simply because he does not appear to have the potential for competitive employment, for there very well may be lower levels of employment—which are still legitimate "gainful occupations"—in which his capacities and abilities will permit him to engage.

Despite the wide range of levels of possible employment objectives that a counselor and his client may choose, the counselor is still faced with making a prediction about the possible effects of the agency's services in (1) "reducing or correcting the disability" and in (2) "lessening the employment handicap." The former is primarily a question of treatment prognosis. The latter is primarily a question of rehabilitation prognosis.

In estimating the possibilities for "reducing or correcting the disability," the counselor must rely on the plan of treatment and prognosis reported by the examining psychiatrist. This plan of treatment should outline the proposed treatment modalities and give some indication of the expected results. It should be recognized, however, that the psychiatrist is also making a prediction, and there are many variables beyond the control of the psychiatrist which can make this prediction inaccurate.

In estimating the possibilities for "lessening of the employment handicap," the counselor is faced with the difficult problem of predicting rehabilitation outcome. Outcome prediction studies involve relating various predictor variables to a predicted outcome criterion. The rehabilitation counselor would be interested in predicting vocational rehabilitation, the outcome criterion, from information obtained in the study of the client, the predictor variables. The question becomes, then, what variables reliably predict successful vocational adjustment for the mentally disabled?

Patterson, in a 1962 review of the research in this area, found that for the mentally ill success in vocational rehabilitation was not related to diagnosis, nor necessarily to the presence or absence of symptomatology, i.e. some clients can be schizophrenic, hallucinating, and delusional, and still be able to perform successfully on a job. He also found that vocational adjustment is not highly correlated with interpersonal or social adjustment. None of these variables is a measure of specific occupationally relevant behavior. Studies using *these* kinds of variables:

> . . . indicate that it is possible, by using measures and ratings of variables that are relevant to performance in the work situation, to achieve some success in predicting later occupational adjustment of psychiatric patients. The results, while encouraging, do not provide adequate methods of selection of individuals, however. Too many of those whom the predictive measures indicate should succeed do not succeed, and too many of those for whom failure is predicted actually succeed.[16]

Patterson concludes that ". . . there is no simple or easy method of evaluating or predicting occupational adjustment of psychiatric patients." Vocational adjustment is not a simple matter, and although whether someone is employed or not is easily determined, the factors affecting his employment status are many and varied. "Even if we were to be successful in evaluating all these factors, our predictions would be less than perfect. We cannot expect 100 percent prediction in any complex activity involving human beings."[17]

16. Patterson, 1969, p. 162.
17. Patterson, 1969, p. 163.

In a recent review of prediction studies done since Patterson's 1962 article, Brian Bolton found that the problem of prediction still had not been solved. He states that: "This limited predictability is not unique to rehabilitation, but rather is the rule in applied psychological research." (Bolton, 1972). Perhaps it is more realistic, then, to suggest that counselors really cannot make *reliable* predictions about the future vocational adjustment of mentally ill clients based on the usual client study data. Why should this be so? The problem is that on the basis of client study data we cannot predict on a continuing basis the motivation of the client; and client study data describes the adjustment of the client at a particular point in time, and mental disability is not a fixed disability.

Gerald E. Cubelli (1970) in writing about vocational evaluation of mentally ill clients observes that:

> The concept of fixed disabilities is a burden which can haunt evaluators of the mentally ill. Historically, rehabilitation was developed almost exclusively with clients who have fixed or permanent disabilities which could be measured (with increasing skill each year) and around which permanent plans could be formulated. When implemented successfully, plans could be counted. This approach can give the rehabilitation worker a comfortable feeling of knowing what he is doing. He can identify more readily which part of the process needs strengthening. Failure can more definitely be assigned to the lack of a community resource or to the client's motivation.
>
> In mental illness there is rarely a permanent cure which remains indefinitely constant. Very often there is improvement to higher levels of functioning. However, the tendency of mental patients to regress, recompensate and regress again is well-known. In any extended evaluation the movement back and forth, up and down, in the functional capacities of the client, can be downright disconcerting. In other words, vocational evaluation conclusions which represent one point in time could be misleading. Therefore, plans based upon evaluation results should take into consideration the transient nature of any particular status.

In other words, a prediction based on data gathered today, may be completely invalidated by the client's behavior tomorrow.

There is often the attempt to make decisions on rehabilitation potential and "reasonable expectation" on the basis of the mentally ill client's *motivation* to participate in a vocational rehabilitation program. Black (1964) suggests that:

The importance attached to motivation seems to derive from two principles: the theory that self-determination is a right of human beings in a democracy, and the maxim that one can lead a horse to water but one cannot make him drink. Experience is gradually bringing those who serve the ill and handicapped to recognize that it may be necessary to employ "aggressive" techniques in offering services, if they are to be used at all; and that for the individual in need, the "right" to decide his own future may not be matched by his ability to do so.

On the basis of our experience at Altro we have reported that ". . . an expression by the patient of positive motivation for rehabilitation for the world of work is rare. Ambivalence is the rule rather than the exception. This seems to be related to the tremendous dependency needs of most of these patients, their fear of any change in their tenuous equilibrium, the threat to the psychic economy served by the psychotic symptoms, and the fear of aggression implied in activity. Though we believe that most people have a basic drive toward health, many of our applicants seem to mask this effectively by their need to hold on to their illness."

The counselor, then, is faced with a dilemma. He is unable to make reliable predictions about a mentally disabled client's rehabilitation potential due to the client's sometimes fluctuating adjustment and ambivalent motivation; however, the requirement that there be a "reasonable expectation" of success is not a demand for certainty on the part of the counselor. Many clients can, therefore, be declared eligible without the counselor feeling any pangs of conscience because of a lack of certitude. The difficulty comes when the counselor feels he must declare an applicant *ineligible* for services because of the lack of a "reasonable expectation" of success. If the counselor, in making his decision, however, is responding to such factors as diagnosis, presence of residual symptoms, present interpersonal or social adjustment, present psychological adjustment, or present motivation toward rehabilitation, he may be doing the client an injustice.

Richman outlined the following positive and negative aspects of a client's attitudes and behavior which may be helpful guidelines in assessing where a client is in his progress toward rehabilitation. "They represent some aspects in the recovery process within the client and should be viewed in terms of cause and the possibility of improvement or modification through remedial effort, guidance and environmental manipulation."[18]

18. Richman, 1964, p. 196.

I. Some Positive Aspects[19]
  A. Acceptance and awareness of emotional problem by client as evidenced by the fact that he:
    1. Verbalizes his hospital treatment experiences in terms of his mental illness or reaction symptomatology.
    2. Does not project his hospitalization or illness as the needless or punitive action of his family, employer or co-worker.
    3. Concentrates on plans for recovery through actual participation in home or vocational activities in the community at a level that he can perform.
    4. Has, or is willing to accept, realistic appraisal of his abilities and employability as a guide to vocational planning, as expressed by:
      a. Vocational aspirations within the limits of his functional ability.
      b. Identification with normal work demands of employment.
      c. Recognition of (or ability to be counseled to accept) the concept of the give-and-take in interpersonal relationships or relationships in a situation.
      d. Employment history suggestive of potential for future stability with appropriate services if necessary.
II. Some Negative Aspects
  A. Poor interpersonal relationship.
  B. Low drive reflecting withdrawal from personal or vocational interaction.
  C. Current overt disturbed behavior (assaultive or destructive).
  D. Supersensitive reaction to noise, dirt, grease, heat and other unpleasant environmental conditions (ever-present in some degree in all situations), suggesting that such reaction is a means of avoiding vocational action.
  E. Poor attention span or concentration, reflecting withdrawal and resistance to change.
  F. Concentration on illness as an excuse when positive action in a vocationl direction is suggested or implemented.

19. Richman, 1964, p. 196.

   G. Denial of illness through:
      1. Projection of his problem on the actions of another
         person in his environment.
      2. Projection of his problem on impersonal environmental
         situations.
   H. Lack of past participation in hospital social-vocational pro-
      grams, if they were available.
   I. Despite awareness of DVR services, an inordinate delay
      in seeking such assistance while making no other socially
      acceptable adaptive effort.
   J. As a resistance to movement or change, consistent failure
      to evidence normal social practice, such as:
      1. Not keeping appointments or not notifying of inability
         to do so.
      2. Failure to follow through a planned activity.
      3. Reporting with inappropriate dress or unkempt.

The more a client exhibits these positive aspects and the less he
exhibits the negative, the more a counselor will feel comfortable in
predicting that there is "a reasonable expectation." The more a client
exhibits these negative aspects, on the other hand, the less sure a counselor will probably feel about success. In view of the uncertainties
in prediction discussed above, it is suggested that the counselor not
declare the doubtful client ineligible for vocational rehabilitation
services, but that he accept the client for a period of *extended evaluation.*

   In *extended evaluation* it is:
   . . . possible for State agencies to provide vocational rehabilitation
   services to handicapped individuals before a determination has been
   made that there is a reasonable expectation that vocational rehabilitation services can fit him for employment. The major purpose of
   providing such services is to evaluate their effect on the individual,
   thus facilitating making a determination that there is or is not a reasonable expectation that vocational rehabilitation services will render
   the individual fit to engage in a gainful occupation (the third condition of eligibility) (*Manual,* 16-1-8 to 16-1-9).

A period of extended evaluation will afford the doubtful client
an opportunity to deal with his anxiety about growing toward independent living and work. If after a reasonable period of time—and

this might be a year or more with some chronic institutionalized psychotic clients—the client is not responding to vocational rehabilitation services by some positive improvement in functioning in vocational behavior, the counselor may have no choice but to close the case as ineligible. Before this decision is made, however, the counselor is obligated to consider whether every possible approach has been tried and whether every possible chance has been given the client to take advantage of the opportunity to rehabilitate himself through vocational rehabilitation services.

A CONCLUDING WORD

The vocational rehabilitation of the mentally disabled can be one of the most gratifying and exciting tasks in the field of rehabilitation if the rehabilitation counselor only realizes that its many uncertainties offer an outstanding opportunity for the creative application of his skills for helping people. The eligibility determination process is not primarily for the purpose of screening ineligible people out, but rather for screening eligible clients in! If carried out in a thorough and skillful manner, the process can help the rehabilitation counselor to better understand the client, his problems, and most importantly, his *possibilities*.

REFERENCES

American Psychiatric Association: *Diagnostic and Statistical Manual of Mental Disorders*, 2nd ed., (DSM-II). Washington, D.C., The American Psychiatric Association, 1968.

Bellak, Leopold: Research on ego function patterns: A progress report. In Bellak, Leopold, and Loeb, Laurence (Eds.): *The Schizophrenic Syndrome*. New York, Grune, 1969, pp. 40-52.

Black, Bertram: Psychiatric rehabilitation in the community. In Bellak, Leopold (Ed.): *Handbook of Community Psychiatry and Community Mental Health*. New York, Grune, 1964, p. 251.

Black, Bertram J., and Benney, Celia: Rehabilitation. In Bellak, Leopold, and Loeb, Laurence (Eds.): *The Schizophrenic Syndrome*. New York, Grune, 1969, pp. 735-756.

Bockoven, J. Sanbourne: Moral treatment in American psychiatry. *Journal of Nervous and Mental Disease, 124*:167-194, 292-321, 1956.

Bolton, Brian: The prediction of rehabilitation outcomes: Review of studies. Arkansas Rehabilitation Research and Training Center, no date.

Bolton, Brian: The prediction of rehabilitation outcomes. *Journal of Applied Rehabilitation Counseling, 3*:17, 1972.

Chalmers, Rives: Panel: Essential differences in vocational rehabilitation of the physically disabled and emotionally disabled. *Rehabilitation Record*, March-April, 1961, p. 16.

Cubelli, Gerald E.: Vocational evaluation with mentally ill clients. In Pruitt, Walter A. (Ed.): *Readings in Work Evaluation—I*. Menomonie, Wisconsin, Institute for Vocational Rehabilitation, Stout State University, 1970, p. 26.

Cubelli, Gerald E., and Havens, Leston L.: The expanding role of psychiatric rehabilitation. In Bellak, Leopold, and Barten, Harvey H. (Eds.): *Progress in Community Mental Health*. New York, Grune, 1969, vol. I, p. 172.

Department of Health, Education and Welfare: Basic and related requirements for determining eligibility for vocational rehabilitation services and for acceptability for extended evaluation to determine rehabilitation potential. In *Vocational Rehabilitation Manual*, revised Chapter 16, Section 1. Washington, D.C., Vocational Rehabilitation Administration, August, 1967.

Department of Health, Education and Welfare: Standards for terminating cases. In *Vocational Rehabilitation Manual*, Chapter 24, Section 1. Washington, D.C., Social and Rehabilitation Service, Rehabilitation Services Administration, June, 1971, pp. 24-2-9 to 24-2-10.

Eichman, William J.: Counseling the emotionally disturbed. *Journal of Rehabilitation*, Sept.-Oct., 1961, p. 26.

Engel, George L.: *Psychological Development in Health and Disease*. Philadelphia, Saunders, 1962.

Glasscote, Raymond M., *et al.*: *Rehabilitating the Mentally Ill in the Community*. Washington, D.C., Joint Publication Service of the American Psychiatric Association and the National Association for Mental Health, 1971, p. 15.

Joint Commission on Mental Illness and Health: *Action for Mental Health*. New York, Basic, 1961.

Kolb, Lawrence C.: *Noyes' Modern Clinical Psychiatry*, 7th ed. Philadelphia, Saunders, 1968, pp. 35-37.

Lewis, Nolan D. C.: American psychiatry from its beginning to World War II. In Arieti, Silvano (Ed.): *American Handbook of Psychiatry*. New York, Basic, vol. I, pp. 14-15.

McGowan, John F., and Porter, Thomas L.: *An Introduction to the Vocational Rehabilitation Process*, revised ed. Washington, D.C., Department of Health, Education and Welfare, Vocational Rehabilitation Administration, July, 1967.

Oseas, Leonard: Work requirements and ego defects: Work dilemmas for the recovering psychotic. *Psychiatric Quarterly*, 37:105-122, 1963.

Osman, Marvin P.: Work: Its potential for therapy of emotional illness. *Newsletter of V. A. Day Treatment Centers*, 2:25-33, Oct., 1965.

Patterson, C. H.: Evaluation of the rehabilitation potential of the mentally ill patient. *Rehabilitation Literature*, 23:162-172, 1962. Also reprinted in

Patterson, C. H.: *Rehabilitation Counseling: Collected Papers.* Champaign, Stipes, 1969, pp. 151-171.
Richman, Sol: The vocational rehabilitation of the emotionally handicapped in the community. *Rehabilitation Literature, 25*:194-202, July, 1964.

CHAPTER XI

SPECIAL PROBLEMS IN WORK ADJUSTMENT OF THE MENTALLY ILL

ROBERT L. GUNN

- OVERVIEW
- THE CLIENT
- STRENGTHS AND WEAKNESSES
- PREPARATION FOR EMPLOYMENT
- THE WORK SCENE
- SOME FINAL CONSIDERATIONS
- REFERENCES

OVERVIEW

THIS REVIEW of the special problems faced by practitioners involved with work adjustment of the mentally ill is approached from a somewhat arbitrary point of view. It will not be a review of the literature in the field of vocational rehabilitation of the mentally ill. Consequently, the succeeding pages will be relatively barren of references to the good efforts of others. It will be as realistic and as down to earth as practical day-to-day experiences can make it. In short, this chapter will represent the ruminations of one practitioner over his experiences and observations gained in the attempt to rehabilitate the mentally ill person to the world of work. These have been gained, for the most part, during the period of 1960 to the present. Although the language is directed toward males for ease of writing, the comments apply equally well to the female client.

It is perhaps a tiresome cliché to point out that any field as broad as work adjustment of the mentally ill could scarcely be handled adequately without filling pages and pages and books and books. Thus an attempt to sketch an accurate, informative and realistic picture of the problem in this area within the confines of a single chapter certainly appears to be an ambitious undertaking. It is clear at the outset that some kind of arbitrary decision must be made as to what to include and what to omit. A desirable outcome would be that a minimum of confusion would result from the selection process that will be at work throughout this chapter and that little will be omitted that is critical to an understanding of the special problems of helping the mentally ill person return to society as a working member, functioning at a level commensurate with his physical and mental make-up.

This chapter will be approached in the following manner: (1) a sketch will be drawn of the client—the mentally ill person; (2) techniques for evaluating the strengths and weaknesses of the client will be reviewed; (3) consideration of special measures that are necessary elements in helping the mentally ill client reach a state where work adjustment is a feasible goal (on the whole, these measures will be drawn from personal experiences within a fairly homogeneous setting); (4) description of the work scene since the end result of all the efforts that will be expended is the eventual placement of the client in some kind of work situation in the community; and (5) some final considerations.

Description of the Mentally Ill

Perhaps the most comprehensive study of vocational rehabilitation of the mentally ill patient was accomplished by the Psychiatric Evaluation Project (PEP) of the Veterans Administration (VA). During the early 1960s, this research unit conducted a follow-up study of discharged mentally ill patients over a period of four years. There were twelve VA hospitals from different areas of the country involved in this study. One of the primary objectives of the PEP evaluation of community adjustment was the ex-patient's work record. At each of the time points used for follow-up, over one-half of the sample of patients were in the not-working category. The bulk of the subjects either were not working (less than five hours a week) or working full time (thirty-five hours a week or more). The number of subjects working part time (from five to thirty-five hours weekly) never exceeded 15 percent. On the average, occupational adjustment of the sample was rated as marginal; and fewer than a fourth of the sample were considered to be making a good occupational adjustment. Out of 1142 subjects who had spent a minimum of thirty-one consecutive days out of an institution and were thus considered as available for employment, 35 percent did not work at all during the four year follow-up period. On the basis of the results obtained, it was concluded that, relative to community norms for the average adult male, the picture of vocational adjustment of the mentally ill patient was not very bright.

A later PEP study of vocational restoration, using a slightly different sample of hospitals and a sample of 3609 schizophrenic patients under sixty years of age, brought out a similar vocational pattern. These patients were surveyed via a mail questionnaire as to the extent to which they had worked in the six months after release from the hospital. Results based upon a 90 percent rate of return of questionnaires indicated that exactly two-thirds reported themselves as not working as much as one month. Only 14 percent reported themselves as working as much as five or six months.

The factor which was judged by PEP staff to be most significant in understanding why patients did not work and/or look for work was, pure and simple, their shaky emotional integration (Psychiatric Evaluation Project, 1965).

THE CLIENT

Let us assume for a moment that there is a discussion in progress concerned with the difficulties of preparing the mentally ill person for the world of work. As the discussion continues there seems to be an implied community of agreement or understanding on the specified kind of person being discussed. However, if we pause to define the mentally ill person, the agreement indicated above becomes somewhat strained. Defining the mentally ill person does not fare any better than defining its opposite, the mentally healthy person. In each case the definition tends toward some kind of arbitrary definition, e.g. "someone who has been confined to a mental hospital," or it becomes weighted down with qualifications and exceptions to the point where no clear-cut image can be obtained of the individual described.

For the purposes of this report, the mentally ill client will be viewed as a person from a wide band of our society who presents one or more extreme examples of "psychologically based behavior." His behavior will be viewed by others as strange, frightening, or at the very least, disquieting. He may have been hospitalized for mental illness in the past, but not necessarily so. The client may exhibit persistent difficulties in such ares of his life as the following.

Interpersonal Relationship

There will very likely be a history of ineffective or inadequate behavior in interpersonal situations. Difficulties arise not only with family, friends and relatives but with supervisors and peers on the job. For example, ideas of reference, delusions of persecution, or inappropriate affect may operate to create a discordant atmosphere between the client and others around him.

Self-Image

The client may have such a low opinion of himself that it interferes with his performance as a man, husband, father, son or employee. He will tend to view himself as having problems with identity, dependency needs, self-confidence, decision making, assertion, etc. Most frequently the mentally ill client occupies a dependent role in family or work situations. It is almost as if the dependent child role has never been resolved. Such a client apparently does not become too uncomfortable letting someone else make decisions for him and order his life. From another point of view, many mentally ill clients have a problem determining or maintaining an optimum life style. Even though their life styles create more problems than they are capable of resolving, they seemingly are unable to make the necessary changes on their own.

Past Work Record

The past work history of the mentally ill client will tend to be very poor or, at best, erratic. He will likely have held many jobs, usually for short stretches of time, or manifests periods of good work performance with a gradual deterioration to the point where he either quits or is fired. There may be records of inability to get along with supervisors or co-workers. Normal pressures of the job are likely to be reacted to in an extreme or disorganized manner, all out of proportion to what might be expected in such a situation. Many mentally ill clients will be seen as having been employed at a level well below what might be expected on the basis of educational background, training, or experience.

The mentally ill person's attitude toward work may exhibit some aspects that are quite different from the attitudes of the "normal" person.

Struening and Efron (1965) conducted a study of the attitudes of former mental patients about work. They conceptualized that work was viewed by the patients as including (1) motivation and the value of work, (2) the opinion climate of the social context, and (3) evaluation of self and relationships with others. They imagined that there were many motives that might inhibit or interfere with the pattern of behavior generally necessary for getting a job. For example, seeking employment may be perceived as reducing guilt, increasing self-respect, or enhancing the ego. It may be positively valued as a way of life, an end in itself, or as a duty. On the other hand, even the thought of attempting to get a job may arouse anxiety, feelings of incompetence, and a deep sense of failure and frustration. Work, especially that available to the mental patient may be seen as a boring, menial and energy-consuming activity with few rewards. The opinions of others in society about mental illness may result in a cynical, resentful, pessimistic point of view or an anticipation of acceptance, friendship and respect. On the job he may expect biased evaluations, menial jobs, and outright rejection; or he may look forward to understanding bosses, interesting work, and just rewards for good labor.

Another study designed to aid in identifying those restored mentally ill patients who would have difficulty in making a satisfactory vocational adjustment came up with a measure of unemployability. The records of patient-clients at the Logan Mental Health Center, Denver, Colorado, who had been successfully or unsuccessfully placed and employed were reviewed. An analysis of the results obtained from a schedule of items relating to various aspects of the work situation classified the items into three categories: (1) motivational, (2) vocational and (3) personal. Inspection of the content of items indicated that they are not necessarily behaviors that are characteristic of mental illness. Many unemployable people are characterized by qualities such as "no work experience" or "lack of education." Therefore the items appear to be applicable to the whole range of unemployable people including the mentally disturbed clients (Searls, Wilson and Miskimins, 1971).

Although there are certain aspects of work adjustment that might be present in either a mentally ill population or a non-mentally ill population, the evidence on the whole indicates that the mentally ill person adds an additional complication on top of the usual complexities that arise when dealing with employment problems.

STRENGTHS AND WEAKNESSES

Determining the strengths and weaknesses of the mentally ill client from the standpoint of work adjustment does not proceed in any direct manner. Various techniques must be put to use in order to arrive at some kind of an impression of the client's capabilities. The counselor may utilize psychological or vocational testing, evaluate the client's behavior in interpersonal relationships, and review past history.

Psychological-Vocational Testing

Psychological testing as used here refers to the process of obtaining indices of the client's personality dynamics. Vocational testing refers to obtaining indices of aptitudes and abilities that could be related to work adjustment. It is clear that there is no sharp line of demarcation separating the two, since personality dynamics might very well affect performance on vocational testing. Among the more frequently utilized measures of personality are the Minnesota Multiphasic Personality Inventory, Thematic Apperception Test, Bender Visual Motor *Gestalt* Test, Edwards Personal Preference Schedule, and the Rorschach.

The General Aptitude Test Battery (GATB), published by the United States Department of Labor, is a very comprehensive attempt to measure aptitudes and abilities as they relate to acceptable performance on the job. This test battery provides measures of intelligence; verbal, numerical and spatial aptitude; form and clerical perception; eye-hand coordination; and finger and manual dexterity. Normative data are provided for practically all occupational groups within the economy. Complete information about the GATB including the utilization of its testing service can be obtained from the state employment service.

There are, of course, numerous other measures of aptitudes and abilities. For those who wish to obtain information about the complete range of psychological and vocational tests, the *Mental Measurements Yearbook*, (Buros, 1972) periodically reviews most tests currently in use.

The results of psychological and vocational tests may need to be evaluated differently with a mentally ill population in contrast to the "normal" population. Some underlying assumptions in most test administration is that the testee will be motivated to do the best he can on the test, not deliberately lie and not be prompted to go too far out of his way to confound the results of testing. Very frequently these assumptions may be subjected to considerable doubt where the mentally ill person is concerned. He may not be highly motivated to do well. In many instances his illness mitigates against optimum performance even when he is personally committed to do his best. Testing, if necessary, may be desirable; however the counselor must be wary of making predictions based simply on the test results. Cross comparisons with non-test measures such as observations of behavior and even a review of past accomplishments can provide an estimate of the level of abilities and aptitudes possessed by the client that could be related to attaining a certain level of functioning. Psychological measures of personality, interest, aptitudes and abilities provide some beginning impressions about the kind of person the counselor will be attempting to rehabilitate to the world of work.

Interpersonal Factors

The ability to get along with others on the job, whether supervisors or fellow workers, will many times be a determining factor as to whether the client succeeds or fails on the job. Evaluations of this aspect of the client's functioning is a continuing process beginning with the initial contact and ending when it is felt that he is capable of making it on his own. At each step along the way the counselor will be forming and reforming opinions about the client's resolution of problems in this area. A review of past history, discussions with significant others, and observation of present behavior in a number of situations are all utilized to assess the client's effectiveness in interpersonal relationships.

Past History

It should not be considered unusual to review past accomplishments and attainments as a basis for determining strengths and weaknesses for a potential job placement. This does not mean that the client at the stage in life where the counselor enters the picture will be able to, or even become motivated to, reenter the same or similar job he was in previously. The use of past history is an attempt to estimate the range of job activities the client could reasonably be expected to perform. Within the limits posted by past accomplishments, the realities of the present, plus the projections of the future will be the job goal the counselor and client will work toward. It is safe to say that a simple, uncomplicated predictor of future accomplishment is what happened in the past.

PREPARATION FOR EMPLOYMENT

Preparation for employment will include all of those activities that the counselor deems essential to modifying the behavior of the mentally ill client so that he is acceptable to an employer. Concurrently, the client must be brought to the point where he is capable of withstanding the stresses of being an employee to the extent that he can apply his abilities and aptitudes to the task at hand.

The author's personal experience and observation is with a population consisting of veterans of military service. Although they present certain unique features, it is felt that the experiences, observations, problems, approaches, etc., should not be significantly different for any population of mentally ill persons.

One element of difference in the mentally ill veteran population should be brought out. Many veterans who are counseled receive service-connected benefits or compensations which may range from hospitalization for their disabilities to 10 percent to 100 percent disabled pensions and compensations. (As a general rule, a 100% service-connected disability pays the veteran $450 (tax free) per month with additional increments for being married, supporting children, or having additional disabilities.) There are numerous occasions where the client concludes that there is little likelihood of obtaining a job within reasonable range of his capabilities that would pay him as much as he gets from the Veterans Administration simply by remaining a patient. Thus, many veterans become "professional patients." This aspect adds another factor to the rehabilitation process. Far too often the counselor feels that he is "spinning his wheels" in helping to motivate the client to enter the world of work.

It may be, however, that the above difference is more apparent than real. This lack of motivation to enter the world of work may very well be a general tendency of the mentally ill client no matter in what setting he may be found. In addition, there are other monetary renumerations to be found in the economy such as welfare, unemployment compensations, and insurance benefits. It has been observed that many of the mentally ill veteran clients who do not receive a VA service-connected compensation are as reluctant to enter the job market for fear of getting their unemployment or insurance benefits cut off as are those who receive a VA pension.

It is clear that work adjustment, as the end result of rehabilitation, is reached only after many stops along the way. If there were a single concept that could describe adequately the efforts that are expended in preparing the client for work, behavior modification would be that concept.

In a figurative sense the counselor begins with a piece of raw material in human form that must be shaped to the point that it finally reaches the stage of a finished product—in this case one that is acceptable to an employer. Very frequently the "finished product" must be returned or sent back for further modifications or revisions. Within a hospital setting such as in the VA, there may be a number of individuals in various disciplines involved in rehabilitating the client. Social work service, psychology, psychiatry, physical medicine and rehabilitation service, and nursing service are examples of the disciplines that might be involved. It can be seen that there may be a fairly extensive remodeling program for the mentally ill client in certain situations. The following are some of the kinds of modifications of behavior that are essential to preparing the client for entry into the world of work.

Interpersonal Relationships

One of the most consistent features of the mentally ill is poor interpersonal relationships. There are many forms that this relationship might take. The individual may exhibit unusual behavior of some kind by inappropriate affect, withdrawal, hallucinations, unusual thought patterns, etc. There may be unrealistic sensitivity to others to the extent that he makes himself the reference point for the attention of others around him, reacting to his interpretations of the meaning of these attentions. Relationships may be poor with authority figures—the client's behavior may range from presenting a deferential, obsequious manner to over-reaction with anger and hostility or outright physical violence. He may be so fearful of others that he withdraws or escapes when faced with such situations. The mentally ill person usually comes to the attention of a hospital or counselor when he becomes such a problem to others in his life situation that they prefer to escape from him through the medium of hospitalizing him or having someone else take over the job of rehabilitation.

Modifications in the area of interpersonal relationships will be usually approached with some combination of individual or group psychotherapy. Drug therapy is frequently used in order to reduce the effects of extreme behavior and to enable the client to profit from psychotherapy. There is no precise measure of the length of time a client may be in therapy—it is purely an individual matter with some clients progressing at a faster pace than others.

The client may progress through group therapy which simply stresses sociability to the involved therapies where highly emotional material is brought to the surface for resolution. The former may try to get the client to relate and simply talk to others about nonthreatening subjects. The end result is to assist the client to become a more socialized being, sensitive to his effect on others and with some insight into his own mental "hang-ups"—a person who is capable of controlling extremes of behavior in interpersonal relationships.

Through individual and group interactions, the staff and/or counselor can evaluate the client's ability to function more effectively or at least adequately with others. Among the behaviors relevant to work that are important to evaluate are: ability to withstand frustrations, appropriate affect, emotional control, elimination of unusual behavior and ineffective thought patterns such as paranoid views or ideas of reference.

Individual Development and Remodeling

The elements that enter into individual development will include improvement in such skills as communication, self-control and appropriate work behaviors as well as the development of a heightened self-confidence and a more effective self-image. A low level of self-confidence is very frequently a major aspect of the mentally ill client's psychological make-up. It occupies a considerable part of the counselor's time and in many instances is resistive to little more than minor changes. A similar comment can be made for self-image. The client may have lived a long time with the notion that he is not a person of worth, not entitled to be respected as a human being. Some of the techniques that have been found useful in heightening a self-image are as follows:

Assertion Training

This is a technique that is designed through training to bring the client to the point where he can assert himself in an appropriate manner when he feels that his basic humanity has been trampled upon. One of the very first steps in assertion training is to teach the client the difference between hostile, aggressive responses and appropriate, assertive responses. For the mentally ill client, his response to situations where his basic humanity has been violated is likely to be an overt striking out or escape to ruminate later (out of range of the offending other) about what he should have done. Neither of these is considered an adequate or effective response to the situation.

It is pointed out that slouching in a chair or furtive glances with an inability to direct one's attention toward others is likely to create an image of an inadequate person in the minds of those who view such behavior. In order to counteract this impression, the client is taught proper posture and techniques to maintain eye contact with others. The client is shown that it is possible to maintain eye contact without ever looking the person in the eye. Given a range from the shoulders to the forehead, attending to such features as mouth, nose, ears and shoulders cannot be distinguished from looking the person in the eye.

There may be occasions when the client indicates hypersensitivity to significant others and which is reflected in inadequate interpersonal behavior. Desensitization is the technique used to counter this problem. This technique proceeds in a similar manner to the process the allergist goes through with a patient who has a high sensitivity to certain substances in his environment. Through repeated role-playing as well as modeling by staff and by gradually increasing the tensions he can tolerate, an attempt is made to desensitize the client to the disturbing elements in his environment. For example, if the client is highly sensitive to supervisors to the extent that he becomes highly anxious or behaves inappropriately when the supervisor is around, repeated role-playing and role reversal may reduce the anxiety and inhibit the ineffective behavior.

Work Attributes

Many mentally ill clients are deficient in the knowledge of the attributes of a good employee. They must be taught that a good employee is dependable, sticks to his assignment, maintains a certain standard of dress and personal hygiene, and behaves in a proper, sociable manner with those who work with him.

In a hospital setting such as the Veterans Administration, many possibilities exist to train and evaluate the client in relevant work attributes. There are assignments in the various divisions and services where he can be placed, and his behavior observed and evaluated. Poor work behavior can receive the attention of the counselor and be modified prior to placement in an actual work situation in the community.

Some improvising may be required where the counselor does not have a hospital handy for training and remodeling purposes. However, there are community resources where clients could be placed as volunteer workers, their performance observed and evaluated.

Some Other Approaches

The mentally ill frequently complain about an inability to concentrate or a preoccupation with certain thoughts that they seem powerless to control. Some may complain of difficulty in relaxing —a constant feeling of being tense and tight. Unless these aspects of the mentally ill client are handled, his tenure on a job is likely to be a brief one.

One can initiate therapies that are designed to teach the client how to relax by a process of control over thoughts and muscles. Specific procedures are repeated over and over by the therapist until the client is capable of carrying them out on his own. Clients have been observed who became quite adept at relaxing when they feel themselves getting too tense.

Since inability to concentrate is also a disabling feature of the mentally ill, exposing the client to methods of concentration and control over the thinking process are extremely desirable.

Still another approach is therapy designed to teach the client to expand his perceptual horizon and to seek out the humor in his life situation, even to the extent of laughing at himself periodically. This technique is an effort to counteract the tendency of the client to become so preoccupied with his own problems that he neglects to attend to many of the events that occur around him. His complete preoccupation with himself will tend to magnify his problems to such an extent that he becomes a humorless, deadly serious individual whose probability of success as an employee would be extremely low. Teaching him how to look for and recognize the humor in his surroundings can contribute toward helping the client become a more social person as well as acceptable employee.

The life style of the client may interfere with adequate functioning in the community. Getting the client to understand his life style, its adequacies as well as inadequacies and contradictions, accepting it or making adjustments if necessary, is another approach to rehabilitation.

Significant Other Involvement

The client in most instances cannot be considered in isolation. Usually there are significant people in his life situation who influence his thinking and behavior to a considerable extent. Most frequently these will be a parent, a spouse or a child. On the other hand the significant other may be a relative or a good friend. Preparing the client for employment may encompass the need to resolve problems between him and the significant others in his environment. Many times there is a lack of understanding as to the client's illness or capabilities—the significant other must be involved if the efforts of the counselor are to be fruitful. At times it may be necessary to schedule afternoon and evening sessions in order to make it convenient for significant others to be involved.

It can be seen that the approaches the counselor takes may vary, depending on the availability of facilities and personnel. If sufficient personnel and resources are available, many approaches can be parceled out to others thus extending the efforts of the counselor.

THE WORK SCENE

A comprehensive involvement in the world of work is a must for the vocational counselor, especially one concerned with placing the mentally ill. To quote the vernacular of the market place, in the final analysis that is "where the action is." The end result of the counselor's labors, the success or failure of his efforts, will be determined in this arena.

The counselor must have at least a working knowledge of the many elements of the community that are involved in job placement or work activities. There are agencies such as the state or local employment services, private employment agencies, business and industry, sheltered workshops, employ the handicapped groups, and committees in Rotary Clubs that assist in job placement. The counselor must be familiar with as many of these groups as is possible within his available time. It is highly desirable that he attend meetings, visit agencies and employment resources, and participate actively in developing sources of work placement in the community.

The state of the economy has a considerable impact upon the efforts of the counselor. For example, when the economy is in a low period with many men out of work, the difficulties of placing the mentally ill person become even greater. A brief reflection will make it clear that during periods of high unemployment most employers can select from a sizeable pool of applicants with considerable talent and a high level of motivation to work. In addition, the employer may need to do some retrenching so that jobs he may be willing to assign to the mentally ill person during the periods of full employment must be reserved for other employees for any of a number of reasons.

It is obvious from the above that the vocational counselor cannot escape being a man of the community involved in many activities that relate to employment.

An example of a comprehensive program in operation in one of the VA hospitals will probably present a clearer view of what is possible for the counselor to do in this area. The hospital has 900 beds with approximately one-half of the patients being treated for mental illness. The program in its major aspects follows.

Job Placement Boards

In the early years of the program, two boards were set up. These boards met periodically at the hospital, interviewed mentally ill clients that were presented by the counselor, and decided whether they could or would assist the client in finding employment. One of the boards consisted of representatives from business and industry and the state employment services. The other board consisted of members of the employment committee of a local Rotary Club. During these sessions a fairly complete work-up of the client was presented to the board followed by a personal interview with the client. Suggestions were made where the client could look for work or if a board member knew of a particular employer who could use such a client, he would be so referred. Following the meeting, board members would contact acquaintances in the world of work for possible job placement opportunities or leads. If a successful placement was made, the counselor made periodic follow-up to see that the client was performing adequately on the job. There were occasions when support needed to be given to the employer as well as to the client-employee.

Failures as well as successes were part of the picture too. In many instances, and in spite of the work done with the client, many did not have the capabilities of doing the job or even remaining out of the hospital. Frequently the whole process began again at a later date.

Employ the Handicapped Groups

Another source of job placement used by the counselor was membership in local groups whose objectives were to seek out job placements for the handicapped. These groups—composed of representatives from community agencies, business and industry, and government—usually met monthly, generally around a noon hour. They were a source of referral or assistance in job placement of the mentally ill client.

Professionally Endorsed Patients (PEP)

The PEP program was a somewhat unusual technique used by the vocational counselor to develop placement outlets for the mentally ill. Through an arrangement with several of the local newspapers, an advertisement was carried in the classified advertising section of the newspaper for selected clients. This was done as a public service by the newspaper at no cost to the hospital, counselor, client or employer. The clients selected for PEP consideration were those who had some kind of saleable skill in a trade, service, profession, etc. The following is an example of the kind of advertisement that was placed in the newspapers:

> "Professionally Endorsed Patient" (PEP) #1072 Veteran experienced in sales 11 years, restaurant equipment and related items. Will work anywhere in Southern California. Licensed commercial pilot. Personable, good health, family man. Interested in any kind of outside sales.
>
> Concerning above-named veteran, contact Vocational Counselor, VA Hospital. Southern California Phone 231-3725.

Sheltered Workshop

The counselor frequently utilized sheltered workshops in the community as a source of job placement. Generally speaking it was felt that the sheltered workshop was a stepping stone to job placement in the competitive job market. It was usually more tolerant of less than desirable employee behavior than would be the case in the competitive job market. Uusally there were staff people at the workshop who were understanding and patient with the mentally ill employees. The goal was to provide additional training in the attributes of being an employee in a work atmosphere. Although it was emphasized that sheltered workshops should be viewed as a temporary assignment, in some instances it became a more or less permanent placement. Some employees never progressed to the point where it was felt that they could move up to competitive employment. On the other hand it was felt that they made a reasonable contribution to the mission of the workshop.

SOME FINAL CONSIDERATIONS

The emphasis in this chapter has been, for the most part, on the mentally ill client. It should be fairly clear that work adjustment of the mentally ill client does not proceed in a steady line toward some future employment goal. All too frequently months of efforts can be washed away in a short time span because the client is confronted with a situation he cannot handle. Even when he is placed on a job, the counselor is aware that the placement may be a tenuous one and that pitfalls of all kinds abound. Very frequently many attempts may be made with a particular client before anything approaching a permanent kind of job placement has been effected. For some mentally ill clients, the goal of work adjustment is never reached—the client cannot be brought to the point, with all of the techniques we now possess, where he can adequately do those things required of an employee either in a sheltered workshop or in competitive employment where the demands are much greater. There are many occasions when the client is placed in a position well below what could be expected of him based upon his work, educational or training background. The counselor must be able to resist his own inclination and objectively view what the client's optimum level of functioning may be at a particular time. It may come as a big surprise to the counselor to find out that many mentally ill clients do not share his views on the need or desirability of work. On the other hand, the fact that the client does share the counselor's view on work may create such a high level of tension that it may interfere with his functioning at a level commensurate with his physical and emotional state.

Thus one sees that matching the mentally ill client to a possible job in the community calls upon so many different skills and abilities that it is questionable whether one person could possess all of the necessary ones. The counselor must be comfortable in an authoritative, all-knowing role at times since he will be looked upon by some clients as the possessor of infinite knowledge and wisdom. He must be a person who can be satisfied with small gains, have a high frustration tolerance level, accept failure when he has put out considerable efforts, maintain an objective outlook, and remain flexible at all times. The counselor will be continually tested by clients who either have adopted, or wish to adopt, a "professional patient" life style. Such a outlook on life will make it necessary for the counselor to recognize and deal with his own biases relative to work and life styles. There will surely be some clients where a "professional patient" life style makes very good sense.

The rewarding aspect of counseling the mentally ill client comes in the form of a human being that the counselor has helped along a confused, rocky road that may lead to a successful work adjustment, but frequently stops with an individual simply functioning within the limits of his abilities in the community.

REFERENCES

Buros, O. K.: *Mental Measurements Yearbook*. Highland Park, Gryphon, 1971.

Psychiatric Evaluation Project: Patterns of mental patient post-hospital adjustment. Washington, D.C., Veterans Administration Hospital, February, 1965.

Searls, D. J., Wilson, L. T., and Miskimins, R. W.: Development of a measure of unemployability among restored psychiatric patients. *Journal of Applied Psychology, 55*:223-225, 1971.

Struening, E. L., and Efron, H. Y.: The dimensional structure of opinion about work and the social context. *Journal of Counseling Psychology, 12*:216-312, 1965.

INDEX

225